BERNIE'S

MITTEN

MAKER

BERNIE'S MITTEN MAKER

a memoir

Jen Ellis

Foreword by Dar Williams

i

GREEN WRITERS PRESS
Brattleboro, Vermont

Printed in the United States

10 9 8 7 6 5 4 3 2 1

Green Writers Press is a Vermont-based publisher whose mission is to spread a message of hope and renewal through the words and images we publish. Throughout we will adhere to our commitment to preserving and protecting the natural resources of the earth. To that end, a percentage of our proceeds will be donated to environmental activist groups. Green Writers Press gratefully acknowledges support from individual donors, friends, and readers to help support the environment and our publishing initiative.

GReen
WriTers
press

Giving Voice to Writers Who Will Make the World a Better Place
Green Writers Press | Brattleboro, Vermont
www.greenwriterspress.com

ISBN: 979-8-9865324-5-5

COVER ART: JULIANNE HARRIS
COVER DESIGN: AMANDA FELLER AND GRACE KENNEDY

Green Writers Press and the author thank the following sponsors:

PRINTED ON PAPER WITH PULP THAT COMES FROM FSC-CERTIFIED FORESTS, MANAGED FORESTS THAT GUARANTEE RESPONSIBLE ENVIRONMENTAL, SOCIAL, AND ECONOMIC PRACTICES.

For Helen, may you always tell your stories.
And for Liz, may every seven years bring us more joy
than the last.

Contents

Foreword

To be clear, this is about more than the mittens! Jen Ellis shows us how she has fashioned so many things—memories, friendships, fabric, and yes, a lot of sweaters—into a deeply wonderful life in a snowy land on a teacher's pay. This is a story for all of us who care about our communities and our planet and utilize the best of what we have around us to "make a living, not a killing," as my fellow folksinger, Utah Philips, used to say.

Like Helen and Scott Nearing, modern homesteaders who wrote *Living the Good Life*, Jen is a resourceful steward of her surroundings, a gardener, beekeeper, and improvisational designer of a Walden-worthy outdoor classroom during the pandemic. In her memoir, she presents us with a recognizable terrain of breakdowns, breakthroughs, and broken American systems.

Some books tell us how to live. Jen lives. Instead of asking myself, "How does she do it?" I found myself nodding and saying, "Yes, this is how we do it." We can be determined. We can muster up our emotional courage and also let friendships help us find the way forward. We can be crafty in all the best ways.

I couldn't wait to finish Jen's manuscript and write this Foreword so the book could come out and I could give it to fifteen friends.

And I know I will place my own copy next to the flowers I put in the now-empty jar of honey from Jen's bees. And next to my jar of flowers, I will put the cedar box I ordered specially to house the mittens Jen made for me. They're from the same sweater she used for Vice President Kamala Harris's mittens.

I will remember that in a country that offers all that is conveniently disposable—our legacy is in what we craft, reclaim, and value enough to redeem.

—Dar Williams, singer-songwriter
and author of the book,
How to Write a Song that Matters

I

Chapter 1
Inauguration Day

*T*oday *should be a holiday*, I thought as I punched my entry code into the keypad of the Westford Elementary School front door, *or at least a snow day.* It was Inauguration Day, and I arrived with just three minutes to spare before my 8 am morning meeting with my second-grade class was set to begin.

The building was dark and mostly empty. We were now ten months into the COVID-19 pandemic. The school year had been splintered by periods of remote and hybrid learning, followed by in-person instruction with students in desks that were supposed to be six feet apart, though the best we could do with the space we had in most classrooms was four. The number of new rules and restrictions made my head spin. I unlocked my classroom door, hung up my coat, and opened the blinds. The bright January morning lit up the room. The fields surrounding our little country school in Northern Vermont were covered in fresh snow.

Most days I loved the quiet online teaching, alone in my classroom. But today, more than anything, I wished I was at home watching the pre-inauguration events with my partner, Liz, and our five-year-old daughter, Helen. In just a few hours, President Biden would be sworn into office and Kamala Harris would become our first female vice president. The ex-president would be boarding a plane and leaving the Capitol. I found solace in the fact that I would be done teaching at 10:45 and would be able to go home to see most of the action.

I logged into the computer and opened my Zoom meeting. There were several urgent doorbell chimes in a row letting me know that students were arriving. I pulled up the participants tab and hit 'admit all.' Their faces appeared on the screen like a Brady Bunch intro. I was delighted to see that no one was wearing pajamas today, even though some were still finishing up with their breakfast.

"Hi, Ms. Ellis!"

"Hi, Amelia!"

"Hi, Reagan, it looks like you're enjoying the last of your muffin! Was it banana or chocolate chip this morning?" Reagan always ate two mini-muffins for breakfast. We had a little game where I would try to guess today's flavor.

"Guess!" Reagan said with a big smile.

"There's chocolate on your chin," Amelia said.

"It's true, Reagan; that kind of gives it away." We laughed. There were more "ding-dong" sounds as kids trickled into the meeting. I greeted every student and called hello to all their cats and dogs by name. Sometimes older siblings would appear, which was always fun for me because I had been their second-grade teacher, too. This window into my students' lives was sweet, and almost made up for the fact that they were at home instead of with me. Almost.

"Let's start the morning meeting with a greeting. Maeve, you're the leader today, which greeting would you like to do?"

"I choose the 'I Wish' greeting!" Maeve always wore her sunglasses to the morning meeting, and today she had a hen wandering around on the kitchen floor behind her.

"Is that a chicken?" I asked.

"Yes. She was getting pecked by the other hens, so my dad

brought her inside to let her heal." I could see the kids laughing, but they were now all on mute. They knew that when the Zoom meeting began, they had to be on mute until it was their turn to speak.

The I Wish greeting was one of my favorites. There were no limitations—the kids greeted a classmate, then could wish for anything they desired.

"Good morning, Dylan!" said Maeve. "I wish for a chocolate donut!" It took Dylan a few seconds to unmute himself.

"Oh, me too!" said Dylan. "Good morning, Ana! I wish for a yellow lab puppy!"

"Good morning, Dylan. I wish it would rain tacos!" This brought peels of muted laughter and many hands signing "connection." We had taught the kids to lift their pinky and thumb fingers in the air and draw them back and forth between the speaker and themselves to indicate "me too," or "connection." This helped them to connect to one another without calling out or hijacking someone else's story. I don't know where this sign came from; maybe it was an easier version of the American Sign Language sign. Probably it was just a teacher trick that seemed to work and was passed along from one to the next.

The greeting went on like this until we got to Grace.

"I wish for there to be no more pandemic," she said with a sigh. There were many nods and more connection signs. Usually after someone wished for the pandemic to be over, everyone else began to wish for that too. This class, like all school-aged kids, had missed one-third of the previous school year. Many of their parents had lost their jobs. Their families had canceled all vacations and playdates. Their birthday parties were also canceled or postponed and then never rescheduled. We all thought this would be over by now. Our patience for the whole ordeal was gone. At the end of the greeting, we moved on to the daily message.

"Alright, Maeve, would you like to read today's message by

yourself, or with everyone's help?" We waited for her to unmute herself.

"By myself."

I shared my screen with my class and pulled up today's morning message.

"Dear Exquisite Second Graders," she began reading, "Maeve is the leader today. We have a virtual art class with Ms. Feller at 10:45 A.M. Make sure you double check your SeeSaw Online Learning Platform to see when your reading group is this morning. We will have a live math lesson at 10:00. Are you going to watch the inauguration at 11:30 A.M.? Today is a historic day because Kamala Harris will become our first female, first Black, and first South Asian American vice president. Have a great day! Fondly, Ms. Ellis."

We went on to have our sharing time and correct our daily sentences before splitting into reading stations. Some kids read independently while others worked on an online reading and spelling program. I began teaching a reading lesson with five students who had completed a chapter book the day before.

Remote teaching required teachers to have every minute of the day planned in advance. Each student had a personalized folder full of "Just Right" books and differentiated spelling and math assignments. Students took home classroom books, supplies, writing folders and Chromebook devices the previous day. I could only hope that the materials would come back. If a student left their school supplies at home, they couldn't borrow anyone else's, not during a pandemic. The student-specific lesson plans needed to be written out and programmed to drop into the student's account by 7:00 A.M. Daily schedules were also emailed to families in case they were available to help their kids with their schoolwork. Many kids spent the day with their grandparents or older siblings if their parents were essential workers and gone during the day. Other kids struggled with limited internet bandwidth as their parents and siblings worked remotely from other rooms, or sometimes in the same room. I frequently could hear my colleagues teaching a brother or sister on another device at the same dining room table. It was very distracting. It was a mystery to me how the students stayed focused on their own schoolwork.

I took a quick break just before 10:00. The snow was falling gently outside my classroom window. I could see Pat Haller's fields filling up with a perfect blanket of white. Pat is the school's friendly across-the-road neighbor who always helps us with our outdoor projects. The dirt road on which my school resides was barely visible. Westford is a rural town with a population of around 3,000 people. There is only one school, grades pre-K–8. There is only one second grade class, and only one second grade teacher: me.

On my way back to my teaching station, I glanced quickly at my phone. My partner Liz had texted me a picture of Trump's helicopter leaving the White House. I breathed a sigh of relief. I was ready for new leadership. Our country was bitterly divided. Just two weeks before, our capitol building had been attacked by a pro-Trump mob. Five people had been killed. I put the phone back in my coat pocket and went back to my computer.

At 10:00, I reopened the Zoom meeting, and there was another flurry of doorbell chimes as my students returned for the math lesson. We jumped right into double-digit subtraction. I turned on my document camera and was writing out an example for my students when I heard the first "ding" on my cell phone, notifying me that someone had sent me a text message. I was slightly annoyed at myself for forgetting to put the phone on silent. I ignored it. We were almost to the end of the first problem when the phone dinged several more times. I knew that if I left my teaching station to check my phone, I would lose the momentum of my lesson.

I wrote another example on my paper beneath the document camera and asked for a volunteer to explain how they would solve the problem. Before I had a chance to choose someone, my phone gave an insistent, "Ding! Ding! Ding!"

I wondered who all the texts were from. It was early on a weekday and most of my friends were at work. I was just about to pick a volunteer when my sweet little student, Sophie, leaned into the camera, unmuted herself, and said, "I think someone is trying to reach you, Ms. Ellis." In that moment, a terrible fear came over me. What if something had happened to my parents? Were my partner and daughter safe? Was my house on fire?

"I need to go grab my phone, friends. I'll be right back." I moved quickly to my coat, snagged the phone, and returned to my remote teaching station. Second graders will not wait long for a teacher to continue her lesson before they start a dialogue of their own about how cute their cats are. Then the conversation turns to meows. It's hard to come back from that. I sat back down and glanced at my phone. The first text was from the librarian at my school.

"Bernie is at the inauguration, wearing your mittens!"

This made me laugh a little. That's why people were texting me? I had made a pair of mittens for Vermont Senator Bernie Sanders after he lost the democratic nomination to Hillary Clinton in 2016. I sewed them out of old wool sweaters, which I cut apart and pieced back together. At the time, I was making a lot of these mittens and giving them away as holiday gifts. I sent them to Sanders via his daughter-in-law, who owned my daughter's preschool. It was very sweet that he had worn them to the inauguration. I was delighted, but I needed to teach so I silenced my phone.

I was eager to finish the math lesson because as soon as it was over, I was planning to rush home and watch the inauguration with my family. We had dug our television and bunny ears out of the bedroom closet for the occasion. We'd put the TV away two years ago in an attempt to limit our screen time—an attempt, I admit, that had been only mildly successful.

Ten more minutes went by. As students mastered the math concept, they began saying goodbye and leaving the Zoom meeting to work independently offline. I was down to two students now. I began wishing the time would go faster, or that they would learn faster, or that I could teleport home to watch the pre-inauguration news coverage. The more I thought about it, the more flattered I became that Bernie was wearing my mittens in Washington, D.C. *It must be a cold day there, too*, I thought.

As soon as my last student left the Zoom meeting, I gathered my stuff and rushed out the door. My car was covered in three inches of fluffy snow, which easily slid off when I engaged the windshield wipers. I dusted off the rest of the windows and was on my way. The Westford roads and woods stretched out before me like a scene from a Robert Frost poem. How could a place be so beautiful every single day? I sped up a little and my car immediately fishtailed. A red, flashing image of a swerving vehicle appeared as a warning on my dashboard. This was going to be a slow drive home.

Liz was making fondue for lunch, and I knew she had bought cupcakes from the new bakery in town. We had the whole afternoon planned out. First, watch history being made as the first female vice president was sworn in! Then, a celebratory lunch. The afternoon would be for snow fort making with our daughter and maybe a walk around the Indian Brook Reservoir now that it was frozen over and there was no chance our dog would fall in. Getting a new administration in the White House felt like the greatest gift to us. We had decided to treat Inauguration Day like a holiday.

I was relieved when Joe Biden won the election. We listened to his speeches on the radio every chance we could. His words were encouraging and peaceful. Our country sorely needed this kind of unifying rhetoric. Never had I seen such bitter polarization in my community. People had lost all sense of what it meant to politely disagree about anything. The local online message boards had disintegrated into community troll networks. The pandemic was raging across our nation, leaving over 400,000 people dead. President Trump told us not to fear COVID-19, while our respiratory therapist neighbor told us that yet another person had been put on a ventilator at the hospital. People separated the shoppers downtown into categories. There were those who wore masks, those who wore masks below their noses, and those who did not wear masks at all. Lots of people had strong opinions about other people's mask-wearing choices, which they freely and loudly shared. Everyone was on edge as the virus quietly stalked us while we moved about our days. Maybe it was false hope, but I thought the change in leadership might help lift our country out of the steaming hot mess in which we were languishing.

Then there was Kamala Harris: a smart, powerful woman about to be inaugurated as vice president. Although I supported our hometown hero Bernie Sanders in the primary, I respected Harris's outspokenness on issues of racial justice in the debates. She had forced Biden to confront his legacy on issues of race. She had called him out on his opposition to school busing, a system which enabled her to get a better education. Harris reminded us all about the dire need to close the opportunity gap in our still-segregated school systems. Then she turned around and accepted Biden's invitation to join his ticket. He knew he needed her to win, and she knew it too.

My heart leapt with joy just thinking about it as my mom-van picked its way over the snowy hills towards home. I turned onto Old Stage, the long road that leads straight into Essex from Westford. After traveling this route every school day for the past nine years, I knew each landmark and every bump in the pavement. The inside of my car was warm now, and my thoughts began to drift from Kamala Harris to past female vice-presidential candidates. Until this election year, I could only think of two: Sarah Palin and Geraldine Ferraro. My memories of Palin were vivid, as her candidacy was recent enough to recall the highlights, most of which I followed on Saturday Night Live. I didn't remember Ferraro's campaign, as I was only six when Walter Mondale chose her as his running mate. The magnitude of that choice was not clear to me until adulthood. In fact, most of my knowledge of that election came from my fifth-grade class play. We acted out the 1984 election, from Mondale's historic choice of Ferraro to their predicted and resounding defeat. At the time, it felt like ancient history to my eleven-year-old self. In actuality, that election was only five years prior. Studying that play was the first time I had ever really thought about politics. It wasn't hard to notice that all the presidents and vice presidents were men, but it didn't occur to me then to question why.

I was very bitter that I didn't get the part of Ferraro in the play. My teacher assigned me the role of a reporter, whom she ironically insisted had to be played as a man. She told me to borrow a tie from my brother. I wanted to wear nylons, high heeled shoes, and blue eye shadow. I argued with her daily over this detail.

"Why can't the reporter be a girl? Isn't that the point of the story? Girls can be anything they want to be! Reporters don't have to be boys!" I begged my teacher to let me just play the part my way. I refused to learn my lines unless I could say them in a dress with puffy 1980s shoulders and pointed high heels. Eventually, my teacher told me that if I didn't play the part as written, she would give it to my classmate Gary, who, in my 11-year-old opinion, was not a very skilled actor.

In the end, I lost the battle and donned a top hat used by someone who played Abraham Lincoln in the previous year's fifth grade play. My paper mustache, scotch-taped to my upper lip, repeatedly fell off, which was probably funny to everyone else. I hoped my brother wouldn't notice that I'd snuck into his room the night before to "borrow" one of his clip-on ties.

It was not the high-quality performance I'd hoped for. Most of my dialogue consisted of interviewing Ferraro and reporting back to the audience how she felt about running. When we practiced the script, I felt a fire in my chest at the injustice of her lost election. The ending devastated me every time we performed it. There was a magical-thinking part of my brain that believed if we just did a better job of acting it out, maybe it would have a different outcome next time. Obviously it never did. No amount of quality grade school acting could rewrite an unjust past. I'm glad my pre-teen self didn't know that it would be thirty-one more years before a woman was sworn in as vice-president.

I pulled into our driveway and raced inside. My partner Liz had left the heat on for me in the mud room. She is always doing thoughtful things like that. Liz is the kind of person I think belongs in everyone's life. She is unendingly generous and supportive—and the perfect combination of Tina Fey and the *Encyclopedia Britannica*. She's a walking canon of both useful and useless information with excellent dance moves and the wit of a stand-up comic. You don't want to go against her at trivia night; she always wins. I had simultaneously been in awe of her and in love with her for thirteen years.

I stepped into the cozy atmosphere of our living room. The gas fireplace was brightly flickering, and the TV was set up on the old steamer trunk with bunny ears reaching halfway to the ceiling. Liz stood up, and the first thing she said was, "Oh my God, Bernie is wearing your mittens at the inauguration!" An athletic woman with short, blond hair and nerdy glasses, Liz was wearing a black hoodie with a picture of a covered wagon on it that said: *You have died of dysentery.*

"I heard!"

"How were the roads?"

"Bad."

It took me a moment to take in the scene on the TV screen. People were sitting in small groups or by themselves. Everyone was masked. An announcer was narrating the events.

"Where is he sitting?" I asked. Liz pointed to the right-hand side of the screen, but I could barely make out that it was him. I sat down with year-old daughter Helen. on the couch. She was clearly brooding over something.

"Mama's being mean to me!" she said with a pout. I pulled her close into what we called a huggle-snuggle.

"Oh, my little love munchkin." I rubbed her back. I was trying to be sympathetic, but gave Liz a knowing look.

"She won't let me play violin!"

Ah, the dreaded argument about the violin. Helen had been playing for a year and a half, and lately her practice sessions had dissolved into temper tantrums every time she made a mistake. I could see that Liz had put Helen's expensive, rented violin away to keep it safe. This was not the rabbit hole I wanted us to go down. It had taken me twice as long as usual to get home, and the inauguration was about to begin. I pulled a blanket over us and made the most comforting little nest for her.

"Come here, baby bird." She nestled into my embrace, her warm body leaning on my chest. Liz rolled her eyes; I shrugged my shoulders.

"Tweet," went Helen's tiny voice.

"Tweet, tweet," I responded. She loved playing mommy and baby bird. I fed her a pretend worm as the trumpets began to sound on the television screen and Vice President-Elect Kamala Harris arrived with her husband, Doug Emhoff.

Resplendent in her purple coat and dress, Harris smiled behind her black pandemic mask. Tears began to stream down my face as she waved her gloved hand. This was the moment for which every girl in my fifth-grade class had waited over three decades. I hoped they were all watching too, wherever they were. There would be a new elementary school play written about the 2020 election, and this one would have a long-overdue ending. I imagined little girls across the world watching this brave woman take the stage. Every woman who had ever burned at the injustice of misogyny could delight in this victory. She represented so many underserved and unheard people in our country. Her confidence was unwavering as she walked arm-in-arm with her husband down the steps to the inauguration platform, giving fist bumps to the Obamas.

I lifted the blanket that Helen had pulled over her head. "Look Helen, there she is!" I said in my most elated whisper.

"Why are you crying, Mommy?"

"Because we've waited too long for this." I looked over at Liz and realized she was crying too.

Through her tears, Liz said, "Mommy and Mama had to live four decades of our lives for this day to happen. These are happy tears because *you* only had to wait half of one."

"Helen, stand by the TV screen! Let's take your picture with Kamala Harris." As I flicked on my phone to take a picture, I noticed I had eighteen new text messages—about as many as I typically get in a whole week. I clicked a few pictures of Helen and Kamala. Helen gladly cheesed for us, not hesitating to upstage our vice president-elect.

I was elated in a different way for President-Elect Biden. I was beyond grateful for the way he had stood up to our former president during the debates. I also deeply admired his wife, Dr. Jill Biden. Having a champion for education in the White House would put a spotlight on teaching.

Even though I was fixated on the inauguration proceedings, it was hard not to notice what was happening on my phone. Texts were pouring in.

"Bernie is wearing your mittens!" *I heard!*

"Are those the mittens you made for Bernie?" *Yes!*

"The mittens that Bernie is wearing look like they came from you!" *They did!*

"Did you give Bernie a pair of your mittens? It looks like he is wearing mittens you made!" The text messages went on and on, and as I read, more continued to arrive.

"Ha ha—Bernie must be headed to the post office after the inauguration! At least his hands will be warm in your mittens!"

In one message, someone forwarded me a Twitter post that identified me as the mitten maker. I could see that it already had a long line of responses. My jaw dropped. *How did they find me?* I wanted to dig in and figure out how the internet had identified me so quickly, but wanted to see the rest of the inauguration more. It's stunning how many events teachers miss because they are busy teaching all the time. I had carved out a chunk of my day to watch the inauguration and was determined not to be side-tracked.

The people chosen to speak and perform that day represented so many different parts of our country. For the first time in four years, it felt like the under-represented voices of Americans might be heard. We live in a very liberal part of Vermont, so it's fairly easy to be a lesbian, and people respect my family. In other areas of our state and country, being anything other than straight, white, and male is still a disadvantage in most situations. When you belong to a group of people often discriminated against, there is a natural affinity with all people who are oppressed. Biden said he wanted to be the president for every American, and I believed him.

I had composed myself by the time Amanda Gorman, the youngest inaugural poet in U.S. history, took the stage. She looked stunning in her yellow jacket and beautifully corn-rowed hair swept back in a bun with a red band around the base. Her clear words lilted off her tongue as she recited her poem, "The Hill We Climb."

"Yes." I said to Gorman as her hands lifted and danced in the air, adding punctuation to her words. Hot tears made their way down my cheeks once more. She was saying the very things I longed to hear. Not a single syllable of her poem was wasted. It was a call to action.

I took a deep breath when she got to the part about the past and how we need to repair it, because I knew she was talking about the disgusting racism in our country: the murders of George Floyd, Breonna Taylor, and many others at the hands of police, and the white supremacy condoned by our ex-president. The pandemic had rendered us all house-bound for nearly a year, and we had watched the play-by-play on the nightly news and social media. Last spring, I'd attempted to teach my students how to respond to the terrible things they had heard and seen on TV, but I was so far removed from them during the school closure that I never knew if they truly understood. Gorman's poem, and her perfect delivery, re-ignited my fury at all the injustices of the past, but it also inspired me to do better; it inspired me to be better.

When it was over, we erupted into applause as if we were there, jumping up from our seats in elation. This really was a new day for us all. It was a day of hope and promise for a better America.

I'm not sure Helen understood our spontaneous rupture of joy, but she clapped and jumped up and down too. When she was a baby, we called her "Little Laugh Along," because every time we laughed, so did she, even when she had no idea what was funny. Living in a house with Liz, there is always laughter. It is our currency.

The camera panned over the audience at the capitol as Lady Gaga made her way to the microphone for the National Anthem. It zoomed in on Bernie Sanders, the Junior Senator from Vermont.

"There they are!" I shouted. "There are my mittens!" The camera stopped on him for what seemed like a long time, before shifting back to Lady Gaga for the start of her performance.

By the time the musical guests had finished, the anticipation of what was next had us on the edge of our living room couches. Justice Sonya Sotomayor stepped up and faced Kamala Harris, while Harris placed her hand on Justice Thurgood Marshall's bible. The oath they spoke was calm and clear. I watched my daughter stand near the TV and witness these iconic women perform a ceremony that was written over two hundred years ago—for men. We had shielded Helen from the last four years of politics. Trump was a name we discussed, but she had no idea what he looked or sounded like. As she gazed at the television screen I thought, *This is where you enter politics, my love. Let this be your first presidential memory. Let these amazing, courageous women be your inspiration.*

While the inauguration transitioned from the swearing in of Harris to the swearing in of Biden, I looked again at my phone. Someone had sent me a picture of Bernie Sanders with the caption: "The pose. The mittens. The social distance." I chuckled. Another text featured Bernie with the caption: "This could've been an email."

I felt a sense of calm come over our home as Biden began his inaugural address. I loved watching him speak, and I appreciated how open he was about his life and his struggles. I found him relatable. This was our nation's chance at redemption. We were turning a new page. Our country had chosen a president and vice president who promised to unite us in the middle of a raging pandemic, social injustice, and economic catastrophe.

When President Biden was finished speaking, we clapped once again. The announcer declared that the code for our nuclear weapons had been changed. The last grip that our ex-president had on America was gone. Fresh, new leadership was here. As Biden, Harris, and the whole inaugural entourage returned to the Capitol building, I turned to Liz and said, "Thank God there were no assassins."

"What's an assassin?" Helen asked. My face flushed. I always tried to be honest in a kid-friendly way, but I didn't have an explanation for this one.

"An assassin is . . ." Would it scare her if I told her the truth? I didn't want to steal her joy. "An assassin is . . ." I looked at Liz with pleading eyes. "An assassin is . . ."

"A bad guy," Liz stated. "Who wants fondue?"

I was starving by the time we sat down for our celebratory late lunch. Liz got out the fondue pot and began mixing the shredded cheese with wine. The phone kept dinging, but now I knew why, and it was funny. The memes poured in: Bernie with the Golden Girls, Bernie sitting with the chorus in Hamilton, Bernie with the cast of Friends.

We decided to do a spontaneous gratitude circle over lunch. Liz was thankful for Kamala Harris; I was thankful for Amanda Gorman; and Helen was thankful that we would be having cupcakes later. We had just about finished cleaning up from our meal when the phone rang.

"Hello, this is Jack Thurston from NECN Channel Five in Burlington. Am I speaking with Jen Ellis?"

"Yes." *How on earth did he get my cell phone number?*

"We're just over here in Jericho and we understand you live nearby. Would you be interested in doing an interview about your now-famous Bernie mittens?" I was completely caught off guard. Was it really that big of a deal? Why on earth would he want to interview me? I had made those mittens for Bernie Sanders five years ago.

"I guess so. Our house is kind of a mess, can we talk on the front lawn?"

Liz and I scrounged around the house for some presentable and clean face masks, got dressed in our winter gear, and headed outside. It had stopped snowing, and the sun was beginning to show. The footprints in our front yard from where we had been playing over the weekend were barely visible under five new inches of snow.

We dusted off Wilhelmina, our snow woman. She sat awkwardly on a vintage bike I'd purchased at the Re-Store last fall. An aspiring bike mechanic, Liz had fixed the bike up enough to be ridden, but it was wobbly. Eventually, a mechanic at the Old Spokes Home bike shop in Burlington confirmed what we feared: the bike had a bent frame, most likely from being hit by a car. The 1961 Columbia Fire Arrow was not safe for humans to ride, but Wilhelmina straddled the wide, two-toned seat with the thunder thighs of a yeti. She had a look of steely determination in her eyes of coal. Her head was adorned with a raw carrot and my old, cracked bike helmet . . . for safety. Our family was particularly proud of this creation, and I secretly hoped she would be featured in our moment of local fame.

Jack Thurston, with his microphone and camera woman, showed up within fifteen minutes. Helen was certain they had come to talk to her. We stood together under the birch tree in front of our house, and Thurston asked questions about how I made the mittens and why I gave them to Bernie Sanders. Helen chimed in with her description of her own homemade mittens, which I'd fashioned out of one of her baby sweaters. I felt a little pang of guilt as she showed them to the camera, because the knit sweater I repurposed to make the mittens had been a handmade baby shower gift. I destroyed it by washing it years before, when Helen was an infant, not realizing it was wool. I hoped no one would see it on the news.

Helen made snow angels and delighted the crew with her stories and laughter. She proudly told Thurston that her hands "weren't going to get cold in these mittens!" Before the reporters left, we found an old pair of the Bernie-style mittens that Liz only wore when snow blowing the driveway and stuck them on Wilhelmina's stick hands. Everyone was laughing so hard by the time the interview was over, it felt like we were all old friends. We watched the news report online later that evening. Helen was front and center through the whole story. She couldn't wait to tell her kindergarten class all about it the next day.

After the reporters left, we went inside, and I checked my phone. There was a message from my principal:

"Your PLC meeting started 10 minutes ago." *Crap.* I had forgotten all about it. I was so completely absorbed by the glory of the day that I'd lost track of the fact that it was still a remote school day and I had an afternoon meeting. There went my inauguration holiday.

I logged on to my laptop and joined the meeting already underway. Our PLC team, short for Professional Learning Community, consisted of the kindergarten through third-grade teachers, the special educators, and our principal. The women in this meeting were some of my closest friends in life, and I enjoyed working with them. However, the excitement and glee of the past few hours drained out of me as we debated to what depth our standards reflected our *guaranteed and viable curriculum*. We began to dig into a document outlining our students' "I can" statements. We spent the first 45 minutes discussing exactly which vowel teams should be taught in the second grade. Then we moved on to suffixes. Meanwhile, Liz was texting me Bernie Sanders memes which I was covertly opening beneath the table. Bernie as the fly on Mike Pence's head, Bernie on a roller coaster, Bernie with Forrest Gump, and Bernie on the New York City subway. How was I supposed to concentrate on the dry and humorless world of phonics?

It didn't stop there. The memes kept coming. By nightfall, my Facebook was overloaded with messages and posts tagging me, talking about my mittens. People were texting me to get the story. I logged onto my email just before bed, and nearly four thousand people had contacted me in the past ten hours. How had they found me so quickly? Then I remembered the tweet someone had forwarded to me earlier in the day. I hadn't been on Twitter in almost a year. I didn't even remember my password.

Right at the top of the email list was a request for another interview. Out of curiosity, I did a quick search for 'media,' and six more requests popped up. I was not a person who kept up with the media. I listened to Public Radio, and that was about it. Scanning down the list I noticed requests from the Washington Post, L.A. Times, CNN. And then I saw it: Ari Shapiro from *All Things Considered*.

I had been listening to Ari Shapiro for years. He was such a good storyteller, and he had a perfect radio voice. I had the kind of crush on him that only a middle-aged lesbian from Vermont would form on a public radio persona. I ran upstairs to where Liz had already crawled into bed.

"You're *not* going to believe this! Ari Shapiro wants to interview me!" Liz was just as stunned. I was beginning to realize that maybe this phenomenon was about more than the mittens.

That night I lay awake for a long time, thinking. In one day, we had waved goodbye to a polarizing and dangerous president and welcomed a new leader whose mission was to unite our country. We witnessed the historic swearing in of our first female, Black, and South Asian vice president. We celebrated the beauty and diversity of our country with music and poetry. And in the same day, on the same stomping ground, a gift I gave received global attention because of a photo that went viral. The fact that I had anything to do with this historic day both delighted and astonished me. I felt enormous joy for the moment and the memes, but I also felt something else. My body felt shaky and slightly nervous. It was hard to put my finger on why, but I was a little afraid.

Chapter 2
Lost and Found

1987—1990

My story starts with something lost and something found. Like most stories of upcycling, the Bernie's mitten meme tale begins with unraveling and stitching back together.

I spent most of my third-grade year painstakingly copying definitions out of the student dictionary in cursive. I still have the scar of a callus on my right middle finger from where I rested my pencil. It was a blister that turned into a callus that grew a blister on top. I remember how proud I was when I finished the A section. My teacher, Mr. Hunter, didn't have very many rules, or lesson plans, or lessons for that matter. I think he was an old hippy. I liked him, and he was nice, but he didn't do a lot of teaching.

Mr. Hunter let us put our desks anywhere in the room we wanted. I found a little corner behind a bookcase and tucked myself away every day. It felt like my own private office, and it allowed me to focus, and work, regardless of the chaos happening in our class; and there was a lot of chaos. It was the first time I was legitimately bored in school. Every time we would ask Mr. Hunter for something to do, he told us to copy out of the dictionary, so that's what we did.

That spring, I had a wonderful idea: I began to plot my escape. On the first warm day, I intentionally left my winter coat at home and came to school wearing a sweater. At 2:00, an hour before school was scheduled to be dismissed, I asked to go to the bathroom. My heart was thumping as I exited the classroom. Instead of turning left to go to the girls' room, I turned right and casually walked down the stairs towards the school's side exit. I passed a teacher, smiled, and said "hello" like I had nothing to hide, though inside, my stomach felt full of dancing ants. The giant wooden doors were relics from its 1930s construction, and it took all my weight to push the metal bar that opened the latch. Luckily, I had grown a couple of inches since the fall, and my height gave me just enough leverage to get the door open.

The sun was so bright that I momentarily stood blinded at the top of the concrete steps. Then I began to run. I had to be quick because if I was caught, there was no excuse for being outside in the middle of the afternoon. I ran directly to the back entrance of the public library next door.

The smell of dusty books and old librarians greeted me like the perfume of freedom. I couldn't believe my plan had worked. I went up the stairs to the main floor and walked directly to the bathroom. My knees were rattling with nerves and excitement. I was always the kid who felt the urge to pee during games of hide and seek, and the bathroom was the perfect place to land after my big escape. For a second, I contemplated waiting there until 3:00 so as not to arouse any suspicion. But I wanted to see if I could really get away with my plan to make it all the way home, so I pushed myself to keep going. I calmly walked out of the bathroom with all the confidence I could muster, waved hello to the librarian behind the check-out counter, who had a very puzzled look on her face, and walked right out the front door. Broadway Road, the main thoroughfare of my hometown of South Portland, Maine, stretched out before me.

I was skipping with glee as I passed the Holy Cross Catholic School and Portland Harbor came into view. Taking in a deep breath of the briny ocean air, I hurried along until I got to my neighborhood. I was home by 2:20, a full hour before my brother. I was so surprised that it had worked that I didn't quite know what to do with myself. I wandered around the house, peeking out of the window like a fugitive.

The following day at school, I expected Mr. Hunter to scold me, but he said nothing. No one had even noticed. I decided to try again a few days later, and made another flawless escape. It was completely thrilling to leave school early. I could only do it on days when I didn't need a coat, and had to be careful not to do it too often. Skipping out on the last hour of school became my favorite trick. I never told anyone what I was doing, and I was never caught.

My fourth-grade teacher, Ms. Alfaba, had a much tighter grasp on the class. I knew from the first day that I would never get away with leaving school early. She was strict and had a habit of keeping the class after school to clean up or serve out a consequence for bad behavior. If a handful of children were caught talking or goofing around, the whole class would have to stay after for five minutes. Sometimes the five minutes would turn into ten or fifteen, depending on how many kids were being naughty that day. Despite my deviousness in third grade, I was not typically naughty in school. I did my work and listened to the teacher. Staying after school because of someone else's misbehavior filled me with righteous indignation.

The thing that put me over the edge was the bussers. Every day at 2:50, Ms. Alfaba would line up the children who rode the bus and send them down to the first floor where they exited out the side door to board the bus. This happened like clockwork, even if the kids riding the bus were the ones who still had messes to clean up or had earned us ten minutes of after-school detention. No one could interfere with the bus schedule, so the bussers were set free.

This led me to my second wonderful idea. My house was over a mile from the school, which qualified *me* to ride the bus. I asked my mother to write a note to add me to the bus list. I had been walking to and from school for years, so I was quite surprised when my mother agreed. I presented my note to Ms. Alfaba like a prize apple. She raised an eyebrow and reluctantly added me to the list. At the end of the day, I skipped to the bus and laughed as we pulled away.

It was woefully disappointing to learn that the bus meandered down every side street in our town dropping kids off. By the time we made it to my stop, forty-five minutes later, I was carsick and still had to walk all the way up Sawyer Hill to get home. The kids on our block had been home from school long enough to already be cruising around on their bikes.

Since I was now a "busser," it was going to be hard to switch back to being a "walker." I had gotten myself into a legitimate mess. The next day, as the bussers walked out to board the bus, I happened to be the last one in line. The teacher who dismissed us at the side door said, "Goodbye Jenny," turned on her heels, and walked away, letting the heavy old door slam shut behind her. I couldn't believe my luck. From the end of the line, I could see that there were no adults outside with us, and no one was watching. I veered off and ducked down behind a cedar bush beside the building. From my hiding spot I watched as the bus finished loading and pulled away. The cedar bushes lined the front of the school, forming a tunnel between the foliage and the building. I skittered down the tunnel to the other side of the school near Red's Dairy Freeze, hopped on the sidewalk, and began walking home. I knew full well that the rest of the walkers were staying after school to finish cleaning up and serve out the after-school detention. It made me feel slightly guilty because some of my buddies were in that group, but not guilty enough to turn around.

My plan worked perfectly for a few days. I felt the same devious thrill I'd experienced the previous year. I wasn't getting home as early as I had in third grade, but I'd tricked Ms. Alfaba into never making me stay late . . . or so I thought. Less than a week later, I emerged from the cedar bush tunnel and made my way out to the sidewalk when the hairs on the back of my neck stood up. It felt like someone was watching me. I turned around and looked up at my classroom windows and there was Ms. Alfaba, looking down at me, one eyebrow raised, wagging an angry finger. I gulped. There was nothing to do but run.

I slinked into class the next day, ready to be yelled at, held in for recess, or made to clean the chalkboard erasers. Ms. Alfaba greeted me with a dangerous smile and didn't say a word. I was on high alert all day, but nothing happened. By late afternoon I was pretty sure she had forgotten about the incident at the window. When Ms. Alfaba called the bussers to line up, I hopped out of my seat and began to stack my chair.

"Jenny Ellis!" boomed a loud and foreboding voice. "Where do you think you are going?"

"To the bus?"

"What makes you think you're a busser?"

"My mom put me on the list?"

"Bussers ride the bus, Jenny, and you haven't been riding the bus, have you?" Her face contorted into a satisfied grin and she cocked her head to the side.

"No."

"Sit down then."

I unstacked my chair and sat down with all the other sorry walkers, quite certain we would be staying after school for a very long time.

I take great delight in remembering that I was once a precocious child who had the confidence to sneak out of school. I navigated the world with trust and a true belief that people were kind.

I had a spark that was bright. I didn't know how valuable it was, until it was taken from me.

That fall, my mother bought a used upright piano. It was enormous, loud, and had real ivory keys. I thought the keys were very special until I found out where ivory came from. I started taking piano lessons and instantly loved it. I would plunk out every song I learned each week and leave the windows open hoping to be discovered as the next Liberace by my neighbors— who were obviously talent scouts and loved hearing a child banging on the piano.

It was right around that same time that I befriended an elderly man in our neighborhood. Mr. Johnson lived in a small, yellow house set back from the road on a large piece of property. I usually walked home from school with a group of neighbor-hood boys, and we would pass his house every day. On the nice afternoons that fall, Mr. Johnson would sit out on his driveway near the street in his lawn chair, his two miniature poodles jumping and running all around him. Sometimes he would call us over to talk to him, and he would give us Hood Ice Cream cups with little wooden spoons. He was especially nice to me; so much so that when the boys moved on to play Wiffle Ball in our yard or hunt snakes in the stone wall behind our house, I started staying behind with him.

When people make jokes about not taking candy from strang-ers, it isn't that funny to me. I was that kid who accepted ice cream cups and attention from a man I thought I could trust. I was naïve, and eager to make friends. I thought old people were kind, like my grandparents. At first, Mr. Johnson would do what seemed like innocent things to me—like invite me to sit on his lap on his lawn chair. Then he started tickling me on my belly, lower and lower, until he was no longer touching my belly. I made a lot of excuses for him in my mind: he was old; he didn't know what he was doing; he would never touch me inappropriately for all to see. I mean, we were outside and very near the street. Gradually, he made more and more sexual advances on me, and because I trusted him, I believed it was ok.

When I think back on it now, I can imagine why he must have considered me to be an easy target. Child predators are very skilled at what they do, and they often have hundreds of victims in their lifetime. My parents were divorced, and I had a single mom who worked full time. I was alone after school and left out of a lot of the neighborhood games because I was a girl and wasn't "cool." When you are nine and powerless, there are no words to describe sexual abuse. I didn't know how to tell him to stop, and I was too ashamed to ask for help. What I did know was that I never wanted to talk about it with anyone.

Mr. Johnson used to walk his dogs past our house and he had heard me playing the piano through the open window. One day he invited me inside his house to play his organ. The sexual abuse had escalated at that point, and I became deeply aware that afternoon that he was committing a crime. I managed to escape from him and ran home in tears. That day, I made two promises to myself: I would never go back to his house again, and I would never tell anyone what happened. I kept both of those promises for a very long time.

By middle school, I had already learned that the world could be a cruel and dangerous place for a girl. One of the few comforts I found after the abuse was eating. By sixth grade, I had put on a considerable amount of weight. I felt fat, out of place, and hated everything about my developing body. The food gave me comfort, and the weight helped me to hide. I was terribly lonely and didn't think I had any real friends. I also walked around carrying an enormous amount of shame. I was embarrassed that my parents were divorced, that my brother was badly behaved, and that my body wasn't the perfect size. All of these things were out of my control, but they were burdens I carried, nonetheless. I also carried with me my dark secret. It was like a shadow that never left. The precocious and confident child who snuck out of her third and fourth grade classrooms had been squashed under the weight of trauma. Thoughts of the abuse occupied my every waking moment and stole the peace from my sleep. I paid close attention to my peers and tried to act the way they acted so that I could blend in and no one would find out. I was terrified that I would say the wrong thing and give myself away. By the time I entered Mrs. Collett's Home Economics class in sixth grade, I had a good handle on how to remain silent.

Mrs. Collett was a short, motherly woman with long brown hair. She had a kind face and a gentle way about her. I instantly liked her and looked forward to her class every day. There was rarely any homework; all we had to do was show up, listen, and create. Those three things were about all I had in my wheelhouse as an insecure sixth grader. Her classroom had rows of sewing machines with neat vinyl covers. They sat like magical sentinels over the students.

When Mrs. Collett announced to the class one morning that we would be starting our unit on sewing, I sat up straight and smiled. I had been looking forward to learning how to sew all year. My mother used to sew all her clothes. When I was young, she made my brother and me elaborate costumes for Halloween. I felt that people who could sew were part of a special club and I was about to be initiated.

Many of the boys in my class grumbled through the lesson. They thought it was a girl's hobby. Even in 1989, the traditional gender roles were clearly defined. Our school, to its credit, required all the kids to take both Home Economics and Industrial

Shop class. By the time I turned twelve, I could operate a table saw, lathe, screwdriver, drill, and sewing machine.

The sewing machines were all uncovered that day, and bins full of fabric scraps and thread were waiting for us. I sat down at my machine, turned it on, and a bright light appeared, casting a spotlight on the needle. Mrs. Collett patiently walked us through the many steps of setting up the thread and showed us how to carefully stick it through the needle. I'm sure there were other instructions and safety warnings that day, but what I remember most is the magical moment when I first pressed my foot on the peddle and my scrap of fabric shot forward beneath the needle, emerging from the other side with an even line of stitches.

Everything about the sewing machine appealed to me. I loved the chopping hum of the needle as it bounced in and out of the fabric, and the perfect stitches it left behind. Nothing else in my life was that measured or controlled. I loved navigating the maze of hooks and wheels along the side of the machine to thread the needle. I loved the zing and spin of the bobbin as it wound up and down in a quick circle with my foot on the accelerator. It was exhilarating and, unlike the power tools I was learning to use in shop class, it seemed unlikely that it would cut off my finger. My friend Erika told me that her brother had sewed right through his thumb a couple of years earlier, in that very same home economics classroom in the basement of Mahoney Middle School. After over thirty years of sewing, I am still puzzled at that feat and vacillate between doubting the truthfulness of the tale and being impressed by his carelessness.

After Mrs. Collett taught us the basics of sewing, she gave us the directions for creating our first project: a pillow. We could either dig through her bin of fabric scraps for the materials or bring in our own from home. I thought about that assignment all day, drawing little pictures of my design ideas in my math notebook. I wanted mine to be the best pillow in the world.

When I got home that night, I convinced my mom to take me to JOANN Fabrics in Westbrook, so I could pick out the perfect fabric. She could have told me to go through the fabric scrap bin in our basement, but I think she knew how excited I was to sew my first project.

My mother had taken me to JOANN's many times before, but never on a mission to pick something out for myself. The rows and rows of colorful fabrics lit up by fluorescent overhead lights were like a wonderland to me. It was almost impossible to choose just one pattern. My mother allowed me to take my time wandering through the aisles. I picked out a blue paneled fabric that had dogs in some panels and cats in others.

I brought the fabric to school and diligently cut and sewed the pillow together inside out, leaving a small gap in the stitching to turn the fabric right side out so that the seams would be invisible. I then stuffed the pillow and carefully stitched up the remaining hole in the seam by hand. I was so proud of it when I was done. I brought it home and displayed it on my bed for years after. I immediately wanted to start another sewing project. I was hooked.

My mother said I came by it honestly. She was the most talented seamstress I knew. One day, in sixth grade, as I was hustling from one class, the wide pocket of my favorite plaid dress caught on the knob of the door to my math class. It tore a giant hole right down the side. There was a loud ripping sound, and I was left standing there with my underpants showing, trying to untangle my dress from the doorknob, while a group of merciless middle school boys laughed at me. My kindly math teacher sent me to the nurse's office, and they called my mom to come get me. I didn't have a change of clothes except my gym shorts, and in 1989, children were not allowed to wear shorts in school. My mom was very sympathetic. I was not only upset by the embarrassment of being exposed in front of my peers, I was also upset that my favorite outfit was ruined. My mom assured me that she could and would fix it. I admit, I doubted her. The material was plaid. Even if she could sew it back together, how would she ever get it to match up?

My mother went into her bedroom closet and pulled out her old Singer sewing machine. She hadn't used it in a long time. She allowed me to thread the needle and was duly impressed with my new skill. I don't remember how long it took, but she fixed the dress that night. It was so perfectly sewn back together that I couldn't even tell where it was ripped. For the rest of the school year, my math teacher would comment on the dress every time I wore it. "Your mother is an amazing seamstress," she would say, shaking her head, and I would beam with pride. For my next birthday, my mother gave me my own Singer sewing machine so that I could create my sewing projects at home. It was a simple machine, but it had all the appeal of the machines I had used in school.

Sewing at home wasn't quite as wonderful as sewing with Mrs. Collett though. Sometimes I would walk to school a little early just to have a few moments of peace with her in her empty classroom and me at the sewing machine. It was a small piece of joy in an otherwise bitter time. Every day in middle school felt like a struggle. It seemed like there would be no end to the corrosive silence of the sexual abuse I had experienced. I walked through my days feeling disgusted by my changing body, my awkwardness, and a secret that was devastatingly hard to keep, yet impossible to tell. My concentration was constantly interrupted by memories of Mr. Johnson. But when I was sewing in Mrs. Collett's class, my mind was focused and I was happy. It was my first glimpse of a new kind of freedom.

Perhaps I was never again going to be the girl who had the gumption to skip out of school early. Somewhere in the trauma, the confidence that girl possessed was lost. But in Mrs. Collett's class, something else was found. Without ever knowing she did this for me, she showed me that there is great healing in the art of sewing. I could sit behind the sewing machine and become consumed in my creations. In my many years of teaching, I have learned that students don't usually remember the things you say to them. What they remember is how you made them feel. When Mrs. Collett entered my life, she made me feel competent. She encouraged me to take risks and try new things. She believed that every child who entered her classroom was capable of creativity. It was in her class that I started to develop the skills I needed to save myself.

Chapter 3
Orientation

1997

Icouldn't wait to leave for college after I graduated from high school. I had memorized every idyllic photo of the University of Vermont brochure and imagined a new and magical life for myself beneath the perfect foliage and sun-lit walkways of the campus green. It was going to be a fresh start in a New England college town four hours from home.

That summer I worked at a wilderness summer camp. On the last day, I went skipping toward my beat-up old Toyota, chomping at the bit to leave, and realized I'd locked my keys in the car. I used the camp phone to call AAA and had to wait nearly three hours for them to drive out to the remote camp to break into my car. Everyone else left and I sat on a fallen tree and waited. The woods were shockingly quiet with all the children gone. I had plenty to think about. I was ready to leave almost everything in my life, everything but Annie.

Annie was my co-counselor, and the week before, she had kissed me one night at our staff retreat. Compared to the sloppy high school boy kisses I had experienced, kissing her was magical. I was certainly beginning to wonder if I was a lesbian, but

I definitely didn't want to be one. Sitting on that tree in the vast Maine wilderness, I decided to set a firm goal. I was going to college, and I was going to find a husband. I just had to cool my heels for three more hours.

Growing up in the 1980s and 90s, we were conditioned to be straight in thousands of little ways: from commercials and sitcoms on TV, which portrayed families as having moms and dads, to billboards on the side of the road, to the textbooks and heteronormative prom culture in our schools. Words and expressions like queer, dyke, fag, and "That's so gay!" were tossed around as insults and not-so-subtle reminders that being gay was bad. Throughout my entire childhood, the deep shadow of the AIDS crisis lurked in every conversation about homosexuality and instilled fear and heightened homophobia in our already intolerant culture. When we learned about sex in school, we were told not to have it, because we might get AIDS, the same logic was applied to any notions we might have about being queer. I viewed my growing love for other women as something that needed to be straightened out, both figuratively and literally.

I made a valiant effort to be straight my freshman year at the University of Vermont. I joined a sorority, tried to dress more femininely, and even tried to flirt with some of the men in my classes, though it felt false. I went on a handful of dates with men who were very sweet and kind; I just wasn't attracted to them. I thought I knew what I was looking for, and when I didn't find it, I began to realize that I was looking for the wrong thing. By the end of the year, I was fairly certain that I just wanted to meet another Annie and stop trying to be something I clearly was not.

At the end of my freshman year, I stayed at UVM for an extra month to work as an orientation leader. There were thirty of us on campus that summer. Our job was to give campus tours to incoming freshmen and help them sign up for classes. There is nothing quite as stunning as June in Vermont. After the bitter, cold winter, summer arrived overnight and everyone threw open the windows and rejoiced. Without the pressure of constant schoolwork hanging over us, we had an unparalleled sense of freedom to spend long nights roaming the campus, talking until all hours in our mostly empty dorm rooms, and making midnight runs downtown for gravy fries at Nectar's. I developed some of the most important friendships of my life that month. For the first time, I felt that I had truly found "my people" in the cohort of orientation leaders.

My boss was a woman named Dani Comey. She reminded me a little bit of Mrs. Collett. She was a mother and a natural teacher. She wore many hats at the university, and it seemed that every time I joined a club or took a new work-study job, she was either my supervisor or the faculty advisor. Dani was unendingly wise. You might think that the training to become an orientation leader was simple and straightforward—here's how you give a campus tour; here's how you sign someone up for classes on a 1997 computer. But the training we received from Dani and the orientation administrative staff was clearly designed to help us form a collaborative team. The goal was to help us grow as leaders and realize strengths we possessed that had previously gone unnoticed. One day our job was to draw a road map on a piece of chart paper of the twists and turns of our lives and present it to the group. Not only was I fascinated by the lives my peers had led, but I felt compelled to share my own life with others in a way that I had never felt comfortable to share before. Dani was a brilliant leader. She was everything I thought an awesome woman should and could be, *and* Dani was an out and proud lesbian.

In 1997, being a lesbian felt radical. I couldn't shake my memories of the night Annie had kissed me the previous summer. It felt so amazing, and so right. Yet the lesbians I'd met so far all had short hair, lots of piercings, armpit hair, and tattoos. I wanted to love women openly, but I didn't see myself in any of the examples I saw around me, until I met Dani. None of society's boundaries seemed to matter to her. She was confident, and powerful; openly gay—but still shaved her legs. She had short hair, but often wore dresses to work. She and her partner frequently attended orientation dinners together. They held hands and made absolutely no secret about loving each other. The thing I found most intriguing and wonderful about them was that together they had a baby girl, whom Dani had carried. I'd always known I wanted to be a mother. Not quite understanding how that could be possible as a lesbian was one of the barriers that kept me from coming out. Seeing Dani, her partner, and their daughter together was the first time in my life that I saw a family that looked like the one I wanted.

One night, Dani and I happened to be walking across campus, just the two of us. It was a warm, beautiful June evening. The lilac and crabapple tree blossoms wafted a perfume into the night air. I had grown to deeply trust Dani. In her earnest and intuitive way, she talked to me like I was already an adult, when inside I still felt like a kid. Coming out felt like an adult decision, so I figured her regard for me put me halfway there. Memories of the previous summer lingered, and that first kiss with a woman still sent shivers up my spine. I had given boys the good ol' college try . . . literally, and I was quite sure it was time to move on.

"Dani,"

A long, long pause.

"Yes?" Dani was a very patient listener. I mustered up the courage and the words that had eluded me for so long.

"I think I might be . . ." I'm sure there was another very long pause here. The thing about coming out is, once you say it out loud, it is so much more real.

"I think I might be . . ." After another very long pause, Dani stopped walking and faced me. Her wispy brown, feathered bangs blew in the wind and her intense eyes looked directly into mine. I wanted to trust her.

"Are you trying to tell me something important?"

"Yes." I looked at the ground and kicked at a little tuft of grass poking up from a crack in the sidewalk.

"It's ok. You can say it."

"I think I might be a lesbian." The words hung in the air and my stomach clenched. I looked up at Dani to see if she had heard me. She looked back with a proud and knowing smile.

"I wondered that about you."

"You did?" I was so sure I'd kept this identity private, how could she have known?

"I did. Sometimes it takes one to know one." We walked in silence for a very long time. I was collecting my thoughts, and Dani, in her infinite wisdom, was giving me space in the silence. When we finally made it back to the dormitory, I felt a sense of urgency. I didn't want her to leave. She was the first person I had come out to. I was afraid that if she walked away, I would have to figure out my next steps alone.

Dani started taking the long way through the parking lot, instead of towards the dorm. We walked for a long time until she finally said, "It's been a long day, Jen. Do you want to sit down?"

I was so grateful for the strength of her presence in that moment. We sat on some steps that led from the parking lot to the dorm, in between some overgrown bushes. No one ever used those steps. It felt like a private, out of the way place to talk.

"Do you have any questions?" My stomach flew into a moment of weightlessness, like the feeling of freefalling on a log flume ride at an amusement park. It landed in a rush, somewhere between embarrassment and relief.

"So many."

"I'm not in a hurry. You can ask me anything, and I'll tell you the truth." It took me a minute to figure out what to ask first. I respected Dani and didn't want to cross any of her boundaries, but then again, hadn't she just offered to let her boundaries down? Was she really inviting me to ask her *anything*?

"The thing I'm wondering the most is: how do you know for sure if you're gay?"

I was so afraid that if I came out, it would be final and I was worried that maybe I was wrong. I don't remember how she answered that question but what I do remember is she gave me permission to move forward despite my uncertainty. We sat on those steps well into the night. She told me how she met her partner, and how they conceived their daughter. She told me about being pregnant and giving birth. Her life made what I wanted for my life seem possible. She honestly and openly recounted her coming out story without shame. I unabashedly asked her every question that young lesbians would probably search online now, but back then, we didn't have quick access to unlimited information. What we had was each other. I loved the way she shared her life with such confidence. She possessed a sense of belonging and was certain of her self-worth. Her truth was a gift. That night she gave me the language to explain myself and a belief that it would all be ok. I clung to her words and memorized the way she spoke.

When orientation was over, I dragged myself back to Maine to spend the rest of the summer at home. I worked at the same day camp as the previous summer. To my great disappointment, my kissing camp-counselor friend didn't return. I stayed in my childhood bedroom, with the pink and white checkered curtains still on the windows, trying to grow into my newfound identity. Everything about my old life seemed childish to me. My dresser was full of old tee-shirts from every play I'd done in high school, and every club I'd belonged to. My closet was full of prom dresses and stuffed animals. Even my room was still painted pale pink. I wanted to clean it all out and get rid of everything, but much of it still held sentimental value to me. I was caught between wanting a new, fresh start, and holding on to my past.

One day, I pulled everything out of my closet and began sorting things to take to Goodwill. Long before Marie Kondo taught us to evaluate our things on the basis of the joy they brought, I picked up each memento of my childhood and measured its place in my new world view. Almost everything ended up in the to-go pile. When my closet was almost empty, I reached deep into the dark and found one last thing. There, in the corner, sat the sewing machine my mother had given to me for my birthday the year I turned twelve.

I sat down on my bedroom floor in-between piles of old clothes and toys and beheld this machine that had once been a saving grace for my hurting childhood self. It couldn't have been a coincidence that in that summer of coming out, moving on, and in general finding a new voice of independence, the sewing machine emerged as a reminder of another time. The old Singer machine was perfectly preserved in its plastic case and still threaded from the last project I used it for. I pulled it out of the case and found the original user's manual underneath.

The last thing I'd sewed was a red and white gingham dress one summer when I was in high school. My friend had a dress just like it, and I asked my mother if she could show me how to make one. I think she assumed I knew more about sewing than I did. She handed me the pattern and told me to start cutting. I made a mess of it and we had to start over multiple times. We eventually had to return to JOANN Fabrics to buy more material. My mother hated to be wasteful and quickly grew impatient with me. Though she was an expert seamstress, she was not a very patient teacher. This was also evident the time she tried to teach me to drive a stick shift. I nearly drove the car straight into the Scarborough Marsh while my mother yelled incomprehensible syllables about brakes and clutches. It wasn't pretty. The process of sewing with my mother was so frustrating that I put the machine away in my closet, and in the hustle and bustle of high school musicals and swim team practice, I stopped sewing. I leaned back against my closet door and took a deep breath. Should I keep the sewing machine or let it go?

Out of boredom and a pinch of nostalgia, I decided to keep it. Maybe I could pass the time by making something useful. One of my college friends had a quilt on her bed that was made out of her old tee-shirts. Conveniently, next to my sewing machine was a pile of *my* old tee shirts (which, because I am a sentimental person, I felt conflicted about giving away). I'd never made a quilt before, but I imagined the stories all those shirts could tell, couched in the colorful calicos of a grid-patterned bedspread. I gathered up the pile of tee-shirts, got out a piece of paper, and started to design.

That summer, after working full days as a camp counselor, I spent the long evening hours sewing in my room. I carefully cut each tee-shirt into 10x10 inch squares, not realizing how impossible it would be to work with the stretchy jersey fabric. As soon as I cut the squares, the ends curled right up. In order to give the tee-shirts enough structure to sew together, I had to iron on a fusible backing. I lay each shirt down on the ironing board and carefully unfurled the edges. My memories of high school plays—A Little Night Music, Oliver, Fiddler on the Roof—flooded back to me as the iron hissed and melted the adhesive interfacing to the fabric. Swim team, softball team, environmental club, poetry festival, summer camps. There was a tee-shirt for every big memory from my childhood. When I was done, they lay in a neat, flat pile of evenly cut squares.

Over the course of the next few weeks, I sat down every night with the quilt. My sun-kissed hands guided the fabrics through the pulsing needle of the sewing machine, stitching it together piece by piece. I loudly sang along with my cassette tapes of the

Indigo Girls and Dar Williams as I spilled all of my lingering homophobia into my quilt project. I asked myself: *Am I normal to love women? Is there something different inside me now? Am I the same girl who grew up in this house? Is this the same heart that beat millions of times under this roof?* Sometimes I would look into the bathroom mirror and whisper, "I am a lesbian," just to try it on for size. It's hard not to laugh at my 19-year-old self when I think about it now, but identity can be a fragile thing as you are growing into it.

As a nod to my coming out, I stitched red, orange, yellow, green, blue, and purple borders around the quilt squares and arranged them in a rainbow from top to bottom. Since the summer was coming to an end and I was running out of time, I sewed a large piece of fleece to the top of the quilt, then turned it right side out. This was a quick way to finish the quilt and hide the seams. It was a similar process to making the pillow in home-economics class years before. I stitched up the break in the seam and added a few stitches to the center pieces, through the fleece, to hold the quilt together.

The nights grew colder in August, and I wrapped the finished quilt around me as I slept by the open window in my childhood bedroom. The fog horns called to each other in the distance. Though I'm sure I didn't grasp it at the time, there was a profound metaphor at play in the making of that quilt. Each of those tee-shirts represented a piece of my past, and in fusing them with the backing, and sewing them together, I preserved them in space and time. I was trying to let go of some of the relics of my past, while embracing what I had suspected about myself all along. When I returned to UVM for my sophomore year of college, I quit my sorority and joined the Gay, Lesbian, Bisexual, Transgender group on campus. For the first time in my life, I felt like myself.

Chapter 4

My Grandmother's Quilt

2001

Iwent into the basement of my mother's house one hot, humid day looking for fabric. It was 2001, and I had just completed my first year of Teach for America. I'd been placed in a rural North Carolina town, teaching high school English. My girl-friend and I had broken up, and so, with no summer plans, I headed home to Maine to help my mom, who was recovering from surgery. It was my first summer break as a teacher, and all my old high school friends were working. Settled into my old twin bed, with the weeks stretching out before me, I had nothing else to do, and my mother was not up for adventure, so I decided to sew a second quilt.

The fabric box had sat under the workbench, perched on a pair of two-by-fours, since we moved into the house in 1985. It was originally a large TV box. Over the years I had mined its contents for various school projects and costumes for plays. The layers of fabric in the box were like a time capsule. There were scraps from the two Halloweens I dressed as a clown. There was some blue and brown fabric from the year my brother was Robin Hood. My favorite fabrics were the psychedelic, neon patterns out of which my mom had made her bell bottoms in the 70s.

I started digging through the box, pulling out the larger pieces and putting them on the workbench. The box had been well picked over and I dug all the way to the bottom. My fingers landed on a clump of fabric. I pulled it up like a hunk of sod from the garden. It had been there for so long, the weight of all the other fabrics had compressed it into a solid block. The years of fluctuating moisture in the basement had stuck the fabrics together so that they were stiff and bound. I brought the pile under the fluorescent light of the work bench and realized that it wasn't simply stuck together: it was sewn. I unfolded it to reveal an unfinished quilt face that I'd never seen before. The fabrics were cut into small rectangular and square pieces and stitched together by hand. It was a collection of many colors of cotton fabric. There were floral prints and solids, pinks and navy blues. It looked like pieces from every homemade dress I'd seen in family photos and reminded me of the patterns on my grandmother's cooking aprons and the brown stripes of my grandfather's button-down shirts.

Time had not been kind to this piece; it had many stains and in two places appeared to have cigarette burns, which was odd because no one in my family smoked. It was larger than a twin-sized quilt, but not quite big enough for a full-sized bed. The quilt blocks were lined with a grid of antique white panels adorned with tiny dark red flowers. The stitching was even, careful, and done by hand. I wondered what sort of school or Girl Scout project had prompted my mother to craft such an intricate quilt and why she hadn't finished it. Despite its poor condition, there was something enchanting about it. It was clearly a relic from long ago, and I could see that with some care, patience, and probably a good washing, it could be beautiful. I carried it upstairs into the sweltering living room where my mom lay on the couch, beneath a ceiling fan, reading.

"Mom, look at this quilt I found. Did you make it?"

"Let me see it." My mother put down her book and lowered her reading glasses to inspect the fabric. "I didn't make that. No, I think my grandmother made it a long time ago for my mother, or maybe for me. I don't remember. Where did you find it?"

"It was in that old fabric box in the basement."

"Ugh." She furrowed her brow, clearly annoyed that I was poking around in her stuff. "I've been meaning to bring that box to the dump. Everything in it is gross and moldy from when the basement flooded."

"Well, this quilt isn't gross. I mean, it's dirty, but I could wash it and finish it. Can I have it?"

I could have taken up any number of old hobbies that summer; I'm not sure why I was so set on taking up quilting. To date I had only completed the tee-shirt quilt I made after my freshman year in college. The expense of new fabric made my desire to create another quilt cost prohibitive. I needed to find old fabrics to use if I was going to be successful. Plus, there was something very satisfying about using material that would otherwise be thrown away. It was one part environmental conservation, one part thrift, and one part feeling like I was getting away with something.

"No. I want to finish that quilt," my mother replied. "Why don't you leave it on the workbench in the basement and I'll take care of it later."

"Mom! It was in a box you just said you wanted to throw away. You've had this for like thirty years! If you really wanted to finish it, don't you think you would have done it by now? Come on, I'm really bored. I want to sew something. Why don't you let me finish it, and I'll give it to you for Christmas." My mother rolled her eyes and reluctantly agreed.

Though I had every intention of finishing the quilt that summer, I worked on it for only one day, then put it down and forgot about it until I was packing up to drive back to North Carolina at the end of the summer. I figured once I started teaching in the new school year, I would be too busy for sewing, but I had a little space available in my car, so I tossed in my sewing machine and the quilt, just in case.

The humidity dripped down the walls of the cabin in North Carolina that I shared with my friend and fellow teacher, Tara. The rental was on a small, polluted lake right off Route 1, the highway that led to Raleigh. There were about ten other houses on the dirt road which stretched halfway around the water. The makeshift neighborhood was situated between an abandoned mobile home park to the north and an active mobile home park to the south. Packs of stray dogs ran alongside the highway, in and out of the culverts, shamelessly mating on the side of the road. It was an eerily quiet place.

We almost never saw people coming or going from the houses on our street, or from the mobile home park next door. The owner of the cabin had named it the "La-Li Lodge." He was a white man who lived south of Raleigh and only rented to Teach For America teachers because: "You people are the only ones who pay your rent on time." I'm sure that wasn't true, but it was one of his many opinions, and since we needed a place to live, we weren't really in a position to disagree with him about anything. He had built a swinging gate across the driveway that had a dopey looking sign attached to it with a frog leaning against a lily pad. He had hand-carved "La-Li Lodge" in the wood next to the frog. Even though we thought this was kind of a silly name, we referred to that house as the "La-Li Lodge" the entire time we lived there and have ever since.

Despite its downtrodden location, the La-Li Lodge had an expansive deck overlooking the lake with stairs leading down to the water. I spent hours on that deck playing cards with Tara or grading papers beneath the pine trees. We bought a hammock and adorned the space with potted plants and strings of lights. It was a little oasis in an otherwise destitute corner of the town of Franklinton, North Carolina.

My second year of teaching began, and I jumped right back into lesson planning. I went to football games (something I never did when I was in high school), tutored students after school, and generally felt that I was about one hundred and fifty percent more prepared than I'd been the year before. I was teaching a slate of classes from freshman to senior English. My students ranged from fourteen to eighteen years old. Though I was twenty-three, I appeared to be the same age as many of them. Sometimes people would come to the classroom looking for the teacher, and they would look around for a good long time before asking a nearby student if the teacher had stepped out of the room for something.

"She's right there," they would say, pointing at me. I never told the students how old I was because I feared they wouldn't respect me if they knew. It felt strange that they called me "Miss." I felt like I was pretending to be an adult. Incidentally, I was also pretending to be straight because I could have been fired for being gay in North Carolina in 2001. After being completely out in college, it was a lot of pressure and a lot of little lies just to stay employed.

I was just about to make flight arrangements for my return trip to Maine for Thanksgiving when the unimaginable occurred. I first learned that a plane had crashed into the World Trade Center on September 11th from a group of my colleagues huddled together in the teacher's room. Their faces had expressions of shock and horror. When I passed by, one of them asked if I'd heard the news. It was so astonishing to me that when I got back to my classroom, I turned on the TV and fiddled with the bunny ears until the picture came in clearly. Stunning images appeared on the screen. Just moments before, a different plane had crashed into the other tower. Anxious news reporters tried desperately to keep up with the unfolding events. They would begin to tell us about one thing and suddenly be interrupted with breaking news about something else. There was confusion and chaos everywhere around them. One thing became clear—this was not an accident.

Shortly after my next class began, the first tower collapsed as I sat watching with a group of freshmen, in wide-eyed disbelief.

"Where are those buildings, Miss?" one of my students asked. "Is that near here?"

"No." My eyes began to sting at the realization of how many people had just died. "It's in New York City. It's a seven-hour drive from here."

"You cryin', Miss?" I wiped a hot tear from my cheek.

"Yes."

We were glued to the TV screen all morning. I had carefully prepped lesson plans for the week, in a unit plan that left little wiggle room for spontaneity, but I let them all go. How does one continue to teach during a national tragedy? People were jumping to their deaths from the buildings. Terrified pedestrians were running for their lives. I almost couldn't bear to watch the images, but I also couldn't shut it off. We watched as the second tower crumbled to the ground. There were reports that other planes crashed into a field in Pennsylvania and into the Pentagon. I couldn't help but wonder what was next. I was the teacher, but in that moment, I was also just a scared kid standing in the back of my classroom, weeping.

When I finally got to the privacy of my car that afternoon, I cried all the way home. Thousands of people had died in one day. I couldn't stop thinking about their families. These were mothers, fathers, spouses, and children. The grief and confusion over what had taken place was everywhere. It was a loss too huge to comprehend. The attack on our country became the new focus of all our conversations. It was the undercurrent of every lesson I taught. All plans for holiday travel were shelved.

When Thanksgiving week rolled around, Tara drove home to

Erie, Pennsylvania to be with her family, and I was left at the La-Li Lodge for my first holiday alone. On the first day, I did all my laundry, cleaned the whole house, and graded some papers. On the second day I began to wallow in my loneliness and sadness. I had a whole week to reflect on the last few months and I sank into the stinging sorrow of it all. I regretted not driving home for the holiday, but it was too late to change my mind. Our country was hurting, and so was I. Even though it was a different kind of heartache, I recognized it. When the wide open spaces of silence, loss, and confusion had spread out before me in the past, I had filled them with sewing. Grief remembers how to heal.

I dug the quilt from my mother's basement out of my closet and laid it out on the living room floor. The hard work of piecing together the quilt face was done. Not wanting to ruin the integrity of it by quickly finishing it on my sewing machine, I decided to complete it with hand stitching, the way it had been started.

I drove to Bernina's World of Sewing in Raleigh to seek some guidance on whether or not I should try to clean it before I finished it, and what materials to use for the binding and backing. The quilt had a lot of antique pink hues. The woman behind the counter looked up the pattern in one of her quilting books and dated the design to the 1910s or 20s. That sounded about right. My grandmother was born in 1922. She discouraged me from washing it because it was so old and delicate it might fall apart in the process.

"The dirt is a piece of the charm," the saleswoman said to me in her Southern drawl. "It's part of the story." She slid her fingers over the cigarette burns and hand stitched squares. "You know, if you want to honor this quilt's history, you could finish it with all cotton fabrics and batting, that's what they would have used back then, before synthetics were invented." She helped me pick out a pretty dusty rose color for the edging and several yards of 100% cotton material for the batting and backing. I realized as I left the store that her suggestion to use all cotton tripled the cost of my materials, but decided not to worry about it. It was my entertainment for the week, paid for by the equivalent of my entertainment budget for three months.

I moved all the furniture to the sides of the living room and stretched the quilt out again. It really was a pretty piece, and in remarkably good condition considering the box in which it was found. I looked out at the lake through the sliding glass doors. I loved how the autumn colors lasted until Thanksgiving in North Carolina. Back in New England, it could snow any day.

It had been ten weeks since the 9/11 attacks and our country was still reeling. I thought about all the families who would be sitting down to their Thanksgiving dinners, missing a parent or a child. My heart broke for them. I threaded the needle and began to stitch. I tried to make my stitches small and even. Within minutes, my pointer finger was sore from pushing the needle through the layers of fabric. This was going to be harder than I thought.

My mentor teacher, Zelma Williams, invited me over for Thanksgiving dinner with her family, but aside from that one meal, I spent the rest of the week alone, painstakingly finishing the quilt by hand and processing the events of the last few months. I would sit on the futon in our living room with the quilt on my lap and push the quilting needle in and out of the cotton material. My fingers were raw and punctured many times over. Even the back of a quilting needle is sharp, and I didn't have a thimble that fit my finger.

I found the places where the aged thread ended, and that is where I began. The old stitches on the quilt face were mostly neat and even, but every so often a stitch would slant to the side—a nod to a momentary distraction from decades ago. The sheer imperfection of the original quilter's hand gave me permission to accept my own. *It's ok if I have some weird looking stitches*, I told myself, *for the sake of authenticity.*

When it was done, I laid it on my bed and slept under it for just one night. It had given me a peaceful week of sewing and relaxing at home. Even though it was fragile, I figured it was meant to be used.

When Christmas rolled around, I drove back home to Maine and we prepared to visit my grandmother. She was spending Christmas in a rehab hospital, recovering from a fall.

"Mom," I asked, "would you mind if I gave that old quilt I found in the basement to Grandma instead of you? I finished it over Thanksgiving. I think it would mean a lot to her."

"I think that's a great idea. She's very excited to see you, Jenny." I was excited to see her too.

My Grandma's name was Helen, and I was her only grand-daughter. My grandpa died of Parkinson's disease when I was young. At family holiday gatherings, my brother and all the boy cousins would retreat after dinner to play video games. My mom and her sisters would command the kitchen, laughing and talking so fast no one could get a word in, and my uncles would drink scotch and talk about whatever middle aged men talked about in the 80s . . . Politics? Running marathons? Computer programming? Who knows. Usually that just left Grandma and me sitting at the empty dinner table or cuddled up on the couch to talk about my life and my friends. Sometimes she would tell stories or recite poetry for me. She knew many poems by heart, and there was always a sparkle in her eye as she spoke the seem-ingly endless lines.

She lived alone in a red ranch-style house in Guilford, Vermont. Before my grandpa died, he used to take me fishing up the dirt road at a little place where a stream dumped out of a cul-vert and rounded out a cold-water pool which I named "The Fish Dish." We would sit on top of that culvert and catch trout after hungry trout with crickets we'd hunted down in the fields behind my grandparents' house. When we got home with a basket full of mostly dead fish, my grandmother would cut their heads off, no matter how tiny they were, and gut them with skill. Her childhood on a dairy farm in Lake Placid, New York in the 1920s and 30s had left her with the grit of a pioneer woman and a no-nonsense approach to life. She ate all her meals with the fine silver inherited from my grandfather's family, because she believed that nice things should be used; and no brook trout was too small to throw in the frying pan for dinner.

Grandma always made me feel like I was the most important person in the room. She asked great questions and would remember details from my responses for years. She was still asking about the sorority sisters I'd brought home for Easter my freshman year of college, and I wasn't even in touch with them anymore. I had grown especially close to her during my college years in her home state of Vermont.

For a fiercely independent woman, being confined to a hospital bed for Christmas was especially disheartening. Despite this, my grandma smiled and was gracious to the attendants who moved in and out of her room on Christmas Eve as we gathered at her bedside and tried to pretend that we were having fun. I wished we were the sort of family that would sing carols together and laugh about the days of yore, but we just sat awkwardly in clunky chairs with plastic cushions and made small talk.

When it was time to open presents, I saved the quilt for last. Wrapped in brown paper packaging and tied with a red bow, it looked like a gift that might have been under a tree in the 1920s. I gently placed it on her lap. The present looked bulky and large in front of her shrinking frame. She carefully opened the package and unfolded the quilt.

"Do you recognize it?" I asked.

"A little," she responded, "but I can't quite place it."

"Isn't that the quilt your mother made for you, Mom?" asked my mother. Grandma unfolded the quilt a bit more.

"No. It wouldn't have been made by my mother. She wasn't a quilter." She ran her hands over the top, her papery thin skin patting the seams of the quilt squares. "I haven't seen this in years. I think it was made by my grandmother, for me." There was a long pause. "She probably died before she had a chance to finish it. See these cigarette burns? She was a smoker." She paused again to unfold the quilt a bit more and marvel at the neatly finished binding.

"I found the top part in Mom's basement last summer," I said. "It was stitched together by hand, so I finished it without my machine. I used all-cotton fabric too, to keep it authentic." I wanted more than anything to impress my grandma. She looked up at me and smiled, showing the large, discolored teeth of a woman who had had little dental care until she was an adult.

"Yes, you did." Grandma's eyes always looked a little teary, the way old people's eyes often do. But this time, I wondered if maybe her eyes were full of actual tears. She had a faraway look as if she was trying to remember something. Then she said with nostalgia, "My mother probably thought she would finish it someday, and I must have thought I would too." She pulled a fabric handkerchief from her bathrobe pocket and blew her nose.

"I think I found it when you moved out of the house in Brattleboro after I got married," my mother said. "I probably thought I would finish it too!"

We had a good laugh over the fact that this quilt had been passed down through five generations of women in our family who all intended, at some point, to finish it. At last, I'd found it in a box marked for the dump eighty years after it was started by my great-great grandmother.

After she returned home from the hospital, my grandmother displayed the quilt on the bed where I always slept, which also happened to be the bed most visible to anyone walking down the hall. It was the source of much conversation and delight for my grandma in her final years. Its creation and completion were like the quilt face and quilt backing of her life, and the stuff in between was a journey of a thousand little stitches of chance and intention, intertwined with love.

I do believe that my grandmother's quilt is the greatest gift I have ever given. It brought such immense joy to the one person I felt understood me better than anyone else. I had no idea, when I was carefully stitching it together, that it would mean so much to her to have this family heirloom restored. It was the first gift I had ever given that had a truly unexpected outcome, but it wasn't the last.

Chapter 5
Liz

After my two-year commitment with Teach For America was over, I returned to Vermont and my college stomping ground. I'd left there in a hurry after graduating in 2000, and it was refreshing to be back with my old friends in the beautiful Northeast. I took a job teaching at an elementary school in Montpelier, the country's smallest state capitol.

Union School reminded me of the elementary school I attended in Maine. It was a two-story brick building built in 1939 by the Civilian Conservation Corps. My classroom had freshly polished maple floors and a wall of enormous windows that stretched all the way to the ceiling. The city streets and church steeples of Montpelier, bedecked in colorful leaves or freshly fallen snow, stretched out beyond my classroom like a holiday card.

On the sunny February day I turned thirty, my coworkers decorated my door and left me flowers and a card on my desk. At lunch, we gathered around my reading table and my teammate MaryCatharine served my favorite dessert—chocolate chip cookies with coffee for dipping. Before the meal was over, MaryCatharine turned to me and said, "I think this is gonna be your year, Jen." I didn't exactly know what she meant, but she was a wise friend, and if she wanted to cast an omen of positive change over my thirty-first year, I was inclined to accept it.

That fall, my beloved grandmother died, and as the year drew to a close, I began to think MaryCatharine had really missed the mark. Then, in December, I answered a personal ad in the *Seven Days* newspaper online. The woman's name was Liz, and in the picture that accompanied the ad she was posing on top of a mountain with a yellow Labrador retriever. She was also single, and living in Burlington.

She responded with, "I think we've met before, on the commuter bus, in college."

It turned out that we had both been in the UVM class of 2000. We had the same major and many of the same friends, but we never took a class together. I went back to the journal I kept in college to see if I had written anything about her, and indeed I had. Liz and I had met once when we were seniors in college, and we didn't like each other! I described her as "curt and unfriendly," and misspelled her last name. I find this endlessly funny now. Our paths had probably crossed dozens of times in our four years at UVM and it wasn't until our last semester that we noticed each other. It was January and I was riding the commuter bus to campus when looked up from my book to see a sporty looking woman with big glasses and short blond hair staring back at me.

"Are you Jen Ellis?" Her tone was flat and apathetic.

"Yes."

"Oh, Lisa Schnell keeps asking me if I know you. I'm Liz Fenton"

"Yeah, she's asked me the same thing." Lisa Schnell was an English professor at UVM. We exchanged pleasantries for a few minutes then we got off the bus heading in opposite directions. We had both applied for Teach For America and she hadn't gotten in. She later told me that she thought I was too bold and obviously gay. I had assumed she was gay too, given her boyish haircut and handsome appearance, but it would still be a few years before she came out.

Part of the reason I responded to her personal ad was the dog in the picture looked a lot like my dog. I figured that if we didn't hit it off, at least our dogs could play. It turned out that the dog belonged to her friend and she actually had a cat. I tease Liz that the first thing I wrote about her was how much I disliked her, and she teases me that she lured me into a date by pretending to have a dog. Despite these early mishaps, we agreed to meet for coffee.

I knew I wanted to marry Liz the day I met her (for the second time). Our first date was at the Starbucks on Church Street a few days after Christmas. As we waited in line to buy our coffees, we talked about our holidays.

"I spent Christmas with my friends and their kids here in Vermont," I told her. "Then I went to Maine and New Hampshire and spent some time with my mom, dad, and stepmother." We ordered our drinks and were paying at the counter.

"I spent Christmas with my father and brother in Bomoseen," was her response.

"Were you able to see your mother too?"

"Well, she's dead, so that would have been awkward." The Starbucks cashier dropped my credit card.

"I'm sorry," the cashier said. "I wasn't expecting that." I looked at Liz and she was smiling uncomfortably.

"I wasn't expecting that either," I admitted.

"Yeh, I'm never quite sure what to say when people ask about my mom. I guess I shouldn't lead with a dead mom joke." We laughed awkwardly. It was not funny, but Liz could cut a block of ice with her humor, and that was the first thing I loved about her. The shocked cashier rang us up and we found a seat near the window.

"My mom died of leukemia a couple years ago, it's actually what brought me back to Vermont."

Even though I didn't tell her in that moment, I was also grieving. In the three months since my grandmother had died, I had combed through all her old pictures and thought of dozens of questions I wished I'd asked her. Christmas had felt empty. It was a struggle to imagine my world without her, but that world was unfolding, and she wasn't in it.

I had a therapist once who told me that she thought grief was the most beautiful emotion. I found that idea very confusing until she explained that we grieve because we love. Grief is the price we pay for opening our hearts to someone else.

"It's worth the price, don't you think?" my therapist asked.

"I guess so."

I've pondered on that idea for years. I had some doubts about it, and yet, there I was, sitting at a coffee shop in snowy downtown Burlington, looking into the eyes of someone I was already beginning to care for. It's hard to see the bright light of love through the fog of grief, but we are wired to look for it anyway.

Liz was an assistant professor in the English department at the University of Vermont. I swooned. I'd always wanted to marry a John-Boy Walton literary type, and here she was, sitting across from me, drinking overpriced coffee. After Liz's unusual ice-breaker, we talked for five hours. I had to stop at the ATM to withdraw extra money to pay for the extended parking time in the downtown garage.

On a blistering hot day in July, two summers later, we were married at Kingsland Bay State Park. Neither of us wanted to somberly walk down the aisle linking arms with our fathers. We weren't that traditional. As a shout out to Liz's epic dance moves, we decided to dance in to our ceremony to the song "TiK ToK" by Ke$ha. I was worried that my dad wouldn't want to do this with me, but in what was probably an enormous act of love, he agreed. Everyone in our wedding party danced in that day and by the time the music ended, all of our guests were dancing too. There were about a hundred other people at the park and it wasn't until Liz and I were standing at the altar that I realized there was a crowd of total strangers cheering for us. We were both overcome with tears at the sheer joy of the moment. Several boats in the bay were honking their horns. We reached for each other's hands and laughed.

We honored Liz's mother at our reception by inviting the organization Be The Match to set up a table. They collected mouth swabs all afternoon from our guests, signing them up for the National Marrow Donor Program. The volunteers later told us that they registered more bone marrow donors that day than at any event before.

We sometimes joke that our marriage is a seven year arrangement. Liz told me once that she thinks it's silly to believe you should love just one person forever.

"I mean, what if you become a serial killer? Am I supposed to just stick it out?"

"For richer, for poorer, in sickness, and in health . . ." I reminded her.

"We never said, *in serial killer, or in not serial killer.*" She had a valid point, but I knew the day I married her that seven years would not be long enough for me to love everything about her.

Chapter 6
How the Mittens Began

I taught in Montpelier for five years before landing a job in Westford, Vermont, a rural town much closer to home. I was the first classroom teacher hired in Westford in a long time. Over the previous fifteen years, the town's population had been steadily declining. Certain areas of the town were zoned so that land previously owned by large farms couldn't be subdivided to less than ten acres, and in some parts, less than five acres. The trailer park closed, and housing prices soared. Owning a house in Chittenden County was already an expensive proposition. Many families with young kids were quickly priced out of the small town. This led to murmurs of closing the school, which was ironically one of the big draws to the town for many families in the first place.

The low enrollment of the Westford School put the school budget under fire every March at Town Meeting Day. It got to the point that when teachers retired from Westford, the school just didn't replace them, and by 2011, the classes at the school had gone from three sections of every grade to just one. Westford had one school and its own school district, so there was a tremendous amount of local control over the school. However, it was a tenuous place to work because all it would take was three to four families with kids to leave town and the school would have to fire another teacher. The only reason they hired me in 2011 was that two teachers retired the previous spring, and that year there was an unusually large second grade class, which created what they called a "bubble year." I was hired to reduce the class sizes for the other teachers. I learned after I had already quit my job in Montpelier that the position was likely to be cut the next year.

The rest of the teachers had been at the school for so long, they were like a tightly knit family. They got together for each other's birthdays and for holiday gatherings. They had been at each other's weddings twenty-five years before, and their children had grown up and played together. I mentioned in my interview the previous spring that I was getting married over the summer. A few weeks before I was set to begin my new job, one of my colleagues emailed me to ask if I was taking my new husband's last name. She wanted to order new name plates for all the doors in the primary wing. I explained that I was marrying a woman and would be keeping my name. I noticed when I started that there was no new name plate beside my door. I tried not to read too much into it, but I was pretty sure I knew why.

I started my job at the Westford School at the age of thirty-three, a newly married lesbian with no kids. I didn't exactly fit in with my new colleagues. Even though some of them were very kind to me, most of them were not my friends. In Montpelier, I was on a team of five second-grade teachers and we had a close bond. We planned together, ate lunch together, celebrated each other's birthdays by decorating classroom doors and making our favorite desserts. Every holiday season we had a big cookie swap and baking competition judged by the slightly quirky tech team. We frequently had potluck luncheons and staff gatherings where everyone was invited. Most of my first year at Westford, I felt like I had made a huge mistake giving up the colleagueship I had in

Montpelier to teach in a school closer to home. I was very lonely in my new school, until I met Lise-Anne.

Every morning Lise-Anne would drop her daughter Anna off at the classroom door and chat with the other parents or with me about all the goings on. She was president of the PTA, head of the eighth-grade class trip fundraising committee, organizer of the school's ski and ride program, leader of the parent-led Nature Program, and the mayor of the town. Actually, that last one isn't true, although if Westford had had a mayor, I am certain it would have been Lise-Anne.

Lise-Anne is a tall woman with brown hair and big glasses. She wore solid colored V-neck shirts with some sort of knit shawl or cowl draped over her shoulders every day. Not only was Lise-Anne in charge of just about everything, but she was an avid knitter and crafter. She showed up to her kids' soccer games with a knitting basket, and within the course of one game, she would have completed half a scarf while socializing with everyone and their dog. I mean this literally, she *loved* dogs. She knew the names of people's dogs before she knew the names of their owners. On the sidelines of the games, she would plan fundraisers for the school, resolve conflicts in the community, and make ten new friends, all to the beat of her clicking knitting needles. She had perfected the act of simultaneously spinning both kinds of a yarn.

Lise-Anne's husband, Scott, was on the school board and was therefore, essentially, my boss. You might think that all the power her family had in the community might go to Lise-Anne's head, or that she might be catty, but she wasn't. In true Vermont fashion, she was just a friendly, down-to-earth woman who cared about her community, didn't wear make-up, and was easy to collaborate with. I knew the first time I met her that I wanted to be her friend.

It wasn't entirely wise or ethical to befriend the parent of a student, but the friendship landscape at my new job was barren. I broke my own professional boundary and forged a friendship with Lise-Anne out of loneliness and necessity, and also the fact that she was incredibly fun to be with.

One winter day when Lise-Anne was leading my class in a nature lesson, we were bundling the kids up to go outside when she noticed my mittens.

"Did you make those mittens out of old sweaters?" she asked. Lise-Anne was very direct, in a non-threatening way. She peered at me from behind her glasses, her highlighted bangs neatly feathered across her forehead.

"No, I bought these at a shop in Burlington. They do kind of look like old sweaters though, don't they?" For years I had been on a quest to find mittens that fit my large hands. Even men's mittens felt too small for me. These mittens were made from colorful knit cotton and were lined with flannel. They were the closest I had come to mittens that fit, and they were still too small. They were also boxy, and the cuffs were too loose. When I went sledding with my students, I almost always ended up with a handful of snow inside my mittens.

"I've been experimenting with making mittens out of wool sweaters, see?" Lise-Anne showed me her mittens and let me try them on. They didn't fit much better than mine. They were too loose around the wrist, and they were so short I had to curl my fingers to pull them all the way on.

"They're a little small for me."

"Oh, I know—it's so hard to find mittens meant to fit larger hands." She was singing my song here.

"Where do you get the sweaters?"

"Lots of places. Yard sales, thrift stores. People don't seem to wear wool that much anymore. Do you sew?" she asked.

"I do, but I'm not really that good at it. I mostly sew quilts."

"You should try this mitten pattern I found online, it's really cool. The mittens turn out a little wonky, so you might have to fiddle with it, but I like using the old sweaters."

Truthfully, I wasn't very interested in doing this. I already had a lot on my plate, but the next day Lise-Anne showed up to drop off Anna, and she brought me a pair of mittens she had made and the pattern she'd found online for free. The mittens fit badly, but the pattern looked doable. I was curious to see if I could make them.

On the way home from school, I stopped at the Salvation Army thrift store in the run-down building on Pearl Street in Essex Junction. They had one wool sweater. It was red with a blue zig zag pattern. Someone had clearly washed and shrunk it. It cost five dollars. While I was there, I also picked up a used fleece pullover.

Liz was very amused by my new project.

"That sweater is so ugly. You're doing the world a favor by cutting it up."

I had to admit, she had a valid point.

I cut the pattern out of the paper and used it to cut the pieces out of the sweater. Then I did the same with the fleece. I assembled the mittens and tried them on. They were so small and misshapen, I could barely put my hands in. I brought them over to Liz to try on and she scowled.

"No offense, Babe, but these are pretty bad!" Liz was always good for honest feedback.

"I know. What a terrible design."

"It's a good idea at least," Liz offered. I looked at the pattern again. This time I retraced it and made certain parts bigger and other parts smaller. I used what was left of the sweater to make a modified pair. The end result was better than the first, but not by much. I realized that making mittens had a steep learning curve.

The next day I brought my second pair of mittens into school to show Lise-Anne.

"You're quick! These are great." Lise-Anne was so positive and optimistic.

"They barely fit my hands."

"Yeah, like I said the pattern needs some work." She mulled over my crafting for a moment and then said, "Do you want to come over to my house this weekend and sew with me? I bet we could fix this pattern and make some cool mittens."

Did I want to go to Lise-Anne's house and hang out while sewing? Of course I did!

"Do you have any more sweaters at home?" she asked.

"No, but I could go look for some more after school."

We made a plan for Sunday afternoon, and she gave me her cell phone number. I was beyond excited to go to her house. She was like a local celebrity, and she was going to hang out with me! For the next couple of days, I scoured every thrift store in the area looking for nice sweaters that we could tinker with. They were surprisingly hard to come by. I found three.

It was a mix of snow and sleet outside on that January day in 2012 when I drove out to Lise-Anne's house. Scott greeted me at the door and helped me to carry in my sewing machine and supply box. I showed Lise-Anne the sweaters I'd found, and she showed me a couple she had. Lise-Anne's house was cozy, and lived in. There was a fire glowing through the windows of the woodstove in the center of the living room. Steam drifted from the spout of a cast iron kettle on top.

"Do you want some tea?" she asked. "How about some chips and salsa?" We settled in at her kitchen table with our snacks and drinks and all our crafting supplies. We only had half of the table because the other half was piled high with yarn, knitting needles, patterns and other projects Lise-Anne had in the works.

"Never mind the mess," she said as she saw me looking around.

"Oh my gosh, don't worry about it. My house is a disaster right now."

Her house wasn't very messy, but it was clear that she hadn't cleaned up just for me. My mother had always cleaned our house from top to bottom before anyone could come over, and I had inherited that stressful trait. Not Lise-Anne though. Her house was casual and comfortable. She had three kids, a dog, a husband, and a crafting addiction. I made a note to myself that it wouldn't be necessary to scrub the floors before she came to my house for the first time.

We cut the arms and cuffs off the sweaters and discarded the parts that were stained or moth eaten. Then we discussed the mittens we'd already made. They were too small in some parts and too large in others. We redesigned the pattern to fit our large hands and got to work. Despite our careful planning, the first few pairs of mittens we made were still not very comfortable.

The whole time we worked, we talked. It was the first time I really appreciated the tradition of the quilting bee. We were join-ing in a sacred history of women crafting together. The peace I felt just sitting there, getting to know Lise-Anne and sewing the mittens was like a meditation. I found myself telling her stories about my life that I hadn't told anyone in years. Her life stories were fascinating to me, too. After a few more adjustments, we finally made a pair of mittens that fit; and they *really* fit. They were warm and comfortable.

"That's amazing," Lise-Anne said.

"I know!"

"I bet we could sell these at craft fairs."

"You mean like church bazaars?" I raised my eyebrows and grimaced. The thought of this brought me right back to the First Congregational Church in my hometown that had a holi-day bazaar every year. It was always a crowded affair with lots of old ladies selling crocheted doilies and pastel baby hats. The only good thing there was the fudge. "I can't really imagine myself doing that."

"There's actually good money to be made at craft fairs nowa-days. I have a pop-up tent at the Underhill Harvest Market every year."

"I love the Underhill Harvest Market!" I exclaimed.

"I sell scarves, hats, and pins made from bottle caps. It's really fun."

The Underhill Harvest Market is probably the Vermontiest thing in Vermont. It is always held the last weekend of September when the foliage is at its peak. The people who live in the houses along Route 15 in Underhill and the neighboring town of Jericho hold yard sales and bake sales. The town green is filled with a huge circus-style tent where community members run a cider press all day. You can buy fresh hot cider, apple cider donuts, and listen to the fiddlers and folk singers performing on the lawn in front of the church. In another tent they sell home-made pies and cheese. Every hour a very large man stands in the center of it all and yells, "We got corn! Fresh hot corn! With butter. And pizza! Support your local soccer team! Hot pizza! Fresh squeezed lemonade, and BEANS! Baked beans!" He always ends with "Baked beans!"

"My spot is in the back of the field near the kids' games," Lise-Anne continued.

"I've actually never gone into the field. I usually go from the hot soup tent to the live music tent and try to hit the Clutter Barn on my way out."

"Ooooooh, I love the Clutter Barn!" she said.

"Me too!" A long conversation ensued about the treasures we had both acquired over the years from the large two-story building known as the Clutter Barn.

"I once found an entire dinnerware set from Pottery Barn at the end of the weekend. Everything was fifty percent off!" I said.

"I've found whole skeins of wool for a dollar a bag!"

"That's amazing!"

"I know!"

"I always stop at the yard sales on my way there for extra snow pants and boots for my students, too," I confessed. "We never seem to have enough."

"And then there's the cookie basement!"

"And the whoopie pies!" We both agreed that the whoopie pies in the cookie basement of the United Church of Underhill were basically the best creation on earth. My mouth was still watering just thinking about them when we finally found our way back to selling the mittens.

"Why don't we make a bunch, bring them next fall, and see what happens?"

"Do you really think people would buy mittens in September?"

"We'll find out."

This was about as far from the stuffy church bazaars of the 1980s as I could imagine, so I agreed.

"Let's get together next Sunday and make some more." Lise-Anne suggested. My first thought was, why not make more right now? Then I looked out the window and saw that it was already dark. I'd been at Lise-Anne's house for five hours. We were having so much fun talking and sewing together that I hadn't noticed the time. As I drove home on the dirt roads of Westford, the blackness of the night was eerie. This sleepy little town, which was so stunningly beautiful in the day, was a barren wilderness at night, with no street lights and almost no one on the road. A deer leapt out onto the road and trotted across in front of my car. I quickly slowed down.

"Where there's one, there's two," my dad used to say. I came to a complete stop and, sure enough, another deer jumped up from the ditch. It stopped and looked directly at me before continuing on.

My grandmother used to watch the deer in the field behind her house in Southern Vermont. The dirt road she lived on was very similar to the one I was driving on now. Deer always made me think of how much I loved her. I've always wondered if deer were a sign that something good was about to happen.

Over the next few months, Lise-Anne and I met every Sunday

to make mittens together. She was literally the busiest person I knew, but she always made time for me. We could easily have made the mittens on our own, but it was so much fun to make them together. We divided up the labor into two parts: I designed the wool combinations and sewed the outer layer of the mitten, and she cut and sewed the inner fleece part. Then we would both do the last part, which we called "stuff and cuff." This was where we put the two parts together and bound them with the cuff of the original sweater.

Lise-Anne showed me all kinds of little tricks for how to use my sewing machine more effectively, and we strategized about our mitten sales.

"We need a name for our product," Lise-Anne said one Sunday afternoon. "Like Vermont Sweater Mittens or something."

"How about Swittens, you know, a portmanteau of sweater and mittens?" I suggested.

"Ooooh, I like that!"

We designed and ordered a business card to attach to the mittens. Everything was starting to fall into place. One spring day I was driving past a yard sale in my neighborhood and saw two old-fashioned Radio Flyer sleds with red metal blades. An idea flashed into my mind. I immediately pulled over. My neighbor sold them to me for five dollars apiece. The next day I went to the hardware store nearby and purchased small metal screw-in hooks. Using the mittens as guides, I spaced out the hooks one mitten's length apart on the wooden slats of the sleds and screwed them in. Then I fashioned a wooden kickstand on the back of each sled with a hinge so that they could stand upright on their own. Each sled could hold up to twenty pairs of mittens. It was the perfect display.

The next Sunday I brought them to Lise-Anne's house and she was dutifully impressed with my ingenuity.

"My mother has some of those sleds in her garage, I could ask her if we can have them. They haven't been used in years. We should drive up to Quebec and visit my mom on her farm!" Lise-Anne had talked about her mother in Canada before, and the thought of driving up to Quebec to meet her sounded like a fun adventure. Over the past few months, Lise-Anne had become one of my favorite friends.

Two weeks later, on a weekend in late May, we went on a road trip to Canada, with Anna in the back seat watching a movie on her Kindle. It was a two-hour drive, but it didn't seem long because we had plenty of Westford news to catch up on. We were getting a new principal in the fall and the next year my class was being switched from a multi-age first and second grade to just a straight second grade group. The big topic of conversation, however, was my class's upcoming camp-out, which everyone was very excited about and had become the talk of the town.

I read in a teaching book once that the best teachers were the ones who found a way to share their favorite hobby with their students. My favorite hobby was camping. Our school was situated on acres and acres of beautiful land, just perfect for a camp out. When I broached the topic of doing an overnight with my coworker Marie, she aggressively squashed the idea.

"I have no interest in sleeping in a tent," she declared curtly. "I want to take the kids bike riding on the bike path. That's what the first and second grade classes have always done."

"But I have a lot of kids whose parents can't take a day off of work; they won't be able to go if they don't have their own chaperone."

"They'll figure it out, they always do," she insisted. That was that. It was frustrating to be starting all over again in a new school where everything had to stay the way it always had been.

Despite Marie's resistance, our principal encouraged me to plan the campout anyway. He thought it was a marvelous idea. Lise-Anne was fascinated by all of this and delighted by my willingness to shake things up and try something new. Anna was Lise-Anne's third child to attend the Westford School. It was clear to her that some new energy on staff would be good for the school. We discussed the elaborate camp-out plan most of the way to Canada.

"I admit—I'm with Marie. I don't camp. I'm making Scott do it."

"I think there are a few other parents in your boat," I laughed. "I've lined up the gym teacher and a couple other teachers in the building to act as chaperones if we need them. But honestly, the only kid whose mom or dad can't come has a family friend coming instead. One girl is also bringing her older sister, who's an adult."

"What are you going to do if families don't have tents?"

"Some families are doubling up in large tents, and I have a spare tent and sleeping bag that I loaned to one family."

"You really have it all figured out, don't you?" Lise-Anne said.

"Well, I can't just wing it! These things have to be carefully planned."

Talking with Lise-Anne about my new job at the Westford School was like a soothing balm to what had been a rocky start. Marie was supposed to be my teammate, but we didn't get along. She disapproved of my desire to be openly gay at school, and I disapproved of her desire to sing Christmas carols during morning meeting. I really wanted to get along with her, but not at the expense of hiding who I was. The further I got into that first year at my new school, the more deeply I regretted leaving my old school. Lise-Anne and I shared many of the same impressions of the school and the town. She always had witty things to say or a keen observation about something.

We had lunch with Lise-Anne's mom and helped plant seeds in her garden. On our way out she gladly gave Lise-Anne the two Radio Flyers hanging in her garage.

"I'm gonna be eighty next week!" she said proudly, "I think my sledding days are over."

We laughed and headed home. In a nearby town, we stopped to stock up on Canadian chocolate.

"You're so funny," Lise-Anne commented, "There's nothing special about Canadian chocolate."

"It's a novelty. They should sell this stuff in the states, I personally would keep their market in the black!"

Riding shotgun in Lise-Anne's big SUV to Canada was one of my favorite days that spring. It was so nice to have a new friend and a new hobby. The next week, I sat with my class on Friday night up on a hill behind the school and watched the sun set behind the forested hills. I was determined to extend my classroom into this natural world. We roasted marshmallows and went on a spooky night walk in the woods. The field behind where we camped hadn't been mowed yet and there were millions of fireflies lighting up the dark. It was magical. For the first time that school year, I felt deeply connected to my new school and community.

That summer, Lise-Anne invited Liz and me to spend some time with her family at their cottage in Maine. We played Spoons with her kids and their cousins well into the night. Lise-Anne sat in a wicker chair nearby, knitting by the lamp light. She had to be the craftiest person I knew. It seemed like she could make anything. She had carefully woven a creative life in every pocket of her existence. Before I met Lise-Anne, crafting had been my way out of sorrow, but I realized that night that Lise-Anne didn't craft out of sorrow, she crafted out of joy. I was actually a little thankful for my feelings of isolation at my new job. My loneliness had pushed me into the orbit of a different kind of teacher.

"You know, if you stick with Westford for a few more years, Jen, many of the teachers will retire. You might find that the new teachers you hire will be easier to work with," Lise-Anne advised. And that is exactly what happened.

Chapter 7
Lifelines

2012

Have you ever been to Portland, Maine? Have you ever stood outside the four-story tall brick buildings on Commercial Street in the Old Port? The wide sidewalk is made of cobblestone and the buildings face Portland Harbor. The people watching is exceptional, and the sounds and smells of the working waterfront district are a step back in time. Long before this area became a trendy shopping district, lobstermen and fishing boats would load and unload nearby, preparing to sell their fresh catch from Casco Bay. Have you ever noticed the parking spots in front of those buildings? Well, I can tell you that those parking spots are a pretty nice place to sit and wait for a delivery of sperm.

In early April 2012, Liz and I sat in one of those parking spots in front of the brick building, waiting for a text from our sperm donor. We had been married less than a year, and we were eager to get started with the baby making because of my age. I had turned thirty-four in February.

"Done!" was all the text from our sperm donor said. I scrunched up my nose and grinned at Liz. This was definitely the strangest thing we'd ever done. I had butterflies in my stomach.

The gift of sperm is perhaps one of the most bizarre forms of generosity imaginable. I mean, as lesbians, we had spent most of our lives avoiding sperm, and yet here we were on the sidewalk in Portland, receiving it as gift. It wasn't just *any* gift either, it was a gift that would create a human life. It was the gift of assistance in making a dream of ours come true. It was a gift freely given by a man we barely knew.

Our sperm donor emerged from a nondescript green door carrying a small brown bag in his hands. He looked relaxed in his sweatpants and coat. I tried not to think about what he had just been doing. He was tall, with dark brown hair and bright blue eyes. We approached him and he gave us a warm smile.

"It's nice to see you again," he said. We had met up with him a month earlier to sign a donor contract that basically stated he was giving us the sperm and wanted nothing in return. We hoped to leave the door open for our future child to know this man, because we liked him so much. In fact, I had known of him for over twenty years, as he was a friend of a friend from high school. This friend had connected us with him after a mini reunion the previous Christmas, when we'd recounted the slightly hilarious failed attempts of trying to find a known donor among our friends in Vermont.

"It's nice to see you too," we said as he handed us a brown paper gift bag from Bull Moose Records, a Portland music store. Everything about him was so cool; even the bag in which he toted his fresh sperm was from an indie music shop. The sterile cup inside contained the murky liquid we needed to quickly put to use. Liz reached inside the bag to hold the cup and keep the sperm warm as we exchanged pleasantries. It was a mild day, the sun was shining brightly, and we stood together on the sidewalk, trying to think of witty things to say. We wanted him to have confidence that his genetic material was going to a good home. We wanted him to think we were loving, kind, and smart. We wanted him to like us.

"Well, I'm off to get a bagel," he declared abruptly, and we said our goodbyes.

Do you know how long is an appropriate amount of time to make polite conversation with a man who has just given you fresh sperm? No? Neither did we. The exchange probably took less than five minutes. As we drove away, we immediately started cracking jokes.

"Can you imagine what anyone watching that interaction might have been thinking?" I asked.

"Yeah—that was a classy drug deal in a Bull Moose bag!" We broke into peals of laughter. Why was this so funny?

"Sperm, the miracle drug!"

"I think sperm may be more expensive than drugs," Liz said.

"But is it as addictive?"

"I'm not sure getting addicted to sperm is in the cards for us." I was laughing so hard now that tears were rolling down my face.

We drove as quickly as we could over the bridge to South Portland and to my childhood friend Jessie's house. Luckily, her family was not home, because the awkward turkey baster moment that happened next was everything you have probably imagined an at-home lesbian insemination to be. It was part hilarity, part disgust. We didn't realize that fresh sperm smelled like bleach. Neither of us had much previous experience with sperm. I expected there to be more liquid in the cup.

"So, what do we do now?" I asked Liz after we were done.

"Wait?" Liz suggested. We lay on the bed for what seemed like a long time. I imagined the little spermies swimming to meet the big 'ol egg that all of my ovulation tests indicated was on her way down my fallopian tube.

"Go for the gold, guys!" I said.

"Are you talking to the sperm?"

"I'm offering them words of encouragement."

"I don't think sperm can hear," Liz said.

"It's not for them, it's for me."

There was a long period of silence before we decided it was time to get up and do something. We had driven all the way to South Portland from our home in Vermont for this one special delivery, and the deed was done. We now had the rest of the weekend to have some fun in Maine. We lived it up that weekend. There were bagels from Scratch Bakery, lobsters from the Harbor Fish Market, and long walks on the beach. It felt like a sneaky escapade to be traveling around my hometown, trying not to be noticed by my mother. We had decided that we wanted the pregnancy to be a surprise for her. Plus, most people don't involve their mothers in their conception adventures.

In between enjoying delicious Maine cuisine and frequenting all the coastal hotspots, we scouted out the thrift stores, looking for sweaters to make mittens. From Goodwill to the Salvation Army, we scoured every clothing section in Southern Maine. The best sweaters were the used L.L. Bean ones. They were thick and warm. They came in handsome blues with Nordic prints. Because it is the home of L.L. Bean, Maine has more of that company's castoffs in its thrift stores than any of the stores in Vermont.

There was something very thrilling about looking for these sweaters, the same something that makes me love yard sales. I once found a hand-knit sweater with the name "Jessie" on the back. It was sky blue and had pictures of tents and campfires on it. I gave it to my stepsister Jessie as a joke for Christmas. It was three sizes too big for her and painfully ugly. When we returned home from that holiday, I found that she had tucked it in among my things in the trunk of my car and sent it back with me. The next year I gave it to my childhood friend Jessie—whose house we were now visiting. She kept it for a couple years before also giving it back.

"You should probably cut this one up for mittens," she

suggested. This poor sweater was very unwanted. I finally gave it to my hairdresser Jessica as a joke. She was too polite to give it back. I am sure she got rid of it.

We drove home from that first baby-making adventure on Sunday night with large bags of thrift store finds in a car smelling slightly of moth balls and dirty clothing. The weekend had been part vacation and part mission. I got up on Monday morning and had to laugh at the memories of it. Despite the peculiar things that had happened, I donned my teacher clothes and went to work.

As I entered the school building, I felt strangely different. I felt pregnant. I imagined that by now the sperm had met the egg, and the zygote was dividing and subdividing its cells to form a complex organism called a blastocyst. I had been researching this for months. It was probably not what I should have been thinking about as I greeted my students upon arrival, but I would be lying if I said it wasn't on my mind.

The days seemed to go by terribly slowly that first week. The following Sunday, I met up with Lise-Anne at her house to make mittens. I walked in and could smell the roast chicken she was making for Sunday dinner. Potatoes were peeled on the counter and ready to be cut, boiled, and mashed. Everything at her house felt so safe and comfortable. I lugged my bins of thrift store finds into her living room. We marveled at all the gorgeous sweaters as we laid them out on her couch.

"This is awesome!" Lise-Anne said

"I know! I really scored."

We started sorting the sweaters into piles. Some of them had to go through the wash to be felted, but others were clean and ready to cut. We got right to work.

"Ok, enough about the sweaters," Lise-Anne said as we began cutting. "Tell me all about your trip. Was it weird?"

"So weird!"

"What was he like?"

"He was nice, I mean, we knew that about him, but he was just extra nice I guess, and SO handsome." I laughed, "If you get to pick the donor, might as well pick a cute one, right?" I recounted the highlights of the weekend, and Lise-Anne asked lots of questions. It felt good to be the expert on something.

"Let me know as soon as you hear the good news!" She called after me as I left.

"I will!"

We had a slew of pregnancy tests lined up for the first possible day that I might get a positive test. We decided to wait until the day I was supposed to start my period to see if it was even worth using one of them. When my period didn't come on the designated day, I rushed home to Liz, who had come home from work a little early, and I ceremoniously peed on the stick. I was absolutely sure that it had worked. We waited and waited, but the red line never appeared.

When my period didn't come the next day or the next day, we repeated this ritual again and again. I am a hopeful person, but by the fourth day, even I was beginning to lose hope. When my period came crashing in, bringing a bloody end to my dream of achieving pregnancy on my first try, I was crushed. It arrived mid-morning when I was at school. I had stepped into the bathroom in my classroom in between our math lesson and writer's workshop, but for me it was in between a hoped-for pregnancy and a crimson defeat. I called Liz on my lunch break. As always, she was supportive and kind, but I could tell by the way she was talking softer than usual that she was crushed too.

We called our sperm donor a few days later to let him know that it didn't work.

"It's ok, we'll try again."

"Are you sure you don't mind?" I asked.

"I'm in if you're in."

His gentle demeanor was reassuring. He was unwavering in his decision to help us. I will always be thankful to that man. He was giving us a chance to try this path to parenthood for free. Not having to pay for the sperm lowered the stakes enough for us to feel less stress in the process. He was generous and joyful throughout.

"I can always make more sperm," he joked. "I don't think I'll run out any time soon."

Men are lucky in this arena. Every doctor I had talked to told me that it's much harder for women to get pregnant after age thirty-five. Women are born with all the eggs they will ever make. Isn't that astounding? After puberty, a woman will release one or two eggs every month for thirty to forty years until menopause, and that's it. She never makes more. I knew I needed to get pregnant soon.

We repeated our trips to Maine in May and June with no luck. By July we were ready to up the ante. I visited my gynecologist, and she prescribed a low dose of Clomid, a fertility drug. There was a seven percent chance of conceiving twins with this drug, as it often stimulates your body to release more than one egg. We decided it was worth the risk.

We met up with our trusty donor on the sidewalk outside his building on a gorgeous July day. He handed us fresh sperm in his signature Bull Moose bag. We raced back to Jessie's house, trying to beat the clock. Sperm doesn't live for very long outside the body. When we were done with the insemination, I lay on the bed with my legs and pelvis propped up on a mountain of pillows hoping gravity might help.

It was such a relief to be doing this insemination during the summer, because we could stay in Maine longer and didn't have to rush home to go back to work. We went to the beach with Jessie's family and had a big lobster bake under the oak tree in their backyard. We went outlet shopping in Freeport and hiked around Mackworth Island. Our old yellow lab, Joey, came with us, and he ran along the beach, chasing seagulls. We found a bench on the island path overlooking Casco Bay and sat there holding hands and imagining ourselves coming back next year with a baby strapped to one of us in a carrier. The thought of showering a little one with love and attention made us giddy with excitement. Liz, of course, imagined all the bikes she would buy for our child, and I imagined the quilts I would sew. Sailboats glided through the shimmering ocean water and the waves crashed on the rocks nearby.

"Shall we head home?" I asked.

"Never," she said with a smile. The summer in Maine was a wonderland to us.

As we drove home, I was once again sure that I was pregnant, but this time with TWINS! The month we used Clomid I doubled my mitten production rate, the thought of potentially having two babies at once gave me so much anxiety. Sewing was my respite. I would turn on the TV in our living room and sew mitten after perfect mitten. It was the one thing I could control, and it was a beautiful, unique creation every time.

There is a term that crafters use for the feeling they get when they are completely engrossed in their projects and everything else disappears. It's called being "in the flow." I spent countless hours that summer trying to stay in the flow at my sewing machine. It was how I stayed calm and hopeful. It helped pass the time and gave me a sense of satisfaction. If I wasn't successful at baby making, at least I had piles of gorgeous cut wool and mittens ready to sell.

The wait was excruciating, and I began taking pregnancy tests daily at ten days post-ovulation. Liz and I had decided to switch to a new, more expensive test kit that read "pregnant," or "not pregnant." We were truly sick of looking for the double pink line. The day my period was supposed to start came and went, and several more days went by. Each day it was late, I was ever more certain that I was pregnant. Liz's expectations were more grounded. She remained optimistic, but had read that the statistics for a successful pregnancy from an at-home insemination are only around ten to fifteen percent. Four days went by, and then five. My breasts were tender and I felt crampy, but still no period, and also no positive pregnancy test. At six days overdue, my period again came rushing in, in a huge burst. It wasn't the slow start of a normal period.

"I got my period," I said as I walked into the living room.

"I'm sorry, babe." Liz got up off the couch and gave me a hug. I began to cry.

"Why isn't this working? We're doing everything right!" We stood in the living room holding each other. "Well, if I'm not pregnant, I'm making myself a cocktail."

"It's ten o'clock in the morning!"

"I don't fucking care."

After another month of Clomid and no pregnancy, we decided to take a different route. I looked online for a doctor's office that would do an insemination with fresh sperm. This was difficult to find because doctors typically want to quarantine sperm for six months to be sure the donor isn't HIV-positive. We suspected that if a man and a woman walked into a doctor's office and said they wanted to get pregnant, the doctor would do an insemination for them without a problem. It's a different story with two women and a cup of sperm provided by a donor. Nevertheless, we called around until we found a smart and funny gynecologist who was willing to work with us. I will call her Doctor Grey, since she may have bent some rules in helping us the way she did. At the very least, she chose to overlook some ethical considerations that had been barriers for us at other clinics.

When we arrived at Dr. Grey's office in early September, she met us with a smile and, after preparing the sample, asked if we wanted to see the swimmers under the microscope. They looked like little sesame seeds with tails wiggling around in a forward moving fashion, yet going nowhere—not yet anyway!

Dr. Grey sucked the sperm up into a syringe with a long tube attached to it. The procedure is called an Intra-Uterine Insemination, or IUI for short. The syringe propels the sperm through the tube, which is inserted through the cervix and positioned right up next to the entrance of the fallopian tube, thereby skipping most of the arduous journey through the uterus. It's like a great big short cut.

The procedure was relatively painless and quick. Like all the insemination trips before, the purpose was quickly accomplished, and we were left with the rest of the weekend to walk along the stunning coast and go outlet shopping. Maine is truly one of the most beautiful places. When I was growing up in South Portland, I used to listen to the sounds of the fog horns on opposite sides of the harbor at night. Every so often they would blow at the same time and in harmony. I think of that sometimes in the night when I am at home in Essex Junction, and I can hear the train whistles blowing. It's not the same, but it's soothing. There is a part of me that will always be rooted in Maine.

When we returned to Vermont, it was the start of a new school year, and I jumped back into teaching. It was my second year at Westford, and we had a new principal named Marcie. I was eager to make a good first impression, and spent many long hours making sure my classroom looked just right and my lesson planning was thorough.

The sugar maple leaves were just beginning to yellow on the day I realized my period was overdue again. I had been disappointed with negative pregnancy tests so many times that I allowed myself to get lost in the hustle of the new school year and not think about the testing until it could really, actually be positive. I drove home from school with the windows down, the cool fall air clearing my head. Liz wasn't home when I arrived. I slipped into the bathroom to pee on the stick. It was one of the *two lines and you're pregnant* kind of stick.

Liz arrived home while I was waiting for the result, and I went out into the kitchen to say hello. She was standing by the sink, drinking from a tall glass of water. She always looked so handsome when she came home from work in her button-down shirts tucked into her neatly ironed pants.

"Oh my God, you are not going to believe who I ran into on campus today."

"Who?"

"Meg O'Brien!"

"No way! I haven't seen her since undergrad." We got lost in our reminiscing about Meg, whom we both knew when we were students at UVM. It never ceased to amuse us how many mutual friends we'd had in college. "One summer night when I was walking home from downtown with Meg, we went swimming in John Hubbard's Tub." That's the name of the water fountain in the center of the UVM campus green.

"That is so gross. Drunk people pee in that tub!" Liz said.

"Well, we were definitely drunk, and we probably peed in it too." I laughed at the thought of our college capers, which were both disgusting and dazzling.

"Oh no! I almost forgot. I did a pregnancy test and left it on the sink!"

We ran into the bathroom and there it was, the very faint pink second line of a positive pregnancy test.

"Is that positive?" I said, holding it up to the light.

"No, it's too faint. Also, it just sat for like twenty minutes, so it probably was a little over-marinated."

"Yeah." I threw the stick away, and we went back into the

kitchen to make dinner. Later that night, we were watching the Bachelor on TV while simultaneously cruising the internet on our laptops when Liz looked up from her screen.

"Look at this web page. It has pictures of positive pregnancy tests." She showed me her laptop screen and we scrolled through the pictures and some of them were just as faint, if not fainter, than my test. "You should take another test."

"We actually only have one test left. I need to pick some more up on my way home from work tomorrow. Do you think I should use it right now?"

"Maybe we should wait until the morning." I was dying to take another test right away, but Liz was right, if it was positive, it would be clearer in the morning.

I woke up early the next morning and tested myself again, and there it was—a slightly darker, faint pink line. I *was* pregnant!

"Yes!" I yelled as loudly as I could, pumping my fists in the air. "Yes! Yes! Yes!" Liz came around the corner and gave me a huge hug. She didn't even need to ask why I was screaming. I pulled away from the hug and could see that she was crying. She has such a tender heart. At the sight of her tears, I began to cry too.

"We did it!" She said as she looked at me with earnest love.

"We're gonna have a baby!" We hugged again and again.

As I drove to school that morning, the whole world looked brighter. It was the last week of September, and peak foliage. The early morning sun shone on the trees and everything was aglow—including me.

I walked into the school that morning with joy bursting from every part of my being. The first person I saw was the math specialist Kelly.

"You have that look on your face," she said with a devilish grin. "What is up with you?"

It's true, I was grinning ear to ear, but I also had been cautioned not to tell people I was pregnant in case I lost the baby. My excitement bubbled over anyway, and I couldn't contain myself.

"I got a positive pregnancy test this morning!"

"Aaaaaah! You're pregnant! You are totally pregnant!" The truth of this was so stunning to me. It had worked! No more sidewalk sperm deals, no more needless syringe inseminations, this was it!

I floated through the next few days and weeks. It was like carrying a winning lottery ticket around and not telling anyone that your life was about to overflow with riches. Lise-Anne was one of the few people we told about the pregnancy. Her excitement for me was nearly as big as my own. She immediately started crocheting baby blankets. At the end of September, we brought our mittens to the Underhill Harvest Festival, and even though it was a terribly hot day, we sold several pairs.

"That's a good sign," she told me. "We should try to sign up for holiday craft fairs now, before the tables fill up." Lise-Anne handled all of the sales that day. I was mostly there to observe how to run a craft fair table. She had lots of products for sale and our tent was full of people all day. We saw many of my students running through the fields and going on hay rides. Their parents would linger at our tent and make small talk while they tried on the mittens. I sat in a camp chair in the shade most of the day. The heat and my early pregnancy had taken all the energy out of me. Every so often Lise-Anne would look over at me with a knowing smile and wink.

I subscribed to weekly baby updates that described our baby as various sized fruits and vegetables. By seven weeks it was the size of a blueberry, by nine weeks, it was a grape. Liz and I started making a list of potential baby names.

"How about Ulysses?" I suggested one night, "Uly for short!"

"Ooooh I like that one! Except I still like Fenton Carlos Fenton the best."

"We are not naming our child Fenton Fenton!"

"I thought you liked my last name?" Liz looked at me with a fake hurt expression.

"You're impossible."

Each day Liz would bring home a new item for the nursery. Her friend Jinny was ready to unload all her baby furniture, as her two daughters were now in preschool and kindergarten. One day we got a crib, the next day it was changing table.

"I ran into Margo Floyd today," Liz said one afternoon, "and I told her we were planning to call the baby Ulysses if it's a boy and she gave me the most horrible look. She said, 'Don't do that to the poor child.' Do you think we should rethink Ulysses?"

"Well, there's always Ira."

"She didn't like that name either."

"Well, it's not up to her. Plus, I am currently in love with Ira Glass, so I think Ira is a perfect name."

"You want to name our child after a Public Radio host?"

"Yes, I do."

The next day Liz brought home four large, black trash bags full of baby clothes from Jinny.

"Well," said Liz, "I hope Ira likes pink!"

We decided that the nursery theme would be owls as a shout out to Liz's Ph.D. program alma mater, Rice University. One weekend while we were out shopping, we found two stuffed owls at different stores and bought them both. I propped them up in the nursery with a baby blanket of Liz's that I'd found in an old box.

Perhaps the most excited for us, of all our friends, was Lise-Anne. Within minutes of hearing our news, she was scrolling the internet looking for baby quilt patterns.

"This is going to change your lives forever."

"Well, definitely, for the next eighteen years!"

"No. Forever. When you have a child, I don't care how old your child is, it's like a piece of your heart is walking around outside your body. You never stop thinking about them and worrying for them and loving them. It's powerful."

"I already feel that," I confessed.

My early-pregnancy food aversions set in, and I started to feel twinges of morning sickness. One morning I woke up and the kitchen smelled of cat poop. I became instantly and irrationally annoyed at Liz for bringing a cat into our marriage.

"Liz, can you please change Teluse's litter box? It smells disgusting!"

"I just changed it yesterday."

It wasn't just the litter box that turned my stomach. Cologne and perfume made me gag. We had a new tech specialist at our school, and he was the nicest, most helpful tech person imaginable. He never made me feel like a total luddite for not knowing how to do things on the computer. Yet I couldn't stand to be in the same room with him, or even pass him in the hall, because his cologne was so strong. It got so bad that when my work computer was malfunctioning, I went weeks before I asked for help because I couldn't bear to have him in my classroom. Finally, I went to see our new principal, Marcie.

"I feel really bad bringing this up to you, but I have to tell you something because I need your help with something else."

"What's up?"

"Well, you know Jared, the new tech guy?"

"Yes."

"I need his help because my Smart Board computer isn't working, but I can't get him to come to my classroom because. . ."

"Because why? Is something wrong?"

"Sort of, it's just that, well I can't stand the smell of his cologne because—I'm pregnant." Marcie leapt from her chair and gave me a hug.

"I'm so happy for you!" I barely knew Marcie, so it felt strange to be hugging her, but she assured me that she would find a way to let Jared know that his cologne was too much so that I could get my computer fixed without getting sick.

Mid-October rolled around, and I started to wonder when

would be a good time to go to an obstetrician. It had been six weeks since our insemination, but since you count the weeks of your pregnancy from the start date of your last period, I was technically eight weeks along. I knew that the baby's heart had probably begun to beat, and was eager to hear that little thumping sound inside me. I made an appointment at a local practice that came highly recommended. The earliest they could see me was in two weeks.

About a week before the appointment, a nurse called and said that it was their standard practice to have women get a blood test before they came in, to be sure they were actually pregnant. There was no doubt in my mind that I was pregnant, but I agreed to get the blood test anyway.

It was the Friday before Halloween, and I was teaching a spelling lesson to my second graders when my classroom phone rang. It had been several days since my blood test, and my appointment with the obstetrician was on Monday.

"Hello, is this Jen Ellis?" A curt voice on the other end of the phone introduced herself as a nurse from the doctor's office. "Yes, I have your blood test results and I called to ask you, how many weeks pregnant are you?"

"Somewhere around nine or ten?" I said.

"Are you sure you're that far along? Is it possible that you and your husband have your dates wrong?" I rolled my eyes. It was 2012, why would anyone assume a woman was straight in Vermont?

"Me and my *wife*," I corrected her. She made a little grunt. By now my students had already started chatting amongst themselves. "And yes, we did an IUI the first weekend in September, so I'm sure about the dates."

"Oh, well your HCG levels are too low for you to be that far along." Her voice was completely flat and unfeeling, and I had no idea what she was talking about.

"Are you saying I'm not pregnant?"

"No, you are pregnant. It's just that your HCG levels are low. That's an indication that there's likely something wrong with the pregnancy."

"So, I'm not pregnant enough?" Tears began to roll down my cheeks, and I looked out at my second graders who by now had totally lost interest in me. I stepped into the hall and closed the door behind me. "Can you explain this to me?"

The nurse sounded put out as she began to give me some more information. I was sobbing and could barely hear her anyway. The school guidance counselor happened to walk by and asked me if I was ok. I asked her to take my class for a little bit. The nurse on the phone went on, and nothing she said made sense. When I asked her to repeat some things, she raised her voice and told me I needed to get another blood test. There was absolutely no compassion in her words. I wondered how anyone could be so unfeeling. It was hard to distinguish one word from the next. My ears began to ring, and I felt dizzy. I put the phone down on the floor and walked away, leaving her on the empty line.

I hurried down the hall toward the front office. It seemed like the longest walk of my life. I needed to leave. I needed to cry. I needed to throw up. I passed two third graders in the hall,

"Hi, Ms. Ellis!" one of them said cheerfully. I looked the other way so they would not see my wet and swelling eyes. How could that nurse have told me there was a problem with my pregnancy in front of my class? Isn't that against some rule of decency somewhere? The first open door I came to was to the office of our school nurse, Janet. She took one look at me as I stepped into her office and shut the door tightly behind me. She guided me to a chair, and I explained to her what had happened in between my sobs.

"Oh Jen, I am so sorry, I didn't even know you were pregnant!" She was very sympathetic as she tried her best to calm me down, but I was inconsolable. "Can I call Liz?"

"Yes," I said as I headed for the bathroom where I began to throw up. When I emerged, Janet handed the phone to me so I could make a plan with Liz.

"Do you want me to come get you? I'm on campus, but I can be there in forty-five minutes."

"No, I don't want to leave my car here. I can drive home."

"Are you sure?" Truthfully, I wasn't sure, but I needed to pull myself together.

"Yes, I'll meet you at home."

By the time I hung up the phone, a student was knocking at the door looking for their noon-time medication, and Janet gave me this terrible look. She needed to open the door.

"I can't go back to my classroom to get my things until my students leave for lunch. I don't want them to see that I've been crying."

"I can't let you wait here," she said, "lunch is my busiest time, and lots of kids are going to come to the door. Can I see if you can wait in Marcie's office?"

"I barely know Marcie. I can't show up in her office looking like this!"

"What about the guidance counselor?"

"She's with my class."

"You have to trust Marcie. She's a good egg, she'll understand."

Janet ducked into Marcie's office to make sure no students were in there before ushering me over. Marcie was sitting at her desk. I sat at the table and put my head down and continued to sob.

"I think I know what this is about," she began, "and I'm sorry." I knew she was trying to be kind, but I couldn't even begin to talk to her. I didn't know her well enough to be awkwardly and uncontrollably sobbing in her office. "Do you want me to drive you home?"

"No, I'm just waiting for my students to go to lunch, and then I'll go back to my classroom to get my things."

"Let me get you a sub," she said, and she left the room to talk to the secretary. My head was pounding as I came to the realization that before I left for the day, I would have to sit down at my desk and write sub plans for my students for the afternoon.

There is a picture somewhere of Liz and me sitting on the ground in front of the steps leading up to our front door. Our jack-o-lanterns are carved and placed nearby, and the grass is littered with dried fall leaves. Our smiles are fake. My arm is wrapped around Liz's waist and it looks like a loving embrace, but I remember when that picture was taken. It was the very next day after I found out there was a problem with the pregnancy. My hold on Liz was more than an embrace, it was my lifeline. It was my only connection with the earth. It was all that was keeping me sane in that moment.

Liz's childhood friend Kim had come over to meet up with us for dinner, and then we were heading out to a haunted Halloween Forest in a nearby town. Kim insisted we looked so adorable, she had to take our picture and send it to us. When I look back at that picture now, it breaks me. We knew that I was carrying a baby that might not survive, and there was nothing I could do about it. We looked deceptively happy. Part of me wants to delete that picture from my computer when I see it now, but I never can. It's the only picture I have of myself in my first pregnancy, and I keep it as proof that before we had Helen, we had someone else. We had a little spark of a life, a beginning, a thousand hopes and dreams. We had an empty crib, a changing table, and four bags of clothes. We had a list of names, two stuffed owls, and a due date.

I have always been a little vague with people about how early in the pregnancy we lost our first baby. I am afraid that people will discount those first two months as not enough time to be as sad as I was for losing it.

We did another blood test the following week to see if my HCG numbers were rising, and they were, which indicated that the embryo was growing, but not enough to indicate a viable pregnancy. The obstetrician became concerned that the embryo might be forming somewhere outside of my uterus.

He asked me to come into the office so that he could retrieve a sample from my uterus to determine if it contained evidence of pregnancy. The procedure was very painful, and Liz nearly passed out while watching. After it was done, I sat there in my hospital gown feeling exposed and vulnerable. The doctor handed the sample to a nurse and moved to the other side of the room. He swung around an office chair and casually sat down straddling the seat. The obstetrics teaching fellow who had been observing the procedure stood nearby.

"So how did you get pregnant?" he asked. It seemed like an abrupt question, but we explained to him that we had used fresh sperm from a friend. I could tell by the look on his face that he did not approve.

"Well, just so you know, our clinic cannot continue to work with you if you are going to try to get pregnant that way again. We wouldn't touch your sperm donor with a ten-foot pole unless he came in here and went through all our testing protocols."

I couldn't believe he was saying this to me. Had he even looked at my chart? It was very clear that I was in his office because there was a problem with my pregnancy, and I was likely going to miscarry. He had also just performed a very invasive and painful procedure to verify that fact.

I felt my cheeks flush. I wanted to yell at him and slam my fists against his arrogant chest. How could he think *this* was the right time to lecture us about how we got pregnant? I tried to remain calm. "Do you say this to every pregnant woman who comes in here, who had sex with some random guy without getting him tested for STDs first, or just the lesbians?"

"Now, now, this isn't a gay thing; I mean, do you have a custody agreement with this guy?" My head was spinning. This was none of his business. I felt like he was trying to blame us for what was happening. Did he think we deserved to lose this baby?

"Yes, we have a contract. He isn't the father, he's just the sperm donor. He won't have custody." My voice was shaking now and I was getting more furious.

"Well, those contracts aren't worth the paper they're printed on, and you know, he could just come and take your baby at any time." That was the last straw.

"There isn't going to be a baby!" I screamed, tears pouring down my cheeks. The teaching fellow looked over at me, wide-eyed and shocked. "How can you say this to me? I'm probably going to have a miscarriage! Who cares where I got my fucking sperm?" I was now yelling. I didn't care who heard.

I could tell the doctor was angry and not used to being yelled at. He stiffened his shoulders and began to yell right back at me. "You can't speak to me this way! You can't use this language in my clinic!"

"We're never coming back to this clinic again! I won't work with a homophobic doctor. You're fired!"

His face turned red and he aggressively pursed his lips. Then he threw my chart down on the counter and stormed out of the room, loudly slamming the door behind him, and leaving me there with a speechless Liz and a stunned teaching fellow. I buried my face in my hands and sobbed.

"I'm so sorry that just happened," the fellow said. "He was completely out of line."

"He's an asshole. I don't care what he thinks. I just want to leave," I said to Liz.

"I'll get your discharge papers," the fellow said and then she apologized on behalf of the doctor several more times on her way out of the room. I got dressed and we left as quickly as we could. We didn't even bother to check out.

Liz and I drove home in silence. When we finally got into the house, she began to cry. "I am so sorry I didn't say anything. I should have defended you. I should have said something!"

"There was nothing you could say. Nothing could have prepared us for that."

We were very gentle with each other that night. It was so rare that either of us yelled at anyone, the sheer magnitude of the shouting match in the doctor's office had taken every ounce of energy we had left.

"Do you think he's like that with everyone?" I asked Liz as we cuddled in bed.

"No. He's a homophobe and an old white guy. He's not used to being challenged or put in his place."

A couple days later, the office called to let us know that indeed there was no evidence of a pregnancy in my uterus. However, another blood test later that week indicated that my numbers had continued to rise exponentially. The teaching fellow took over my case because I refused to work with the doctor again, and she explained that all signs pointed to an ectopic pregnancy. It was likely that the embryo was forming in my fallopian tube and was now rapidly growing. She suggested we terminate it as quickly as possible, or I risked rupturing one of my fallopian tubes. We begrudgingly went back to the doctor's office, where a nurse gave me a shot of methotrexate to terminate the pregnancy. Later that night, doubled over in agony on the toilet, I passed a large and painful blood clot, which I immediately flushed away. I went out into the kitchen where Liz was doing the dishes. She turned around and looked at me.

"It's gone," was all I said. She wrapped her arms around me and we cried into each other's embrace.

Sometimes when I think about the salient moments in our little house, I remember that night. I remember holding Liz in the center of our kitchen as we sobbed. I remember where we stood, and the breathless way I gasped for air. I'm not sure if I could have remained standing in that moment without her. If a house can hold a memory, our house holds that one with tenderness and reverence.

Chapter 8
Craft Fairs

November 2012

After the miscarriage was complete, I could see no clear path forward. I canceled my subscription to the emails telling me what fruit was equal to our baby's size. Before I could press unsubscribe, I saw that at ten weeks, the baby was supposed to have fingers and toes. Like a cruel joke, other emails kept coming. The first company had clearly sold my information to lots of other expectant mother websites. I received internet solicitations at various times over the next year offering me vitamins for a growing fetus, pregnancy photos, Pampers, and cloth diapers. The real kicker was a package of formula that arrived at our home address right around the time I was supposed to give birth. I didn't even know how they got my address. It was a stinging reminder of what we had lost.

My co-workers urged me to take some time off work and I did take a couple of days, but I just wallowed in my grief at home. I would spend hours agonizing over my sub plans, trying to create meaningful work for my students at school, and wondering why I didn't just go in and teach them myself. I tried to do the "self-care" things people suggested. I took a hot bath, went on a walk, tried to read a book, and none of it worked. I quickly realized that the sadness I felt was permanent. I know that sounds drastic, but even now, I still feel that way. I have learned to live with the grief of losing that pregnancy, but the sadness was like a little puddle of rain that never evaporated, even on the warmest summer day. It was a puddle one could drown in, and honestly, for a little while, I did.

On the Saturday after the miscarriage, I was scheduled to sell mittens at my first solo craft fair. Lise-Anne had a craft fair at a school in Williston, and one of Liz's work friends had offered me half of her table at the Cozy Nook Craft Fair in Essex. We decided we would split our inventory and go to both. We worked relentlessly to create enough mittens so that we both could have full tables.

I woke up to my alarm early that Saturday. It was a crisp November morning. There had been a deep frost the night before, and the trees were crystallized in white. I drove to the beautiful, historic library building where the craft fair would be held. I'd never been there before. There were lots of other crafters unloading their goods. I walked inside and found Liz's friend, Kathy, who showed me to our table. I didn't know Kathy very well. She is a poet, but she had a side hustle selling fabric napkins and tablecloths made from fabrics she purchased in Ghana. Many years before, her son had died in a tragic accident while on vacation. He had one child, and Kathy sent the proceeds of her small crafting business to the child's mother.

I set up my mittens on my half of the table. We were on the first floor of the library. Behind us were rows of books and above us was a wraparound balcony where more crafters were stationed. Light poured in through the tall leaded glass windows. There was quiet Christmas music playing and a gaggle of pre-teen girls meticulously setting up a bake sale nearby. I sat behind my table and began to chat with Kathy. She was a thoughtful, middle-aged woman, with dark brown hair and a pretty but serious face. I instantly felt at ease with her. We had the entire day to get to know one another. It felt nice to talk to someone new.

"We open in five minutes!" one of the organizers called out.

"I'm going to run to the bathroom real quick," I told Kathy.

"I'll watch your stuff."

As I walked past the other crafters, I wanted to stop and look at everything on their tables. There was a woman selling hand-made, coffee-scented soaps with coffee grounds as the exfoliant. Someone else had hand-painted Ukrainian eggs. People sold pottery and paintings and raw honey. I began to think I could get all my Christmas shopping done in one place.

The opening bell rang just as I returned, and people flooded in. Ours was the second table on the left; we had a great spot. People started trying my mittens on right away.

"These are so soft! Is this made from a sweater?"

"Yes."

"How much are they?"

"Twenty-five dollars." This was our original price-point.

"That's a great price! I'll be back!" Then, as quickly as they had stepped up to my table, they were gone.

"Do you think they'll really come back?" I asked Kathy.

"Yes, I do. They probably brought a limited amount of cash and want to be sure your mittens are their favorite thing at the fair before they buy them."

"It's kind of exciting," I said.

"It's totally exciting." Several more people perused the table before a woman with a baby slung in a carrier stopped and admired the mittens for a long time. She picked out two pairs and handed me fifty dollars in cash. Surprised, I looked at Kathy with a giant grin on my face.

"Oh my gosh, did you see that? My first sale!" The fifty dollars were crisp and new. It seemed like so much money to just be handed by a stranger. Within minutes one of the first people who had stopped at our table was back. She picked up the pair of mittens she had tried on.

"I'm so glad you haven't sold these yet, I love them!" She handed me twenty-five dollars too. As soon as she was gone, I turned to Kathy.

"I can't believe how fun this is!" Then I instantly regretted it, for she had not yet sold anything.

"You're going to sell out, you know." Kathy had a gentle countenance, and her kindness spilled out in every way that day.

"I hope so." And she wasn't wrong. The mittens sold left and right all morning. By noon, I'd made four hundred dollars. I took out my lunch box and pulled out my peanut butter and jelly sandwich. Kathy had brought a sandwich too. We sat behind our table and chatted as we ate.

"So, I can't remember, do you and Liz have any kids?" I choked on my bite of food and managed to chew it a few more times to get it down. I took a deep breath.

"Not yet."

"Are you planning on it?"

"Yes." My eyes filled up with tears and Kathy looked at me with a concerned face. "I'm sorry." I looked away and tried to gather myself, but it was no use. I got up and walked down to the end of the row of books and cried as quietly as I could. I was having such a fun time selling the mittens that, for whole minutes at a time that morning, I hadn't thought about losing the baby. It had been such a relief to be part of this joyous event and not be at home or at school; both places made me sad. I took some deep breaths and went back to my seat. I wasn't hungry for my lunch any more.

"I didn't mean to pry," she said. "I'm sorry I made you sad."

"It's ok. You didn't know. We recently lost a baby."

"Oh, I'm so sorry. That's hard."

"It has been hard," I managed to whisper. I squeezed the fingers of my left hand together with my other hand as hard as I could. The tips turned dark red and began to ache. I just wanted the pain to be somewhere other than inside me.

"How far along were you?"

"Ten weeks."

"That's rough. Will you try again?"

"I hope so."

"I lost my son, did Liz tell you?" I tried to swallow the lump in my throat.

"Yes, she did. I'm sorry for you too." Though her loss was exponentially greater than mine, she never made me feel like my grief was any less. We sat there for the rest of the day amid the great joy of the holiday craft fair holding our own private griefs and the griefs of each other. I didn't know it at the time, but I was learning how to feel both sadness and joy simultaneously, and with dignity. Kathy was a perfect model for how to walk through the world, carrying your grief, but not as a heavy burden, just as part of the load of life. At the time, my grief felt like an albatross, but it wouldn't always be that way.

At the end of the day, I had only four pairs of mittens left. I texted Lise-Anne. I'd made almost six hundred dollars. She was so excited. Her table hadn't done as well, but between the two of us, we had made a lot of money.

"I don't think I'll do this craft fair again next year," Kathy said as we were packing up. "But because you sat here with me today, you should go to the organizers and claim this table for next year. It's hard to get into this craft fair and they give preference to people who've been here before."

"That's a good tip." I followed her advice and Kelli, the organizer, who had purchased two pairs of my mittens herself, wrote me into her book in pen.

"We can't wait to have you come back!"

"Me either!" It was such a positive way to end the day. My first solo craft fair was a huge success. I drove directly to the bank. It was thrilling to deposit so much cash. When I got home, I skipped into the house and told Liz all about the day.

"This is the happiest I've seen you in two weeks!" she said as she wrapped her arms around me. "It's nice to have *you* back."

"I know." I looked into Liz's steady, hazel eyes. It always amazed me how unwavering she was. I actually was happy. It felt so strange and wonderful.

Later that night, I got online and began searching for other craft fairs in the area. I wanted to do it all over again. I sent inquiries to every craft fair director I could find to see if they had any tables available. Craft fairs typically begin booking their tables for the holiday season in the summer and give preference to returning crafters. This was going to be a tough market to break into. Lise-Anne was booked at two more, and I could see the benefit of our splitting up and selling at more than one venue. I did manage to find two more fairs that had tables available, but only because other crafters had backed out. The first one was the Richmond Holiday Market.

Many craft fairs will have multiple locations in one town on the same day, making it an event for the whole town. This is what the little town of Richmond, Vermont did on the first Saturday of December every year. Richmond is a quintessential Vermont town. That day it was covered in new snow, with candles in every window. It looked like the pictures I'd seen in my grandmother's Vermont Life calendars. I parked in the back of the Holy Family Church at around 7 am and began unloading.

I had spent every night between that first craft fair and this one making mittens. Lise-Anne and I gathered on the weekends to sew together. When we got together, we combined the various parts of the mittens we had been working on and completed the process by adding the cuffs. The part we did together was the most fun because each mitten was unique and we were so proud of our product. I looked forward to these sewing sessions all week. Liz was my true love and my support, but she was also grieving, and sometimes our compounded grief was too much for either of us to bear.

Lise-Anne was a wonderful distraction. She always had interesting stories to tell, and her outlook was positive and encouraging. Sharing a crafting hobby with a friend is a powerful bond. It's a way to be together and share delight in something productive. It's a good thing those mittens couldn't talk because we shared everything while making them: our fears, sorrows, and achievements. And I'll admit, we probably gossiped a little more than we should have.

When I wasn't with Lise-Anne, Liz and I would watch reality TV in the evenings, and I would sit at the dining room table and sew. I needed to prevent myself from sinking into depression. If I could just stay busy, I could keep my mind from slipping even farther. We had to wait three months before we could try to get pregnant again. The pressure to have a baby by thirty-five is real. Everything I had read said that your chances of getting pregnant after thirty-five are drastically reduced. It was a process of hurry up and wait.

I was thankful to have the mittens to focus on. Creativity is a healing force that is often overlooked in modern society. Being in the creative flow is a meditation. It helps your brain feel lighter and unburdened. Creativity releases dopamine and serotonin; it makes you happy. Making mittens was literally saving me from my sadness.

I was also thankful to have the craft fairs to look forward to. As my collection of mittens grew, I could also see the dollar signs adding up. I thought that maybe this year I would actually meet my goal of paying off my credit card by the end of December.

On the day of the Richmond Holiday Market, I set up the old Radio Flyer sled display on my table and began hanging mittens on the hooks. This was the most expensive craft fair to enter, which was probably why they had a table available at such short notice. There were five craft fair locations in the town, and each one held a special attraction. The Holy Family Church, where I was selling, had Santa Claus.

The lady at the booth next to me told me that the man who played Santa was ninety years old. He arrived on a horse-drawn wagon and gingerly made his way inside. He looked exactly like the story book version of the man. He had a real white beard and rosy cheeks. He told me during his lunch break that he had been playing Santa in Richmond for over forty years. I jokingly told him that if I had grown up in this town, I would have sat on his knee!

"Oh, I've heard the Christmas wishes of just about everyone in this town," he let out a jolly chuckle, "And their children too!" He had the most perfect red velvet Santa suit, with bright white fur cuffs. "My wife made this suit for me many years ago," he said. "She's been gone for almost a decade. When she was alive, she used to play Mrs. Claus right along with me." He paused and pulled out a bologna and cheese sandwich. "I miss her."

"I bet you do." I pulled out my peanut butter and jelly sandwich and decided to join him for lunch. We sat in silence for a long time, eating. A middle school band had arrived and fumbled through some Christmas carols. They were painfully bad. I saw Santa reach up and turn his hearing aid off. *Lucky*, I thought.

I had brought a book with me to pass the time, but I never got it out. There was a steady stream of people stopping by. Sometimes someone I knew would appear and we would give each other a big hug and catch up a bit. Sometimes other people would see someone they knew and they would hug and catch up. Vermont is a small place, and events like these remind you that your friends are many and your neighbors are near. When no one was at my table, I sat and enjoyed the scene. It seemed to me that things probably hadn't changed much since the first year that old man played Santa.

Our mittens sold steadily, and at the end of the day I went again to the bank. I couldn't believe how easy this was. I truly enjoyed making the mittens, and I truly enjoyed selling them. I also didn't mind a reason to just sit in a happy place with strangers, friends, and neighbors for a day.

A week later, I drove to Montpelier for another craft fair. This was going to be the last one before Christmas, and Lise-Anne and I both stayed up every night until midnight the week before, furiously sewing to be sure I had enough inventory to pull it off. This last fair was called the Solidarity Craft Fair. I only knew to look it up because many years before, when I taught at the Union Elementary School in Montpelier, I had attended it. I had driven all the way from Burlington to work in my classroom for the day that Saturday, as many teachers do, and on my way home, I stopped in to see what the excitement was about. The fair was at the Unitarian Church. Up on the stage they had hot soup and locally made bread. I walked around and eventually found a potter who had the most stunning purple mugs. I bought one and have treasured it ever since.

On the day of the Solidarity Craft Fair in 2012, I arrived early to set up. I found my table toward the front of the community room in the historic church. When I taught in Montpelier, I could see the spire of this church from my classroom window.

After I was done setting up, I noticed a potter sitting directly in front of me. I walked over to her table, picked up a familiar looking mug, and looked at the insignia on the bottom.

"I think I bought a mug from you many years ago."

"It's possible," she said. "I come here every year."

"Do you want to trade a mug for some mittens?"

She looked over at my table and said, "Give me a few minutes to finish setting up and I'll come look." A few minutes later, she came over and started trying on the mittens.

"These are seriously the best mittens I have ever worn!"

"Thank you!"

"Will you set these aside for me?" She handed me four pairs of mittens. I couldn't believe I was now trading wares with someone whose art I had admired for years!

"All of them?"

"Yes, we can work out the trade and payment later, but I love them and I know they won't last long on your table." She was completely correct, too. The Solidarity Craft Fair was the busiest craft fair I'd been to. It was also the one where I knew the most people. All day I was greeted by former students and their parents. We chatted and caught up. My former students all looked so big and mature. It had only been a year and a half since I'd left Union School, but that is a long time for a growing kid. They told me they loved me and missed me. I felt so appreciated. If there was ever a time when I needed to just be affirmed all day, it was that year. You never know what someone has been through or what your kind words mean.

In the last few weeks, it seemed like everyone I knew had announced they were pregnant. We would show up at a holiday party and someone from our softball team would show up with a growing baby bump that wasn't there last summer. The preschool teacher at my school announced that she was pregnant, my step-sister got pregnant, even my high school friend Jessie, in Maine, was pregnant again. I knew that I needed to be happy for all of these people. I genuinely cared about them, but an irrational and depressed voice in my head was angry. Then I was angry at myself for feeling that way. It was a cycle of despair. I started hiding pregnant women from my Facebook feed and ignoring calls from my step-sister. I just wanted to disappear.

The craft fairs were a little vacation from my life. They were a place of good cheer and happiness. It was a respite I desperately needed. By the end of the day at my first year at the Solidarity Craft Fair, I had sold all but eight pairs of mittens. There were five minutes left and I could see that some crafters were beginning to pick up, even though the rules for vendors explicitly asked us not to pack up before 4:00. I didn't want to break the rules and not be invited back. I also didn't want this lovely day to end. I had squared up with the potter and had a pile of beautiful new mugs to give as Christmas gifts. I'd also enjoyed a lovely lunch of hot soup, bread from the Red Hen Bakery, hot cider, and a Christmas cookie. I wanted to hold on to this happiness for as long as I could.

Right as I was about to start packing up, an elderly woman walked up to my table with a push walker. She greeted me kindly.

"How many pairs of mittens do you have left?"

"Eight."

"I would like to buy them."

"All of them?" I had never sold eight pairs of mittens to a single person before. I'm sure she registered the total shock on my face.

"Yes. I have four grandkids and they are all coming for Christmas with their girlfriends and boyfriends and spouses. I don't know if I'll make it out again to do more shopping, so this is a perfect gift. What do I owe you?" She owed me two hundred dollars, but I couldn't imagine charging her that much. I figured she must be on a fixed income.

"How about $150," I said.

"Oh, thank you, dear." She handed me a pile of bills which I didn't bother to count. I was in awe that I had sold every single pair of mittens off my table and couldn't wait to tell Lise-Anne. It was so exciting.

"Would you like a bag?"

"No, I think I can put them in my bag," she said, and she tucked them away in a basket that hung on the front of her walker.

"Merry Christmas to you, dear."

"Merry Christmas to you, too." I sat down and counted out the money she had handed to me. It was two hundred dollars! I looked up to thank her, but she was gone. Some people brush into your life, sprinkle their magic, and go. She was one of them. I looked for her the next year and the year after, but I never saw her again.

The craft fairs gave me adrenaline and hope. They made me love Vermont and my community even more. They filled me with a Christmas spirit in a year when I felt empty. I was so proud of the mittens. Sometimes when I feel like I am at a loss, I list the things I have. That year, I actually wrote out the list in the back of a notebook. It started with Liz. I drew a little heart beside her name. I hadn't been the best partner in the past month, but her love was steady and loyal. I wondered how I got so lucky. The list went on to include: our dog Joey, my job at the Westford School, our house, our family, friends, good health, and car. At the end of the list, I added: Lise-Anne, mittens, and craft fairs. Then, at the very bottom of the paper, I added: "And my credit card is paid off!"

Two-thousand-twelve was not my best year, but somewhere, buried in my boxes of sentimental things, that list still exists as proof that all was not lost. We spent New Year's Eve at Lise-Anne and Scott's house, sitting around their dining room table with their kids, playing Apples to Apples. Their kids were so clever and funny, we laughed until we had tears spilling from our eyes. Lise-Anne roasted potatoes and cheese on a tabletop Canadian Raclette. By 10 pm, everyone was exhausted and Liz and I drove home and went to bed. We didn't bother to wait up for midnight.

The deep freeze of January brought a new kind of low. I no longer had the holidays to keep me afloat. By day I would teach my class, and by night I would sit at my sewing machine and cry. The thought of starting all over again with our sperm donor, Dr. Grey, and Clomid filled me with dread. It was all I could think about. The only thing I looked forward to was crafting with Lise-Anne. I drove out to her house in Westford every Sunday, and we sat by her wood stove and sewed mittens.

"You will have a baby someday, Jen," she said. "I just know it will happen for you. It may not be the way you want it to be, but it will happen."

"I know. I just want it to happen now. I'm ready now."

Lise-Anne's home was peaceful and warm. She had such an easy way of managing it all. Her beautiful children filtered in and out of the room, and she would fix them snacks in between bouts of sewing. She generously shared all of it with me. I wanted what she had so badly, but I wasn't jealous of her. There was enough of her kindness and care for everyone around her. "You are going to be an amazing mom," she would say, and I believed her.

Chapter 9

Motherhood

MAY 2015

I sometimes feel that if I don't tell the story of our first baby, it didn't happen at all. Society rarely recognizes the mothers of unborn babies. It only recognizes me as a mother because I went on to have Helen. When people ask me how many children I have, I always say one, but in my heart, I remember that first little being who was the start of something that never happened.

Several months went by before we tried to get pregnant again. Now that we knew the complicated heartache that could come, our trips to Maine were a little more subdued. Our trusty sperm donor remained dedicated and hopeful for us. After two more failed attempts with him, we decided to try a different course of action.

Over the next two years, we tried nearly every fertility treatment available. I felt terribly guilty about how much money we were spending. We used all our savings and sank into credit card debt. I never wanted to see that wretched Burlington fertility doctor again. He had only succeeded in teaching us that one way to make a miscarriage worse is to throw in some homophobia.

Vermont is a small place, though, so our choices were limited. We began to look out of state. To our immense surprise and good fortune, there were two clinics in Albany, NY. It was a three-hour drive each way, but totally worth it to get the high-quality care we ended up receiving at Albany IVF.

It took us two and half years to conceive Helen. It was September of 2014 when I went in to get a blood test to see if I was pregnant. We arranged for the nurse to call me and leave a message on my phone with the news. The message arrived when I was at school and I saved it because I wanted to listen to it with Liz. I arrived home from work and we sat down on the couch.

"Whatever the outcome is, I love you," she said.

"I love you, too," I said, as I put my phone on speaker and played the message. I'd had some heavy spotting over the last two days, so I was sure my period was on its way and I was not pregnant. I had shared this with the nurse the day before. She urged me to go get a blood test anyway.

"Hello, Jen and Liz!" Her voice was chipper; this was sounding good. "I know you think you are not pregnant, but you are! Congratulations!"

It took me a second to realize what she had said. I'd never been more shocked. I put down the phone and fell into Liz's arms, sobbing. I cried so hard that I began to hyperventilate. We were going to have another chance at motherhood! My eyes swelled shut from the flood of tears. Liz had to get a cold wash cloth to put over them.

The day we found out I was pregnant with Helen felt like the shattering of a mysterious infertility glass ceiling. All of the books and advice I had read about "achieving" pregnancy made me feel like a failure every time we tried, until the last time, when we tried and it worked. I refused to think of the pregnancy in terms of "achievement" though, because it was actually just a miracle. All pregnancies are miracles. When you consider the microscopic cells that unite and multiply to form a human being, it all seems so implausible, and yet, it happens all the time. The profundity of it for me, though I am not a religious person, was that this literally was an immaculate conception.

The first time I got pregnant, I followed the advice of many other women and didn't tell anyone. The reason for this is that so many pregnancies end in miscarriage in the first trimester. The idea is that it's easier to wait until the second trimester to tell people, because there is a much greater chance that the pregnancy will last. The problem with that mindset is, if the pregnancy doesn't last and you have a devastating miscarriage, no one knew you were pregnant to begin with, so no one understands why you are suddenly heartbroken. I didn't want to make that same mistake again, so I immediately called my mom to tell her.

"How far along are you?" she asked.

"About five minutes!"

I then called my dad and stepmother and shared the news with them too.

"That's great, Jen," my dad said. His voice was hesitating. I was so clearly excited, but the last time I'd talked to my dad about being pregnant was the night I found out our first pregnancy was likely going to miscarry. My dad had been a doctor before he retired, and growing up I used to think he was a miracle worker. He gave us our vaccines at the kitchen table and literally handstitched my step-sister's knee up in the dining room once after a particularly bad rollerblading accident. Dad could fix anything. When I had called him nearly two years before, in tears because I was having a miscarriage, it was my last hope.

"Isn't there any way to move the baby into the correct place to save it?" I sobbed.

"No, Jen, this one can't be saved." His voice was gentle.

"Please Dad, please tell me how to save it," I begged. There was just silence. What could he say? My dad usually gives good advice about all medical-related situations. If he had any wisdom to share, he would have spoken up. His silence was the moment I realized there really was no hope for that first baby. Now, here I was on the phone, telling him that I was pregnant again. While I knew he was happy for me, I sensed he was concerned. Parents never stop worrying about their kids. As Lise-Anne said, your children are pieces of your heart, walking around outside your body.

Truthfully, Liz and I were both worried throughout the whole pregnancy. I was thirty-six when I became pregnant with Helen. When doctors referred to me as a "geriatric mother," I laughed. "Oh, sorry," they would say, "the new term is Mother of Advanced Maternal Age."

"That term is no better than the first," I would argue. "Plus it's repetitive."

Most doctors would laugh along with our jokes. Liz and I had a tendency to be light-hearted. I will never forget the poor intake nurse who was collecting my vitals for my appointment one day late in the pregnancy (long after we'd learned the baby's sex). She said something like, "Your daughter's heartbeat is nice and strong," and when I replied, "Wait, it's a girl?" Her face turned to ash.

"Oh my god, I'm so sorry, you didn't know?" Then we broke out laughing. That was probably a mean joke.

Right away at the start of the pregnancy, I began to feel sick. I had what I called, "all day sickness." It was like morning sickness, just all day. Actually, the mornings were the easiest part of the day. By the time I got home from school, I would lie down on the couch and fall asleep. Liz would wake me up to ask if I wanted dinner.

"No, no dinner."

"I'm headed to the library," she would call out. Then the next thing I knew, she would be walking in the door.

"I thought you were headed to the library?" I would say groggily.

"I was there for two hours! I'm making dinner."

"I don't want dinner."

There were many times when I was glad for the sickness, though, because it reminded me that the pregnancy was real.

At ten weeks, we did an early pregnancy screening that revealed what the baby's sex would be at birth. We'd received so much bad news regarding fertility over the last three years, any piece of information about a healthy baby growing inside me was welcome.

We arranged for the nurse to call and leave a voicemail message on my phone so that we could find out together, just as we had when we found out I was pregnant. The early screening came back normal and then the nurse excitedly exclaimed, "She's a girl!"

We named her Helen after my grandmother, on the very same day we found out. We would have called her Peter if she had been a boy; the names Ulysses and Ira had long since been retired with the loss of the first baby. Peter was a fine name, but the name Helen rolled off my tongue and felt like bells ringing in a village square. It was perfect.

That Thanksgiving, we ordered a cake from Mirabelles Bakery, with dark chocolate frosting on the outside and bright pink frosting on the inside. I know it's uncommon to have cake for Thanksgiving dinner, but who ever heard of a gender reveal pie? We let my mother cut into it before the meal even began. She jumped for joy. My mom's two sisters, Aunt Jane and Aunt Sue, were there too.

"We're going to call her Helen, after Grandma," we told them.

"Oh, I told your Aunt Sue that I thought if it was a girl, you would name her Helen, I just knew it!" Aunt Jane said.

"I didn't know, or even guess, but I think it's perfect," Mom said. We all hugged and went on with the meal. I cherished every ounce of joy that my pregnancy brought, both for myself and for my family. I missed my Grandma so much that day because I knew she would have been proud to have her first great grandchild named after her. My friend Jenna Lindbo wrote a song with a refrain that said, "I'm gonna love you when you're gone." That was exactly how I felt about Grandma. It was a love frozen in time. There would be no new memories to make with her, but naming our daughter Helen would be another way to love her even though she was gone.

Lise-Anne and I were busier that holiday season than we had ever been before. We had mittens in five craft stores across Northern Vermont, and were both doing as many craft fairs as we could. I was planning on taking the next school year off to stay home with Helen, so I was trying to save as much money as possible in anticipation of not having my teaching salary.

There were so many people at my craft table buying mittens who were repeat customers. Over the years, I had watched their families grow. The woman with her baby in a sling one year came back with a toddler the next. One of my favorite joys of craft fairs is the community connections made while discussing which pair of mittens is the best fit. I was delighted to share with all my old crafting friends and customers that I was expecting a baby; and disheartened that at this point in my pregnancy, still, no one could tell. Even though I was now almost five months pregnant, because of the all-day sickness, I had barely put on any weight.

At twenty weeks we headed in for a 3-D ultrasound. I was still struggling with terrible all-day sickness and desperately searching for anything to make myself feel better. So many foods had made me sick at that point that the only things left I could eat were breaded baked chicken and broccoli. I also had intense cravings for milk which was funny since I'd always been a little lactose intolerant. When I was pregnant, I could drink a pint of milk. It tasted sweet to me, and never made me feel sick. They say you crave what your baby needs, and I surmised that Helen was a baby who needed calcium.

We didn't have the same excitement and anticipation about the 3-D ultrasound that some parents have. I think this was because we already knew Helen was a girl, whereas most people find that information out at this point. I couldn't imagine waiting twenty weeks to find out our baby's sex. We had named her Helen and had been talking to her in utero for over two months at that point. It felt like we knew her.

The radiologist took lots of pictures from every angle. A few times she furrowed her brow. She moved me into several different positions and asked if I could shift the baby's position. I did a few jumping jacks and got Helen to turn over. She continued to take lots and lots of images. Her brow furrowed again. I began to realize that something was wrong.

"Is it normal to take this many pictures?" I asked.

"It is. We don't want you to have to come back because we missed an angle. And," there was a concerning pause here, "I'm seeing some abnormalities in your baby's formation."

Liz and I looked at each other. I was immediately worried that I'd caused the baby to be malformed because of my inability to eat enough.

"You see, this is the bottom of your child's left foot," she pointed to the cute little image of a tiny foot on the screen. "And this is the top of your child's left knee right beside it."

"Her left knee, or her right knee?" I asked.

"Her left knee."

"How is that physically possible?" Liz asked.

"It's not," said the radiologist. "It's an indication that your child has talipes, or what is more commonly known as clubfoot."

Liz and I looked at each other in utter confusion. I knew what children with clubfoot looked like and I began to panic.

"I'm trying to get enough pictures so that our orthopedic specialist will be able to see what's going on." She left us alone in the imaging room while she went out to check on the photos. I had forgotten my phone in the car, but Liz was already googling clubfoot.

"This is very bad," she said.

"I don't think it's that bad," I said, "I think my brother had something like that, it's fixable."

"Not in all cases. She'll have problems her whole life." Liz was lost in her phone. I knew this was her response to anxiety, but I grew resentful.

"I think you're overreacting. My brother can walk just fine." Liz didn't look up. Her concern cast a shadow of doubt over my optimism. Maybe our child was really going to have problems with her feet for life. My cheeks flushed. I laid back on the exam table and looked at the ceiling. *Couldn't we just have one easy path?*

When the radiologist returned, she told us that she had enough images. She arranged for us to meet with a doctor right away. I was astounded at the speed of this. Apparently, they have a doctor on call for these ultrasound appointments to spare expectant mothers from having to leave the hospital, hysterical, with the news that there is something wrong with their baby. As author and researcher Brene Brown says, "Clear is kind." The more information we could take with us, the less stress it would cause us. I come back to "Clear is kind" all the time in my life, especially when teaching. The times when I have been unclear about my expectations or my feelings with kids or their parents are the times that have caused them the most stress. We appreciated this spontaneous doctor's appointment more than we could express.

We waited in a small room with a circular table for what felt like a long time. Liz was furiously researching on her phone. I was getting frustrated that I didn't have my phone too and couldn't look this up for myself. Liz would occasionally share little bits of information with me. My anxiety grew.

When the doctor finally arrived, he started by asking if there was a history of clubfoot in my family. He was an older man with a kind and studious face. I hadn't really thought about my brother's deformed feet since I was little. He used to have braces to correct his feet and after he outgrew them, my parents left them in the toy box for us to play with. I used to try them on and hobble around the playroom. They were terribly uncomfortable.

The doctor was very interested to know that someone in my family had had this before. He was collecting research for a new study that was trying to determine the extent to which clubfoot is hereditary. For the most part, though, he admitted that as far as they knew, it was a random malformation that occurred in about one in one thousand children. That seemed like a lot to me. I didn't know any children who had clubfoot. He peered at me from behind his wire-rimmed glasses and gave a gentle smile.

"You don't know they had clubfoot because we have amazing doctors who use the Ponseti treatment to fix clubfoot in infancy. By the time children enter your classroom, they've been walking on normal feet for so long, it's a distant memory."

We left the hospital that day full of hope and despair. We were hopeful that Helen's feet could be corrected. But the doctor said the talipes appeared to be bilateral and quite severe. After all we had been through with the infertility and the miscarriage, couldn't the universe give us just one break?

Lise-Anne came over a few days later to stuff and cuff our latest round of mittens.

"How did your ultrasound go? You didn't find out that Helen is actually a Peter, did you?"

"Nope, she's a Helen."

"Well, that's good, you wouldn't want to have to order your mother another cake."

All things considered, having a child with clubfoot was not the worst thing that could have happened. When you open your life to having children, all sorts of unexpected things occur. We had a child coming who was going to need some additional care, but her feet could be fixed and we were grateful. Because we found out about Helen's feet at twenty weeks, we were able to start making plans to help her as soon as she was born. There was a doctor in our area who specialized in the Ponseti treatment. This was a process of casting and braces that started soon after birth and gradually trained the child's growing feet and legs to be correctly positioned. It would take three to five years of braces, but she would most likely be able to walk and not require surgery.

We were also able to find mentors in our community whose children had gone through the Ponseti treatment and had worked with Dr. Lisle, the local specialist. It turned out we knew plenty of people whose children had been born with clubfoot, but just as the doctor at the ultrasound had said, we just didn't know it because they had all been fixed.

The night Helen was born, I went into labor at around ten o'clock. I was nine days overdue and had an induction scheduled for later in the week.

"We don't let the geriatric mothers go past forty-two weeks," the doctor had told me.

"Yes, I wouldn't want to give birth after I become a member of the AARP."

By now, my geriatric jokes were landing a little better with the team of midwives and doctors at our feminist obstetrics practice. "I prefer Mother of Advanced Maternal Age," I reminded her. "Or just, Expectant Mother Who Happens to Be Thirty-seven."

I'd had no Braxton Hicks contractions, no cramping of any

kind, and literally no indication that Helen had any intention of arriving ever. When my contractions finally started that night, I had four contractions that were exactly ten minutes apart. I was certain that this was it. Liz called the midwife to give her a heads up and she said to call back when they got to five minutes apart. As soon as she hung up the phone, I was having another contraction.

"How many minutes has it been since the last one?" Liz asked.

"Three?" We set the timer again and the next one came at two and half minutes.

"There has to be some mistake, you just had a contraction." We let two more contractions go by at two and a half minutes before we called the midwife back. She seemed kind of shocked. Apparently first deliveries don't typically go this quickly. She advised us to drive to the hospital and come in through the emergency room for an expedited admittance.

Helen came into the world so fast that none of our friends or family even knew I had gone into labor until after she was born. During her delivery there was a small hang-up at one point, and the midwife asked me to stop pushing for a moment.

"Something is obstructing the birth canal," she said to one of the other attendants. She pushed and prodded a bit to see if she could free the obstruction. "Woah! There it is!"

"What? What happened?" I said between pants.

"It was a fist!" Liz said. "Leave it to you to deliver a baby fist first!"

"She's gonna be a wild one!" I said, and with a couple more pushes, she arrived!

The midwife put her under the warming lights, which I thought must have felt kind of harsh to a little being who was used to total darkness. I held off asking for a long time as they stitched me up, but I was dying to know.

"How are her feet?"

"Her feet?" asked the midwife.

"Yes, her feet. She's supposed to have severe clubfoot."

"Well, they look fine to me."

I wasn't sure I believed her, but was too tired to question her further. Over the next twenty-four hours we were visited by our pediatrician, who also thought her feet looked fine, and by Dr. Lisle. She told us that yes, one of Helen's feet had a mild case of clubfoot and the other was just a little inverted. She was confident that both feet could easily be fixed.

My mother told me once that she remembered nursing me in the early morning of her thirtieth birthday. She was looking out the window, and a big, fat bunny hopped by. It was late April, 1978. I don't know why that particular memory of hers stuck with me. There was something so sweet and simple about that moment; a moment that I experienced, but obviously could never remember. As mothers, we are the memory keepers of so many precious little moments.

The spring Helen was born was stunning. The flowering trees in our neighborhood had exploded in purple, pink, and white. Their perfume wafted into the open window of Helen's nursery. Everything felt so alive and fresh and new. I would nurse her for hours on end, sitting in the reclining chair, looking out her bedroom window. Sometimes a bunny would go by just as the sun was coming up and I would think of my mother and how history repeats itself. Helen would eat until she fell asleep at my breast. Then her head would fall back a little, her mouth still agape, lips puffed and swollen from sucking. I never got tired of gazing at her perfect little face. Sometimes I would look up to the ceiling and cry tears of overwhelming happiness to the universe. I'm not even sure if I believed in the stars or a deity of some sort, but I believed enough in something beyond myself to whisper my deepest gratitudes.

"Thank you," I would say. "Thank you for this moment. Thank you for this breath, this body. Thank you for this perfect little miracle, asleep in my arms." Everyone's advice was: "Don't blink! It all goes by so fast!" In those moments, it didn't go by fast. I reclined in that arm chair by the window and dozed with the warm little bundle of Helen in my arms. Then she would wake up and nurse some more. I saw many sunrises from that window, and every single one went by slowly, and I never blinked. I cherished every moment of my baby and had no regrets.

Over the next few weeks, Helen's leg and foot were casted and re-casted five times. Each time, Dr. Lisle moved the foot closer to the correct position and casted it in place. Helen was such a compliant and placid baby, she never seemed to mind. The skin behind her knees grew raw from the casts, but she slept through the night and ate like a champ.

Sometimes we would post pictures on Facebook, and people would ask how she broke her leg so young. There were a lot of teachable moments as our entire friend and family community began to understand the Ponseti method and our choice to use it. In the end, Helen did have to have one small surgery to correct the clubfoot. It was an Achilles release. I couldn't believe such a surgery even existed. They cut Helen's Achilles tendon clear through and casted her leg with her foot flexed. Then, like another miracle, her body grew a new, longer Achilles tendon. Amazing.

After the surgical cast came off, Helen graduated to boots and bar braces. She had to wear them for twenty-three hours a day. They held her feet pointed out at what looked like an impossibly uncomfortable position. She never seemed to mind, though. Humans are made to adapt.

Every time I felt overwhelmed by the doctor's appointments, or the constant stares of children and the not-so-discreet sidelong looks of strangers in the grocery store, I would sit down and sew. The repetitive motion of cutting the wool and stacking the neatly cut pieces in piles on our dining room table was so satisfying. When everything else was out of control, sewing mittens was within my control. I would get lost in my crafting. My anxious new mother mind was able to completely rest in the state of creative flow. I felt like I was part of the magical, powerful machine that is generations of women crafting. Long before we had medication and psychotherapy, long before we had iPhones and Facebook, we had each other and we had creativity. It was, and always had been, a force for healing. It was *my* therapy. I would put Helen down for a nap, pull out a beautiful sweater, and start cutting. The more difficult the Ponseti treatment became, the more beautiful mittens I created.

When November rolled around, I had more than enough inventory to go back to the Cozy Nook Craft Fair at the Essex Free Library. Lise-Anne and I had made so many beautiful pairs of mittens, I couldn't wait to sit at that booth and sell them to everyone. I laid them out on my table and took pictures of my display. It was my final goodbye to our creations. They looked so perfect all together, neatly lined up, waiting to be taken home and loved by someone other than us.

About halfway through the day of the craft fair, I was reaching record sales. My cash box was overflowing. I knew Lise-Anne would be so psyched. I had left Liz at home with Helen and a fridge full of breast milk, but we planned for her to come to the craft fair anyway, just for a visit. I wanted to show her off to all my crafting friends. Kelli, the organizer, came right over and oohed and aahed.

"When did you have a baby?" my customers asked.

"In May!" I proudly told them.

Helen was wearing her boots and bar for twenty-three hours a day at that point, and we had carefully planned her one hour of freedom from the braces for the hour she was at the craft fair with me. When it came time to feed her, Liz watched my table and I walked to the back of the row of bookshelves behind where I had set up, for some privacy. I sat in a chair and Helen latched right on. I looked at the wall and remembered that this was exactly where I'd stood three years before, with my uncontrolled tears over the miscarriage, my broken heart, and my empty arms. My eyes filled with tears as I looked up at the ceiling and once again said to whatever omniscient being was listening,

"Thank you."

Chapter 10
The Gift of Mittens

2016

In the early spring of 2016, after a very busy and successful winter selling mittens, Lise-Anne and I squared up our finances and had a heart to heart about Swittens. I confessed that even though I loved making the mittens with her, the holiday season had run me ragged. I no longer wanted to make the time to sew hundreds of mittens each year. Helen was napping less often and soon my maternity leave would be over and I'd have to go back to teaching. I wanted to spend all my time with Helen. Lise-Anne also confessed that as her three kids were getting older, she too was being pulled in a lot of directions. We decided to stop working together and to go our separate ways. We both agreed that we could make the mittens separately and both use the name Swittens. Lise-Anne wanted to keep selling mittens at craft shops and I wanted to occasionally sell at the craft fairs. It was an amicable parting.

At the time, I really thought that we would keep spending time together as friends, but we never did. We were both so busy, and our lives were moving in different directions. Her kids were now in middle and high school. Our daughter was almost one. Our new friends mostly consisted of other parents with small children with whom we could arrange playdates and share hand-me-downs. I always felt that if I needed Lise-Anne I could call her and we would pick right up where we left off. She was like that, and so was I. I will always adore her for the guidance and friendship she gave me during those terrible years of infertility and for the beautiful gift of being my crafting buddy. She taught me a lot of valuable things. Sometimes when I look at our dining room table, covered with fleece and wool, I think of her. There really is very little time to clean when there are beautiful things to create and family to love.

That fall I returned to my teaching job in Westford. I dropped Helen off at daycare and cried all the way to work. She had grown an untamable head of bright blond hair over the summer and had a great big toothy smile. At fifteen months, she was running around the house, babbling, and laughing. Everything delighted her. It was heartbreaking to leave her in someone else's care while I went into the classroom to teach and care for other people's children.

On my first day of school, a little girl named Sarah arrived in my 2nd grade class. She also had a full head of blond hair, and brown eyes, just like Helen. She was crying because she missed her mom. I did my best to comfort her, then asked an instructional assistant to watch my class so that I could use the bathroom. I locked myself inside the teacher's bathroom in the hallway and sobbed. What if Helen was crying to one of her teachers that she missed me? My guilt and anguish about going back to work tied knots in my stomach. I pressed a cold paper towel to my eyes and tried to recover quickly. It was the first day of school, I couldn't spend the day in the bathroom.

Making mittens was very low on my list of priorities that holiday season. After school, I would rush home to get Helen and try to make the most of what was left of the day. At daycare, Helen made friends and played with new toys. Every day she seemed to learn something new and time moved too quickly. I was grateful to Essex Hollow Playschool for teaching Helen and loving her every day. Sometimes I would show up to pick her up and she didn't want to go home, she wanted to stay and finish playing. Her daycare teachers were wise and experienced caregivers who gave us wonderful advice on parenting and different ways to help Helen grow as a confident and loving child.

I walked into Essex Hollow Playschool in December of 2016 with my hands full of gift bags. There was a pair of my homemade mittens, a holiday card, and a gift card in each one. Now that my child had her own daycare teachers, I was excited to give holiday gifts to them. I always appreciate holiday gifts from my students' families. Some are unbelievably generous. I have received everything from a dozen eggs and a pound of bacon from a student's farm, to a traditional kente dress from a Ghanaian family. Some of the gifts have been funny, too. One year, a student gave me a silky slip for my birthday. She thought it was soft and pretty and I might look nice in it. Another family brought in a giant box of home-brewed hard apple cider, at the beginning of the school day no less, and left it right on my desk in plain sight. It was a good thing the principal didn't happen to visit that morning because I didn't notice it until lunch.

After handing out the gifts and saying goodbye to Helen for the day, I headed out the door. Liza Driscoll was heading in. I had gone to college with Liza, who was the owner and director of the daycare. We exchanged pleasantries and then quickly found our way to my favorite topic to discuss with her: her father-in-law. I can't say that I know most of my friends' fathers-in-law, but Liza's is Vermont Senator Bernie Sanders.

"Oh my gosh, did you make mittens for everyone?" she asked as she peeked inside her bag.

"I did!" She pulled her pair out of the bag and put them on.

"I love them!" she said.

Right then, as I was talking to her, it occurred to me that I thought Bernie Sanders would like a pair of mittens. He was probably getting close to retirement, and I knew he liked to go on walks.

"Do you think Bernie would like a pair of my mittens?" Liza's eyes lit up. I knew she loved her father-in-law.

"Oh my gosh, he would love that!"

"If I made him a pair, would you pass them along to him for me?"

"I definitely would."

It hadn't been a great year for Bernie. He'd lost the Democratic nomination to Hillary Clinton, and then Clinton lost the election to Donald Trump. Every time the topic of the election came up, a deep shadow landed on Liza's face. My family was still reeling in disbelief that Trump had won. Liza said almost nothing about it, but I imagined it had been a far more difficult fall for her family. I turned to leave, then as an afterthought, I asked,

"What color is his coat?"

She laughed. "I think it's brown, but I'm sure he would love anything you make for him."

"Ok, well, I'll look for something that goes with brown. See ya later!"

"You too!" With that I headed out the door and drove to work. It was a quick conversation. I drove away from the daycare trying to think of what pieces of wool I still had left that might work. I was excited to make a pair of mittens for my favorite senator. It was a small gesture of kindness to do for Bernie after all the tireless ways he had advocated for just about everyone I know.

I sat down to make the mittens for Bernie towards the end of the holiday season. I spent a long time looking for the perfect pieces of wool. I didn't have a lot of sweaters left, and most of my inventory had been sold at craft fairs. I looked through some old wool that I'd put aside. There were several sweaters that were too loosely knit to look good in mittens, and a few that had shrunk so much when I washed them that they were basically cardboard. In the back of the closet in the guest room, I spotted a plastic grocery store bag and pulled it out. Inside was a brown sweater given to me years before by the grandmother of one of my students. She knew I was repurposing old sweaters, and she left it for me on my desk one day while I was outside at recess duty. It was the right color, but it was in rough shape. I laid the sweater out on the bed and studied it. The elbows were worn completely through, and there were several places where the wool was torn or stained. There were also a bunch of little holes scattered throughout, most likely made by moths. I decided to cut it up and see if I could salvage enough material to make the mittens.

First I cut off the arms. Then I cut the cuffs and the rim off the bottom of the sweater. I cut the front away from the back and looked closely at the inside. The moth holes were actually quite small. I decided to sew them shut with a needle and thread. The wonderful thing about knit wool is, it's actually very forgiving. I found some old brown thread in my grandmother's sewing box and got to work. After carefully sewing shut four or five moth holes, most of the back of the sweater was in surprisingly good condition. I found a piece of wool I'd cut for a different mitten and used it as a pattern to cut out the two pieces that would make up the back of the mittens. Compared to the tattered old sweater they came from, they actually looked quite nice. They were definitely the nicest pieces of wool left from that sweater.

It gave me a lot of satisfaction to repurpose this nice brown wool from a sweater that I never thought I would use. It was a coffee brown color with white, tan, and dark brown zig zags. There was a line of what looked like diamonds across the middle, but I later learned they were *fleurs-de-lis*. I found a nice piece of blue wool from an L.L. Bean sweater that I'd collected on one of our many trips to Maine and used it for the palm of the mitten. Then I found a piece of cream-colored wool with a green diamond design for the heel. Since the brown wool was kind of thick, I looked for a thinner brown cuff from another sweater to finish it off.

I thought a lot about Bernie while I was making his mittens. I don't actually follow politics that closely. I find them stressful. I look the candidates up before I vote and that's about it. Bernie was different, though. I actually did follow him, at least a little. The previous February, when he was on the campaign trail, he'd had a rally at the fairgrounds in my town. Liz and I hemmed and hawed about going. Neither of us like crowds and we knew it would be noisy. Helen was about eight months old at the time. However, something about Bernie compelled us to just go for it. He was traveling the country, and we thought it might be our only chance to see him in person.

We put Helen in the stroller and wheeled her through the fairgrounds to the enormous set of buildings where the rally was being held. Thankfully, there were two rooms; a packed room where Bernie was speaking and an overflow room that was less crowded. There were lots of people with kids in both spaces. Huge screens were hung from every wall so that people could see Bernie speak. The energy was electric.

It felt like a pep rally with all the cheering, chanting, and music. When Bernie appeared, the crowd went wild. We covered Helen's ears so that she wouldn't be afraid, but she didn't seem to mind. She was smiling from ear to ear. Everything Bernie said was a testament to social justice.

"I want to go into the big room for just a minute to see him in person," I told Liz, and I headed off into the crowd. I stood way in the back where there was still space to move around, and there he was. Speaking in his Brooklyn accent, waving his hands, and stopping every thirty seconds so that people could cheer, he had the crowd rapt. I'd never been to a political rally before. It reminded me of a rock concert. This scene was too good to miss. I hustled back to where Liz and Helen were standing in the overflow room and convinced Liz that we could leave the stroller behind and carry Helen into the big room with us.

By the time we got back to the big room, Bernie's speech was almost over. The cheering was deafening. Soon everyone began chanting, "Bernie! Bernie! Bernie!" We chanted too as we bounced Helen up and down. She was squealing with glee. It was such a joyful moment.

When the rally was over, we made our way home and got Helen ready for bed. She went down easily and Liz and I sat in the living room and turned on the TV. We had the baby monitor nearby. Helen was playing with her little stuffed owl in her crib and babbling to herself. She was an early talker. At ten months she had a total of seven words:

1. Mama
2. Kit (kitty)
3. Da (dog)
4. Chi (chickadee)
5. Beebe (Aunt Brigid and Aunt Betsy Beebe)
6. Ba (ball)
7. Bed (bed)

We hadn't been watching TV for very long when the staticky sound of the baby monitor turned on. Ours was a video monitor, so we picked it up and looked down at little Helen lying in her crib. She was chanting something.

"What is she saying?" Liz asked.

"I don't know." I turned up the volume while Liz clicked off the TV. Then we heard a little voice calling:

"Buh— nee! Buh— nee! Buh—nee!"

"Is she saying 'bunny?'" I asked.

"It sounds like it."

"Buh— nee! Buh— nee! Buh—nee!"

"That's amazing!" I said.

"It's clear as a bell."

"I wonder where she picked that up?" That is when we both looked at each other.

"Oh my gosh. She's not saying 'bunny,' she's saying 'Bernie!' She's repeating the chant she heard at the rally!" We sat there mesmerized for several more minutes as Helen chanted "Buh—nee! Buh—nee! Buh—nee!" until she eventually fell asleep. Her eighth word was "Bernie," for my favorite senator.

I was thinking back on that night as I finished the mittens and tried them on. I always try on my mittens to be sure they fit just right. Not only did they fit perfectly, but I was pleased with how nice they looked. I pulled out a little greeting card and wrote a quick note to Bernie thanking him for being an awesome senator and for running for president. I told him I'd been voting for him since I was eighteen. I added, "I hope you run again." I knew it was unlikely, given his age, but if he did run again, I'd vote for him.

The next day I brought the mittens to Essex Hollow Playschool and dropped them off for Liza. She wasn't there, but I left them with someone on staff. A few weeks later, I saw Liza in the parking lot while picking Helen up.

"Jen!" she called over to me. "I've been meaning to thank you for the mittens you gave to Bernie! He loves them! He wears them every day on his walks."

It made me so glad to think of Bernie walking somewhere in the woods of Vermont, wearing the mittens I made for him. That is the way I imagine him when he *is not* being a politician. I have never met Bernie, and it may seem odd to send a stranger a gift like mittens. But I have a lot of reverence and gratitude for him. Somewhere in the archives, there is a picture of him speaking at a gay pride rally in Burlington in 1986. I would have been eight years old that year. That is the way I think of him when he *is* being a politician. Long before I came out, Bernie Sanders was advocating for my rights. It wasn't popular in the 1980s to stand up for gay rights, but he did it anyway. That's why I gave him the mittens.

Helen turned two the following spring. Her glorious, blond, fluffy hair matured into a legitimate toddler mullet. She woke up happy and laughing every morning. Something inside her loved the world and everyone in it from the moment she was born. There was nothing "terrible" about her twos. She was cheerful and engaged in everything. I wanted to make the most of every moment of her childhood. We would read to her from a stack of board books and sing her to sleep at night. Then Liz and I would cuddle on the couch and watch some TV, or read. The time that Helen was sleeping became the precious time we had together as a couple.

I remember that Lise-Anne seemed to craft all the time, even when she was on vacation, but not me. Each year I made fewer and fewer mittens for holiday craft fairs. Sewing was my respite, my meditation, my healing. Sometimes I needed it, and sometimes I didn't. The joys and challenges of being Helen's mother and Liz's partner filled every piece of me. Several years went by and we used the money I made from the occasional craft fair to rent a small beach house in Maine for a week each summer.

By the time Bernie Sanders' mittens reappeared, I had all but forgotten about them.

Chapter 11
The First Meme

"Did you make these mittens?" Liz held up her phone from her side of the couch and I leaned over.

It was a frigid January night, almost exactly a year before the Biden/Harris inauguration. Pictures of presidential candidate Bernie Sanders were swirling around the internet. He was speaking at the Women's March in Portsmouth, New Hampshire. In his very Bernie way he was gesticulating with hands adorned by mittens I had made for him. As if by some cosmic rehearsal, someone had taken a picture and created a meme of Bernie's mittened hands, splashed with rainbows and sparkles

"Here, I'll send it to you." Liz was much more up on pop culture than I was. Helen was in bed and we were watching reality TV on my laptop. Liz was surfing the internet on her phone. I'd like to say we were doing something more exciting on a Saturday night, but it had been a long day of trying to occupy a four-year-old, and we were spent. Parenting is often a less-than-glamorous endeavor.

"Someone wrote on Twitter that those mittens were knitted by Bernie's grandmother for Christmas," Liz noted.

"There are so many things wrong with that statement."

"Maybe you should go on Twitter and set the record straight. Well, as straight as you get." The doldrums of January in Vermont had admittedly eroded our humor.

"I don't think I even have a Twitter account."

We cleaned up from dinner and settled into bed. Curiosity seeped into my brain. I did want to see what people were saying. Before I turned off my bedside light, I tried to create a Twitter account, but it turned out that I did already have one. I jumped through a few hoops to reset my password and began to scroll. Most of the posts I saw were talking about Bernie's "oven mitts."

"His mittens don't even look like *oven mitts!*"

"Oh my gosh, are you looking at Twitter?"

"Maybe."

"I'm trying to sleep." I angled the phone away from Liz's side of the bed.

"I can still see the light." I could tell by the tone of her voice that she was more amused than annoyed.

"Ok, sorry. It's just funny that some random person made a meme out of this. I mean, who would think to do that?"

"Someone with too much time on their hands."

"Thousands of people are talking about it."

"And tomorrow they'll be talking about something else."

"I know you're right. It's just a funny moment."

"Maybe you can make some mitten sales?"

"Maybe. How do you make a post on this thing?"

"You're impossible. It's called a *tweet!*"

"Right, I knew that."

"No, you didn't, that's the problem. If you're going to be internet famous, you need to know what a tweet is."

"I do, look, I'll prove it to you." Through a little trial and error, I figured it out and made my first ever Twitter post.

Jen Ellis @vtawesomeness 1/20/20
I made Bernie's mittens as a gift a couple
years ago. They are made from repurposed
wool sweaters and lined with fleece (made
from recycled plastic bottles)
#BerniesMittens

"There. I even did a 'Pound Bernie's Mittens' at the end."

"That's called a *hashtag*."

"It's always going to be a *pound sign* to me." I couldn't see her face, but I'm pretty sure Liz was rolling her eyes at me.

My first tweet was retweeted 3,031 times, and over twelve thousand people liked it. I was a little embarrassed that my Twitter name was "vtawesomeness." I didn't think many people would actually see that handle when I made it. The next day, an old college friend called me to ask if I was "sure" I'd made those mittens. She was a writer for our local Vermont newspaper, *Seven Days*, and had seen my post on Twitter.

"Yes, I'm sure."

"Like, do you have proof?"

"Well, I still have some pieces from that sweater, I think . . . You could call Bernie and ask him."

"I'm only asking because we'd like to do a little article on you for the paper. Would you mind talking to one of our reporters?"

Later that day, Sasha Goldstein called and I gave a brief interview for *Seven Days*, Vermont's weekly newspaper. He wrote a short article and published it online. *Seven Days* later listed it as one of their most popular stories of 2020, which was impressive considering it was the year of the pandemic!

Earlier that winter, I had sold mittens at two holiday craft fairs. I put up a picture on Twitter of the inventory I had left, along with my email. Right away, my inbox was flooded with requests. My report cards were due on Friday (a scene that would be eerily repeated one year later), so I had to put off fulfilling all the orders for a few days. But over the next few weeks, I responded to every person who wanted mittens and coordinated sales through the mail and PayPal.

It was through this little burst of sales that I made my favorite pair of mittens. A mother named Heather in Cincinnati contacted me about making custom mittens for her daughter, who was a huge Bernie fan. The daughter, whose name was Carolyn, was unable to walk and had contractures in her hands due to cerebral palsy. Heather sent me the dimensions of her daughter's hands and a picture for me to go by. I made Carolyn smaller, thumbless mittens with a tighter cuff so they wouldn't fall off.

Heather was so incredibly grateful. It meant Carolyn could go outside with her caretaker through the winter without the danger of her mittens falling off when she was being pushed in her wheelchair. Heather was diligent about removing every barrier so that Carolyn wouldn't be house-bound. I sympathized with Heather. There were times when Helen was an infant that she needed modifications to her clothes, too. Her braces were awkward and bulky. I would have done anything to make her more comfortable. I understood some of Heather's struggle, but I admit, only some. Carolyn would need modifications for her whole life. It was a small thing for me to do to help her.

My guess is that lots of people think the mittens I made for Bernie Sanders were my best creation; but they are wrong about that. Carolyn's were never famous, but they were the most extraordinary mittens I have ever made.

Within two months of that first meme, we were mired in the first few weeks of the COVID-19 pandemic. The world as we knew it was shattering and no one knew how or when it would be pieced back together.

By April, Bernie Sanders had withdrawn from the race for the 2020 Democratic Presidential nomination and endorsed the senator from Delaware, Joe Biden. Like every elementary school teacher, I transformed part of my house into an at-home Zoom classroom overnight. For me, it was the craft room. I boxed up what was left of the wool and stored it in the basement. The craft room became an elaborate set-up of lights and white boards. Before they closed the school down, I brought home my Judy Clock, dry erase markers, a phonics puppet, and piles of read-aloud books.

There was endless speculation about when school would open again and people would be able to go back to work. A six-week hiatus from in-person teaching stretched to the end of the school year. Spring unfolded in a daily routine of talking to the neighbors from across the fence and riding our bikes around the block over and over again. We started doing the grocery shopping every other week, and thoroughly disinfected everything that came home. It was unclear how the virus was being transmitted, so we spent a lot of time taking every precaution. There was a tangible level of fear floating in the air, along with the smell of spring blossoms. I hung the little *Seven Days* article on the wall next to some of Helen's art work. It was a sweet little reminder that for a brief moment, my mittens were Vermont famous.

Chapter 12

The Outdoor Classroom

FALL 2020

W hen the school district administrators emailed the teachers in July of 2020 to tell us that we would be returning to the classroom in person in the fall, I was shocked. COVID-19 cases across the country were rising at a staggering rate. Thousands of people were dying every day. The argument for returning to school in person was that children were not considered to be vectors for the virus, and when children were infected, they weren't dying. There didn't seem to be much concern or care about the teachers who would also be present in the school buildings. I found it ironic that decisions about whether or not to return to school were being made by district administrators in remote meetings. *They* didn't feel safe to meet in person, but they didn't mind if *we* met in person. Stories rolled out over that first summer of the pandemic of outbreaks at summer camps and daycare centers. As schools in the southern U.S. started back up in August, there were outbreaks in schools too.

I thought it was a terrible idea to return to school. I was sure we were heading for disaster. No amount of mitten-making could calm my anxiety about this one. To add to the angst, Helen was starting kindergarten in the fall. We had requested she be placed in my school for child care purposes, but really I just wanted to keep her close. It broke my heart to imagine her first foray into public school would be spent with a mask over her face all day. I couldn't imagine teaching with a mask on my face all day either.

I needed to find a way to make attending school safe for my students, and for me. If we had to go back, it was safest to be outside. So, I came up with a plan to build an outdoor classroom. I applied for a land-use permit from the town of Westford and was granted a parcel of land in the woods adjacent to the school. Marcie, my principal, agreed to rent a porta-potty for my class to use so that we could limit our trips inside. Every roadblock I encountered with the formation and building of the outdoor classroom, Marcie plowed down. She made it possible for us to have a firepit and take our meals outside. She allowed us the flexibility to adjust our schedule to fit the weather. If I needed to move math to the afternoon because it was too rainy to get out all the counting supplies, fake money, and Judy Clocks in the morning, she gave the green light. Her support for my outdoor classroom project was partly because she recognized the safety and ingenuity of it, and partly because she understood my constant struggle with anxiety. If teaching in the forest was the only way to get me to return to the "classroom," then the forest could be my classroom, and that was that.

Marcie and I had now worked together for eight years, and time had been kind to our relationship and friendship. We'd come a long way since that day in her office when I sat sobbing with the news of my terminal pregnancy. I was thankful for Marcie's steadfast leadership and wisdom. She was the first boss I ever had who allowed me to accept my mistakes as opportunities for growth instead of situations for blame and shame. When you work in an environment where it's ok to make mistakes and grow from them, you open yourself up to a whole different kind of professional improvement. I didn't always agree with Marcie, but I respected her.

My outdoor classroom came together so beautifully that the kindergarten and first-grade teachers followed suit and built their own teaching spaces just across the field. Sometimes I would be sitting out beneath the trees, leading a reading group, and the kindergarteners would walk by and wave as they went to their spot in the woods. Then I would see the shining face of my own little Helen, skipping along with her friends, completely in love with her teacher and our little country school.

I refer to the second graders I taught in the 2020-2021 school year as my "Pandemic Class," even though the pandemic started when they were still in first grade and continued after they went on to third. It was the year I had my Pandemic Class that we wore masks for the whole school year. We had to be flexible to adjust to the many changes in our situation. One week we would be learning in person, the next we would be learning in some hybrid form of in-person and online. There would be long absences of students who were "close contacts" to someone with COVID-19. Sometimes we would start the day inside so that a quarantining student could Zoom in from home, their image appearing on the Smart Board as they greeted someone during morning meeting.

The kids wore masks all day, even on the playground. When they sat on their carefully socially-distanced stumps around our campfire, they could take their masks off, and I could see their beautiful faces. Parent volunteers built a teaching kiosk in the center of the outdoor space for me to hang flipcharts and store white boards and teaching materials. One parent even took some of the small trees we'd cut down for the clearing to make a beautiful, rustic arbor for the entrance, on which she wound grape vines in intricate patterns. It was like a portal to another world. And it was another world. Teaching outside was quiet and peaceful. Even the loudest voices couldn't fill up the forest. Each day after morning meeting, the students would take their folding camp chairs and find a sun-dappled spot beneath a tree to read. I conducted phonics groups in a little clearing next to the ring of tree stumps. I fell so in love with teaching outside that I never wanted to teach inside again.

Parents donated three tarps which we hung over clearings to sit under on the rainy days. It was a surprisingly dry fall. The first rainy day didn't occur until the beginning of October. It was cold and wet. Several times I asked the class if they wanted to go inside, and they unanimously voted to stay out every time. They said they liked the sound of the rain pitter-pattering on the tarps. Plus, they had come prepared with rain pants, hats, and coats, and they wanted to test them out. Our books got wet and wrinkled, the students turned in math work on tattered, damp, and dirty sheets of paper, and we lost plenty of supplies; but it didn't matter. We were safe, and the kids were happy. They knew it was safest to be outside, and they didn't want to risk a COVID-19 outbreak that would send us all back to remote schooling.

For the first two months with my Pandemic Class, we had a hybrid schedule. Half my class would come to school Monday and Tuesday, and the other half would come in Thursday and Friday. When the kids were not physically at school, they were participating in online learning. On Wednesdays I had the whole class together online. I tried desperately to build a whole-classroom community on those days, but it was hard. The Monday-Tuesday class became one community, and the Thursday-Friday class became another. When the kids in the Monday-Tuesday class had recess, specials (like art, physical education and music), and lunch, I would run inside to my computer and log on for online lessons with the Thursday-Friday class. It was nonstop work all the way through the day; there was never a break. Some days I would have so much work to do to plan for the next day of remote teaching that I would put Helen in front of a movie in my classroom after school. Then I'd stay until five or six o'clock at night to write the remote plans, create all the work, including the differentiated work for kids who were above or below grade level, and collect and organize all the supplies needed for every at-home lesson. The strain was unbearable.

Even though I knew I wasn't going to be doing any craft fairs, I tried to make some time for sewing. I knew it would be helpful to be creative. When the pandemic first began in the spring, I had taken the clothes my mother saved from my grandmother's house after she died and combined them with the fabric from my wedding dress and Liz's wedding clothes to make a stunning quilt for Helen's fifth birthday. Then, in the fall, a local woman asked me to turn her deceased mother's cashmere sweaters into six lap quilts for her siblings for Christmas. The project kept me busy for months and gave me great joy to complete. My stress and worry over everything related to the pandemic and remote teaching made me feel, at all times, on the brink of insanity. My doctor had prescribed an antianxiety and antidepressant medication the previous year, and she doubled the dose that fall to keep me from going off the rails.

Everyone seemed to be carrying a tremendous amount of stress, especially as the election day drew near and the debates became more and more divisive. One day I noticed a particularly large amount of distraction and angst amongst my class. It was late October, and kids were coming to school repeating things they'd heard at home. They were being bombarded with negative political ads on TV, and many of them were worried about relatives who'd been hospitalized due to COVID-19. The tension was palpable. I was having trouble keeping the kids focused on our math lesson. Finally, I looked out at them and said, "Who wants to learn how to use a cordless drill?"

This shifted the mood considerably. I told them a story about a time when my stepmother had shown me how to build a sailboat out of sticks and birchbark one summer when we were staying with friends on Lake Memphremagog. It had taken forever to carve a hole in the bark to insert a stick for the mast, but once the boats were crafted, we tied strings to them and let them sail away off the dock before pulling them back to us. This entertained us for hours.

I happened to have a cordless drill in the outdoor classroom that day, and I figured it would be fun to teach the class how to use it. I threw the drill into my backpack and we set off on the trail through the woods to the river. I figured if creativity worked to relieve my stress, then it could relieve theirs too. We spent the afternoon finding birchbark and drilling holes into it to build sailboats. Then we launched our boats into the Browns River, and chased them down the riverbank. We raced the boats and figured out how they could catch the most wind. The next day I used examples of birchbark sailboats in their math lesson and we easily made it through the material from both days.

Sometimes when it was raining, we would go for long walks in the woods, not caring how wet we got. We explored the waterfalls at the southern end of the forest, along Roger's Brook. At the end of those days, we'd return to our indoor classroom so the kids could change into their spare clothes before boarding the bus to go home. The rainy days were always our favorites. I would look out over their rosy-cheeked faces and soaking wet hair, and think: *this is what childhood is supposed to be about.*

My Pandemic Class insisted on staying outside well into the winter. On the very cold days, we built in extra time to go for longer and longer walks in the Westford woods to warm up. We frequently hiked up to the beaver ponds behind Pat Haller's farm across the road from the school. We walked across the frozen water and noted the place where we'd spotted a beaver in the fall.

As it got increasingly colder outside, the chickadees became hungrier and we decided to see if we could train them to eat birdseed out of our hands. I had read about people doing this, but wasn't sure seven and eight-year-old kids could sit still long enough to earn the trust of these friendly birds. You'd be surprised at how peaceful and calm a child becomes when they have fresh air all day and are not confined to the four walls of the classroom. The first time a chickadee landed on a child's hand we could hardly contain ourselves. After it flew away, the whole class cheered. We fed the chickadees so often that when we walked around the field outside our outdoor classroom, they would call to us and swoop down above our heads looking for handouts. One winter day, we migrated out to the field to stay warm in the sun, and the chickadees were certain we had emerged to provide them with afternoon snacks.

"I'm trying to teach spelling!" I yelled when a chickadee flew so close to my head that I had to duck. The students laughed so hard about this that I eventually gave up on the lesson and started laughing too. Soon we were laughing at each other's laughter as the greedy chickadees continued to swoop over our heads. It was completely ridiculous and completely joyful.

I was afraid that the class might score poorly on their mid-year assessments because I had taken such liberties with their lessons, but their scores were just fine, even slightly better than previous years. Where I lost teaching time, I made up for it with investment and commitment. The kids told me that every day felt like an adventure and they couldn't wait to come to school. It was some of the best teaching I had ever done and I knew this would be a school year they would never forget.

In November, ten days after election day, President Biden was declared the winner. People in Vermont flooded the streets in impromptu parades and celebrations. Liz and I set up our projector on our front lawn and showed the acceptance speech on my grandmother's old slide screen. Several of our neighbors joined us with lawn chairs and champagne. I was beginning to feel that everything would be ok. There was talk of a vaccine on the brink of approval. I had my outdoor classroom, and my community of friends and neighbors. I did wish it was Bernie instead of Biden up there on the big screen, but I was deeply thankful it wasn't Trump. We all cried when Kamala Harris took the stage. I was left with the feeling that even though progress seems to take forever, big change was finally here.

Chapter 13
The Dings (that's how it started)

"What was your first sign; like, what was the first moment that you knew something was up? What was the first meme you saw?" People always ask me these questions. They want to recount the glory with me, the awe of sudden internet fame.

"It started with the dings on my phone. I was remote teaching in my classroom, it was a very snowy day. I was alone."

"So did you immediately go online and see all the memes?"

"No. I was teaching. Teaching is a one-lane track. You can't be online looking at memes and teaching at the same time. It's all-consuming." These facts surprise people.

"So, what did you do when your phone started dinging?"

"I silenced it."

"You silenced it?"

"Yes." I did a lot of explaining in these interviews about the nuances of online pandemic teaching and the need to present for your students . . . remotely.

"So, the memes were flying around the internet, someone found you on Twitter, Bernie was walking around the inauguration with a mysterious manilla envelope, and you were teaching?"

"Yes. I didn't think it was a big deal."

I don't know how many times I told this story. After a while, all the interviews blended together. Internet fame is a little like being struck by lightning, except the odds of survival are probably better. It used to be that in order to become famous, you had to first be noticed by a particular kind of person, like a talent scout, agent, producer, or publisher. But the beauty of the internet is that those gatekeepers of fame are now being usurped by the general public. Ordinary people rise to fame just for being noticed by other ordinary people. I love the shattering of a glass ceiling—or gate in this case. However, by 2021, nearly a year into the pandemic, I had grown to cherish the privacy of my life. I didn't want to be famous. People talk about the phenomenon of FOMO—Fear Of Missing Out—but I jokingly told everyone that during the pandemic, I had discovered JOMO: the *Joy* Of Missing Out. I just wanted to stay home and spend time with my family and our friends.

People asked me in interviews over and over if I knew Bernie was going to wear my mittens to the Inauguration: *No.* Was I surprised when this happened? *Yes.* Could I have ever seen this coming? *Not really. I mean, the mittens went viral once before, but I thought that was the end.* Can any of us see what is beyond our imagination, as it barrels towards us in the dark?

In the summer of 2009, I flew out to Skagway, Alaska to visit my brother Ryan. He was working as a train conductor on the White Pass and Yukon Railroad. Ryan is an industrious man, eight years younger than me. He had endeared himself to just about everyone in that little town. He was known for picking up odd jobs on the side. He frequently traded his carpentry services for delicacies such as moose meat or home-brewed beer. That year he had acquired a shrimping permit and kept two shrimp pots in Nahku Bay.

One sunny afternoon after he got off work, Ryan asked if I wanted to go with him to check his shrimp pots. A friend had lent him a canoe. We come from a big canoeing family, and I thought this sounded fun. We drove out to Matthews Creek and parked the car near the sandy beach at the head of the bay.

The ocean was still and calm as we paddled out to the empty plastic laundry detergent bottles Ryan had tied to the rope attached to his shrimp pots. I could see the makeshift buoys resting on the water. They were way out near the entrance to the bay, almost to Dyea Point. Luckily they were colorful and easy to find.

When we reached the buoys, I steadied the boat while Ryan began pulling up the line. The wet rope was heavy and awkward in our canoe. We were wearing life jackets, but I really didn't want the canoe to tip and dunk us in the frigid, glacial water of the bay. We were a long way from either side of the shore.

The haul from Ryan's first shrimp pot contained at least thirty giant shrimp and two Dungeness crabs.

"That's dinner!" Ryan called. His goofy little-brother smile beamed in the sunlight.

He was almost done pulling up the second trap when we saw the first blow from the whale. It was maybe twenty-five feet off the starboard side of the canoe. It was loud, like the air dryer at the end of a car wash, but brief. At the end of the spray of water that forced up from the back of the whale was an almost human-like grunt.

"Shit! Shit! Shit!" Ryan's panicked voice sent a shocking fear response through my veins.

"What should we do?" I asked. My knees turned to jelly and my feet were anchored to the canoe, as if about to run. Realizing that there was nowhere to go, I squeezed the handle of my paddle with a fierce and fearful grip.

"I can see the shrimp pot," Ryan said. "I almost have it."

"No. Drop it! We need to get out of here!"

"Steady the boat," Ryan called, and in one large heave he pulled the second shrimp pot up into the canoe. He was working quickly now, hands shaking and red from the water as he dumped the still-wriggling shrimp out onto the space around his feet.

"Oh my god!" I held my breath and watched as the dark shadow of the whale approached the side of the boat. One flick of its powerful tail would send us careening into the air. We hadn't seen another person all afternoon. There would be no one to save us once we landed in the icy water.

"Oh my god!" I repeated. It was all I could think of to say. I gently put my paddle down and held on to the gunnels of the canoe as the silent creature slowly passed below and the water beneath us turned black.

"Don't panic. I'm almost done," Ryan whispered, trying not to aggravate the giant mammal below. My knuckles turned white as Ryan put some more bait in his trap and prepared to throw it overboard.

The strange thing was, despite the whale's proximity to our boat, the surface of the water remained calm. As suddenly as the water went black, it turned back to the turquoise blue of the glacial runoff. I wasn't sure if it had really passed, or had just dipped deeper into the endless depths. It looked like the coast was clear.

"Do you see it?" Ryan asked.

We peered over both sides of the boat, half expecting the giant to rise up like Old Faithful beneath us.

When Ryan was little and I was a pre-teen, we shared a room for a few years. In the morning, he used to get up before me and play quietly with his toys. He wasn't allowed to wake me up, but sometimes he would creep up to my bed and look at me. I could hear him breathing and feel his face inches from my own. I would open my eyes and go "Boo!" He would squeal and laugh, his blue eyes shining.

He looked up at me now with those same blue eyes, a hint of a smile on his face. He lived for moments like these. He saw this situation as an adventure. I saw it as a calamity. I figured I might be a strong enough swimmer to make it to the shore, but I knew Ryan was not a strong swimmer, and I would never leave him. If this whale flipped our canoe, Ryan would die of hypothermia, and I would die trying to save him. I spent those moments with the whale beneath us steeped in the kind of fear and love an older sister has for her much younger brother. Ryan experienced the whale as a thrill. This was how we were intrinsically different.

We hesitated for another moment before we saw a second blow in the distance off the port side, heading back out to the sea. In one quick toss, Ryan hurled the shrimp pot over the side of the canoe, the coiled rope whipping out from the bottom of the boat after it.

"Let's get out of here," he said as he returned to his seat at the back of the canoe. We paddled directly toward the shoreline near Dyea Point and followed the coast back to the beach at Matthews Creek. The paddling was slow as we worked against the tide. We constantly scanned the horizon for signs of the whale.

When I think back on that day, I replay that experience in my head as if I were watching it from a plane overhead. Ryan and I look like two tiny dots on a sliver of a boat, and the whale, the size of twenty-five elephants, swims ominously below. The sheer majesty of it is breathtaking.

There have been very few experiences in my life that matched the fear and awe of that moment. If I had to compare it to any other one thing, it would be the quiet chaos that ensued in January and February of 2021 when, out of the blue, my quiet life was shattered by the mass media frenzy around Bernie Sanders at the inauguration wearing a pair of mittens I'd made for him.

Chapter 14
Inauguration Aftermath

For weeks after my grandmother died in 2008, I would wake up in the morning and have a few blissful seconds of forgetting. My mind would be clear and content. Then, just before remembering, I would have a brief moment of panic. The panic was narrated by the simple thought, "There is something terrible that I am supposed to be remembering." I would then remember, and my world would go back to the shattered reality that my life would never be the same without her. On the day after the inauguration, that was the progression of my waking: the blissful forgetting, the panicked recall, and the dreadful remembering.

The difference, of course, was that no one died, and what happened at the inauguration was something between fantastic and unbelievable. I didn't wake up excited and happy about it, though. I was filled with dread and fear because I had no idea what to do. I turned on my phone and opened up my email. The list of people who had contacted me overnight had swelled to over eight thousand. Most people said the same thing: "I'm sure you are overwhelmed with requests, but I want to join the queue, I would like to buy a pair of Bernie mittens." Then they would detail the numbers and styles of mittens they wanted. A Buzzfeed reporter, Ruby Cramer, who found me on Twitter, had retweeted a tweet of mine from January 2020. It contained a picture with mittens I had for sale at the time. Each one had a little number on it so that I would know which pair people wanted to buy. The emails I found most off-putting were the ones that just said: "#15 please."

Even more dreadful than the thought of dealing with eight thousand emails for mittens and media interviews was my next thought, which was: "Shit! My report cards are due tomorrow."

I didn't even realize I had yelled this out loud until Liz turned over in the bed beside me.

"Good morning to you too."

"I'm sorry, I can't believe all that stuff happened yesterday. I don't have time to deal with it today. I have to finish my report cards. Can you pick Helen up from school so I can work late?"

"Sure."

"The whole meme thing doesn't even feel real," I said.

"Well, it is." I couldn't tell if Liz was amused or annoyed by the sudden media burst. Liz is an introvert. She didn't want any attention. I'm somewhere in between introvert and extrovert. I didn't mind the attention at first. I also considered the possibility that this might be a way to earn some extra money. We needed a new roof for our house and our car was on its last leg. I could sell *some* mittens—but I couldn't possibly make 8,000 pairs. How would I decide who got them and who didn't?

I dragged myself out of bed and made a strong pot of coffee. Liz made Helen's lunch and we said our goodbyes. Our school district had briefly gone to five days a week in person before the holiday break, but as COVID-19 cases surged across the country and the American death toll surpassed half a million, we were down to four days a week with Wednesdays online. The day after the inauguration was a Thursday, and I drove to school with Helen bundled up in the back seat. The fields were covered with fresh snow. Lots of people were still digging out from the storm. January in Vermont can be relentlessly cold, so my class had temporarily moved inside.

As soon as we got to school, Connie, our school librarian, stopped by my classroom door.

"This is unbelievable, you are so famous!"

"Really? I think it's gonna blow over pretty fast." Connie was much younger than me, and much more technologically savvy.

"No, you should see how this is all over Twitter. You need to get blue-check certified."

"What's that?"

"It's something that people get to verify that they are who they say they are, so people can't impersonate you."

"Why would anyone want to impersonate me?"

"You'd be surprised what people will do."

"I don't want to get certified. I don't have time for this. Plus, I don't want to be famous."

"But you are famous!" Connie rushed off to take temperatures in the kindergarten classroom, and Helen wasn't far behind her. During the pandemic, all students had to have their temperatures checked upon entering the building. The pandemic safety routines had become so commonplace that we no longer gave them much thought.

My students lumbered into the classroom in their bulky snow suits and boots.

"I saw you on the news, Ms. Ellis!" said Jack.

"So did I!" said Grace. "And Helen too!"

"Wait, you were on the news?" asked Charlotte.

"Yup, I was. I'll show everyone at morning meeting." On my way to school that day, I wondered if my students would have heard about my famous mittens. If they hadn't heard, I wasn't planning to tell them. It seemed like it could be a distraction. A large portion of my job as a teacher has to do with minimizing distractions. Many of them clearly had heard, so I called up the clips of news reports on YouTube and showed them on the Smart Board.

It was somewhere in the middle of morning meeting when the classroom phone rang for the first time. I answered it and a polite British accent chimed through the other end.

"Hello, this is Stephanie, I'm a reporter with the BBC, am I talking to Jen Ellis?" My students started to meow at each other.

"Yes?"

"Yes, hi, I was wondering if you are the maker of Bernie Sanders' mittens?"

"Yes." Now the two Maddies were out of their seats and heading for the cubby space. "Hold on—Maddie and Maddie, you need to stay in your seats." They gave each other mischievous grins and turned around.

"I was wondering if you have a moment to discuss the internet meme sensation caused by your mittens?"

Three kids in the back were now simulating what looked like a playful cat fight, while a shy girl nearby was pretending to lick her paws.

"I'm in the middle of teaching right now." I excused myself and hung up the phone. We continued with our morning meeting.

"Ring, ring!" Now we were doing a reading mini-lesson. "Ring, ring!" This was starting to feel strangely similar to the text message dings from the day before. This time the caller ID said Toronto. I let it go to voicemail. However, someone from Toronto proceeded to call my classroom phone every fifteen minutes for the rest of the morning. There were calls coming in all day from other places: Australia, Germany, Dubai. My school's secretary, Betty, was fielding many of them. During my lunch break I went down to the office and asked her not to let any more phone calls go to my classroom. It was too distracting. But reporters are a relentless bunch, and they quickly learned how to bypass Betty and call my classroom phone directly.

By the end of the morning, I was on the phone with our district's tech department trying to figure out how to make it stop. We decided that I would turn my ringer off but keep my classroom radio on, which I primarily used in my outdoor classroom.

The Maddie who sat in the front row was in charge of listening for the name "Jen" when it was called on the radio. The radio sat on my desk nearby.

"Who's Jen?" asked Maddie.

"That's my first name."

"Oh, ok, Jen." Maddie laughed.

"No, you call me Ms. Ellis. Everyone on the radio will be calling for Jen. If you hear them call 'Jen' and I don't hear it, let me know, ok?" Maddie agreed.

When my students went to recess and lunch, I glanced at my email and noticed a journalist from Jewish Insider had reached out to me. I decided to call him back. His name was Matthew Kassel, and he seemed surprised to hear from me. He asked a slew of questions, and I tried to give him thoughtful answers. I'm not Jewish and I didn't know much about his online magazine. His was just the email that appeared at the top of my swelling list of incoming messages. I answered a few phone calls and gave another brief phone interview before I realized thirty minutes had passed and I needed to quickly eat, or lose my chance.

I sat down to eat my sandwich and check my email. I now had nine thousand emails. It was impossible to even read them. I would try to read the subject line of an email and the screen would automatically refresh and the subject line would disappear under ten new emails. They were not only coming in on my personal email, but also on my school email. There was a knock at my door. My colleague Marie poked her head in.

"I just heard on the radio about a business opportunity for you.

You really should call these DJs and hear what they have to say."

"I don't really have time, Marie. I need to work on my report cards." Marie gave me the look a mother would give a disobedient child.

"You are missing a great opportunity here."

"I can't, Marie, thank you for letting me know, but I can't." A feeling like acid reflux churned in my throat and burned down the veins in my arms. It was the same feeling I'd had when my college girlfriend cheated on me; like something really good was getting away and I had no control over it. I had a single goal for that day and it wasn't to sew mittens, or give any more interviews; it was to finish my report cards.

"I really think you should pursue this," pushed Marie as I waved goodbye to her and closed and locked my classroom door. I tried to take another bite of my sandwich and gagged. Eating would help me make good decisions and I knew it, but I couldn't manage to chew and swallow. The pressure of the situation had a physical hold on me. I didn't know it at the time, but over the next two weeks the stress would cause me to lose eleven pounds.

I used what was left of my lunch break to write a few more report card comments. The previous Monday we had the day off for the Martin Luther King Jr. holiday. I came to school anyway and sat in my empty classroom for nine hours straight writing my report card comments. My family used the day to go sledding and watch movies on Liz's laptop while curled up by the fire. Teachers are rarely given time to write report cards, and this year was no exception. The expectations for the elaborate content of these documents grows every year, turning Martin Luther King Jr. Day into one of the most stressful "vacation" days of the year.

In the 1980s, our elementary school report cards were a single eight and a half by eleven-inch piece of pastel-colored card stock folded in half. Our school's logo was on the front, and inside was a mimeographed set of standards. The teacher gave us varying grades, from E for exceptional to S for satisfactory to U for unsatisfactory. She wrote them out by hand in blue or black ink. There were no comments. On the back of the document there was a place for my parents to sign four times each year indicating that they had read the report card.

When I started teaching elementary school in Montpelier in 2006, the report cards looked much the same as they had in 1986 except we now had a space at the end for comments. I painstakingly handwrote a summary of every student's progress each term; a process that left my hand aching and me second guessing everything I'd written. Not long after I started my career in Vermont, my school moved to digital report cards. With the introduction of the Common Core, a set of learning standards adopted by most public schools in the US, our digital report cards became more and more complex.

By 2021 report cards took about twenty hours for a teacher to produce. They were done on a computer program where you click through all the standards and give kids a rating of beginning, approaching, meeting, or exceeding the standard. For every standard, the teacher had to have evidence to back up the rating. In addition to the ratings, there were comment boxes for every subject, with a place to detail what the whole class had been working on, and a separate place to detail what the specific student was working on. If a teacher didn't leave a comment in a particular box, the box didn't disappear, it just appeared as an empty box in the report, like a wagging finger chastising the teacher for not being more thorough. When all was said and done, the printed report cards were ten pages long and very, very thorough. There was no place for parents to sign. I often wondered if they even bothered to wade all the way through them.

I was about seventy-five percent done with mine from my marathon of report card writing on MLK Day, but I still dreaded the night ahead. I knew I was going to stay at school until they were printed and ready to go. At the end of the school day, when Liz arrived to pick up Helen, she handed me a lunch box packed with dinner.

"I know how this goes," she said. I loved her so much in that moment. It takes a special person to be married to a teacher.

"Thanks."

I strapped Helen into the car seat in Liz's car. Due to the pandemic, most of the kids were no longer riding the bus. Parents would line up in their cars and classroom teachers would stand outside and dismiss kids one at a time. It was a tedious process. There were days when I sat outside for an additional twenty minutes after school, waiting for parents to arrive to get their kids. It made me feel resentful. It was little things like this that made my job extra hard.

The day after the inauguration was no exception. I stood out in front of the school, freezing, with one of my students as we waited for her dad to arrive. Every minute I sat there waiting was one more minute I would be at school tonight, trying to finish my work. As soon as her dad arrived, I dashed back to my classroom and furiously started writing the math comments section. Two hours later, I started the literacy comments.

As the hours went by after school, my feelings of angst grew. I had been cutting wool for a few weeks now in preparation for next year's craft fairs. I could go home after this and make three or four more pairs of mittens tonight. Then what would I do with them? I used to sell them for thirty dollars a pair. Would I raise it to fifty? Should I sell them for more? It was true that some people probably would buy the mittens for much more, but was it right to take advantage of this internet sensation and price gouge people? Thirty dollars was plenty to spend on mittens. All evening, my mind kept wandering off on tangents like these and I would have to reel myself in to focus on my report cards.

The sun set and my classroom cast a beacon of light out the

window into the blackness of the Westford schoolyard. The afterschool program ended, and the building was now quiet and empty. Somewhere in the lonely building, the custodian, Jeff, was mopping the floors. He was probably the only other person there.

When it was time to print a draft of my report cards and check them for spelling and other mistakes, I realized that the printer near my classroom was broken again, so I walked down the hall to the main office. My eyes burned from looking at the computer screen, and my hips ached from sitting at my desk. The empty Westford School was creepy at night. The sound of my footsteps in the hallway rang like the soundtrack to a horror movie. If I thought too much about it, I began to panic. *There's no one here,* I told myself. *Mind over matter.*

The light was on in the teacher's room and I cautiously looked around the corner of the open door. A man turned around and jumped when he saw me. I let off a little scream. It was just Jeff, mopping the floors.

"Sorry, you scared me!" he said.

"You scared me too!" I was a little embarrassed about screaming. It was completely involuntary. I did it on rollercoasters too.

"You're working late."

"Yup. Report cards are due."

"You gonna make some more mittens to sell?"

"I don't know." I rolled my eyes and shook my head. Jeff took the hint and the mitten conversation was over. My report cards were pumping out of the printer. I stood impatiently nearby, trying to avoid any more conversations. I truly liked talking to Jeff, but wanted to be done with the day. I gathered up the stack of report cards and warmed my hands on the hot, copied paper. I said my goodbyes and walked back down the long hallway to the primary wing.

My mind was racing. Should I make more mittens? Am I losing valuable time to seize this moment for profit? I could hire people to sew for me and start a cottage industry, then earn enough to buy a factory. These thoughts were overwhelming. They made me feel like I *should* stop teaching, or I *should* be pursuing this to make money, or I *should* be frantically making mittens in every moment of spare time. I didn't want to surrender my life to mitten making, but I didn't want to miss an opportunity that could be great.

In the back of my mind, there was another nagging voice that grew louder every year, especially during report card season. For several years I'd been wondering if I should look for a different job. Sometimes being an educator sucked all the life out of me. It was endlessly frustrating. Maybe it was time to move on from teaching? However, the outdoor classroom had been so incredibly fun that thoughts of looking for another job hadn't crept into my mind in months. I honestly didn't know what to do. The only thing I knew I *had* to do was finish my report cards.

Liz had made me korma curry with rice for dinner, one of my favorite meals. I knew I was hungry, and desperately wanted to eat it, but after a few bites I began to gag again. Some people eat when they're stressed; I can't even chew. A terrible angsty feeling was rising in my gut. I threw the rest of the dinner away and began proofreading the one-hundred-seventy-page report card document, ten pages for each of my seventeen students. I highlighted the mistakes and painstakingly corrected them in the computer program. At around ten o'clock, I was finally finished. I pressed print and walked down to the main office again to pick them up. I would need to staple and fold them tomorrow.

Helen had long since fallen asleep by the time I got home. I was so thankful to fall into Liz's arms. She gave me a big, sincere hug.

"Thanks for the dinner, Babe, I needed it."

"How was your day?"

"Bad." I explained about my stressful interaction with Marie and how my inbox was beyond full with mitten requests.

"What should I do?"

"What do you want to do?"

"I want it all to go away. I'm just so tired. I don't want to make mittens for anyone."

"Then don't." She made it sound so simple.

I stumbled up to bed and pulled my homemade quilt over me. I looked at the wall for a long time, then the ceiling. Liz came to bed shortly after, and I tried not to toss and turn too much. I didn't want to keep her awake. A sliver of moonlight peeked in from the side of the window shade. Liz's breathing changed and I could tell she was asleep. I envied her. She always fell asleep more quickly than me.

After several hours of alternating between studying the wall and studying the window, I got out of bed and went downstairs. I turned my laptop on and googled "Bernie's Mitten Memes." The images went on and on: Bernie was playing chess in *The Queen's Gambit*, Bob Ross was painting Bernie into a peaceful mountain scene, Bernie was being pulled by a dogsled, sitting at a restaurant, and inserted into photos of holiday gatherings. I pulled up my email and could see that I now had ten thousand requests for mittens. It had only been a day and a half since the inauguration. People were not just requesting one pair of mittens, they were asking for three or four, or more. They wanted them for everyone in their family, for all their coworkers, and for gifts. In addition to their requests, people were writing incredibly kind things to me.

"Thank you for giving us such a laugh, we needed it."

"You gave us something to smile about!"

"I just want to tell you that I love your mittens and I saw you on the news, you are great!"

I wanted to answer each one of their kind notes, but I needed to try to sleep. It was past 3 A.M., but I figured that a couple hours of sleep were better than nothing so I returned to bed. After another restless hour or so, I finally fell into a deep, dark sleep in which I had a terrifying dream. I dreamt that I was sitting on our couch and heard a noise in the kitchen. All of a sudden, a figure was moving toward me very quickly. It flashed back and forth like a strobe light, oscillating between a person who resembled Liz and a large male intruder. It was approaching me so quickly, I didn't have time to think. Was it good? Was it Liz? Should I open my arms and embrace the person I love most in this world? Or was it a dangerous thing? It came at me so fast. The intruder had no face and my heart was pounding, but then it would turn into Liz and I wanted it so badly. Before I knew it, the heavy weight of the being was sitting on top of me and I was startled awake. It's funny how our minds process events in real life through our dreams. I was wide awake and it was Friday. I was starving, exhausted, and dreading the day ahead. At least my report cards were done.

It was close enough to morning now that making coffee seemed like "the next right thing" to do. I laughed at myself for quoting Anna in the movie *Frozen II*. That was the answer, though: I didn't have to know exactly what to do in this situation, I just needed to do the next right thing. How could anyone know how to handle this kind of media blitz? I just needed to do the next right thing. I opened my laptop and did a media search through the emails that had come in. I set up two more interviews for my lunch break and after school. I now had thirteen thousand emails, and more and more people were also emailing me at my school email address.

The past forty-eight hours of being bombarded with media and business offers had exhausted me. There was definitely a part of me that wished Bernie had never worn the mittens to the inauguration. I wanted my quiet life back. When I told all of this to Liz on Friday morning, she said, "Me too."

"I don't know how to make that happen, though."

"Well, you could start by not talking to the reporters." There was an element of snark in her voice that led me to believe she was irritated by all of it. I looked over at her and let out a slow, deflated breath. I knew she didn't mean to hurt me, but that stung a little. I was doing the best I could.

I arrived at school and found a slew of handwritten messages from Betty on my desk. Someone from Saudi Arabia wanted an interview; so did reporters from France, Australia, Poland, and a spattering of places in the U.S. I put them in the top drawer of my desk and began to set up my classroom for the day.

That morning, I shared with my second graders some honest truths about the situation.

"As you know, our classroom phone is shut off, and we have a radio system in place if people want to contact us. Maddie is listening for my name on the radio. But I also want to tell you that it's possible that some reporters will come out to the school to try to find me." The snow storm from Inauguration Day had lasted into Thursday as well, and the roads were fairly difficult to navigate, but Friday was a bright, sunny day. If the reporters wanted to find me in person, this was the day they would do it. I stared into the innocent, wide eyed faces of my students.

"I want to remind you that you should not talk to anyone you don't know."

"Will they come into the school to talk to you, Ms. Ellis?" Amelia asked.

"No. No one can get into the building because of the pandemic. All the doors are locked and no one is allowed in. If someone approaches you, it would most likely be on the playground. Just remember, there is always an adult nearby, and it's important not to talk to people you don't know."

I felt very bad saying this to my class. I didn't want them to be afraid of strangers. Lots of people we didn't know parked at our school to access the walking trails in the Westford Woods. At the same time, I was worried that an eager reporter who had not been able to reach me via phone or email might just take a chance and drive out to the school. The thought scared me. I didn't want this to affect my work or my students. They already had an exhausted teacher who couldn't keep a meal down and was stressed beyond belief.

After morning meeting, we began transitioning to our reading workshop. Some students were browsing for books in our classroom library and I was gathering with a small group at the reading table. Suddenly, our classroom door opened and a man I had never seen before walked right in. He was a tall, imposing man with a black wool hat pulled low over his brow. Everyone stopped in their tracks and a hushed silence fell over the room. How on earth did this man get into our building? Every door was locked; no one, not even parents, were allowed in the building.

"I just wanted to say, congrats on the mitten fame!" His voice was goofy and light-hearted. "How exciting for you! How is it going?" My heart was pounding and a tingle ran up my spine. Who was he? If he was a reporter, where was his camera crew and why was he being so casual?

"I saw you on the news. That was a great interview with Helen." My eyes grew wide. I immediately regretted that I had included my daughter in the news interview. Now everyone knew who she was, and her privacy was ruined too.

"I really love your mittens, I bet you're selling tons of them now!" He shuffled from one foot to the next, holding his winter gloves in one hand and a briefcase in the other. He was talking to me like he knew me but I was sure we had never met before. I walked closer to him and positioned myself between him and my students. I wasn't sure what to say, but in case he wasn't sane, I wanted to keep my students safe.

"I'm sorry, but who are you?" My eye began to twitch involuntarily as it does when I am exhausted and stressed. There was a nervous pause.

"Oh, I'm so sorry! I'm Alan Chapin." He removed his hat, tucked it under his arm, and reached a friendly hand out to shake my hand. Then laughed at himself and turned his outstretched hand into a wave. No one was shaking hands anymore.

"I work for the school district. I was here for a meeting and I thought I'd stop in to say hi to our world-famous teacher. I should have introduced myself!"

I did recognize his name from district emails. We had been so secluded at school during the pandemic. It was kind of astonishing to see an unknown face in the building, much less in my classroom. No one was allowed in anyone's classroom during COVID-19. I sometimes went days without seeing even my closest colleagues.

"I'm sorry, Alan, but I have to ask you to step into the hallway, we're not supposed to have anyone in our classroom."

"Oh yes, well, I just wanted to say hello. I'll head away." With that he left. I closed the door behind him and waited until he was out of ear shot. Then, for the second day in a row, I locked the door.

"Who was that?" Jack asked. "Was that a reporter?"

I was worried that they could see the panic on my face.

"No, he was just a person who works for the school district."

"I've never seen him before."

"Me either," said Dylan.

"Are you really a world-famous teacher?" asked Ana.

"No, I'm definitely not!" But even then I was beginning to wonder.

"Did you know who that guy was, Ms. Ellis?"

"No, he just wanted to say hi. Let's move on," I said, and we continued on with the morning.

As I went about teaching my reading groups, I began to realize what the terrible feeling was, the one from the night of the inauguration. It was the fear of being *known*. I had been living my life as a fairly low-profile person. I could walk down the street and most people didn't know who I was, and I liked it that way.

I could make mistakes, state my opinions, fumble through life and be imperfect, and most people just forgave me and paid little attention to all my faux pas.

Lots of people choose to be public figures. They run for political office or become movie stars. They have agents and publicists to manage their fame. I didn't choose this fame and didn't know how to manage it. And now, millions of people knew who I was. There is a terrifying pressure and responsibility of being known. It is a platform and an opportunity, but I didn't quite see that part yet. All I knew was that the quiet privacy I appreciated about my life was over, and I was scared.

Chapter 15
Darn Tough

I am a confident but sensitive person, a combination that makes me an easy target. I knew that about myself. I felt assured that I could talk to reporters, but I knew that hundreds of internet trolls would be at the ready to pick apart everything I said. A great deal of my anxiety after the inauguration came from wanting to do the right thing and being deeply afraid I wouldn't. By the end of the first week, I was so full of stress over what to do that I felt like I was walking around with lead in my shoes and rocks in my gut. I had talked to so many reporters, I'd lost count. It was a little embarrassing to be on TV. I hadn't had a haircut since the summer before, when Vermont had COVID-19 more under control. My eyebrows hadn't been waxed in almost a year. On top of that, like everyone else, I'd packed on a few extra pounds during that long, cold, pandemic winter. Then there was another part of me that insisted it didn't matter. Everything was happening so quickly that I had no other option but to show up as myself. If the internet trolls wanted to discuss my weight or unibrow, wasn't that a deeper reflection of their insecurity? Wasn't that more about their fear?

There was always the possibility of making more mittens and selling them online. Neighbors suggested to me that I could list them for sale for as much as one thousand dollars apiece. Every time I seriously considered doing that, though, I felt that same fiery feeling like acid reflux pulsing through my veins. The stress of starting up the mitten business again in full force overwhelmed me. It's one thing to sell your mittens at a few craft fairs, where people can try them on and choose which pair they want, it's another thing to sell them online. I very rarely make two pairs using the same wool sweater for every part. If I opened an Etsy store, I would have to list and picture each mitten individually, and it would take forever.

Then there would be the element of customer service. When selling mittens online, people have LOTS of questions about size. Many customers want you to measure the mittens and take pictures of them from every angle. I had learned this the year before, when I'd tried to sell a few pairs online to customers who found me on Twitter after the first meme. Sometimes a customer would hem and haw over a particular pair, and in the meantime someone else would swoop in and purchase it. Then the original customer would be annoyed that I sold the pair they wanted. If I didn't have a job as a school teacher, and I wasn't the mother of a five-year-old, it *might* have been possible for me to open an Etsy shop and engage with customers in this way. It *might* have been possible for me to go to the post office every day to mail out the orders and handle returns. But all of that would consume me.

I considered the possibility of opening my own brick and mortar for a brief minute. That thought passed quickly. I'm not really a business person, I'm a teacher. Owning my own shop sounded nice—I would never again have to write report cards—but the actual day-to-day of sitting in that shop, with my livelihood completely dependent on the people who might or might not walk through the door, was too risky. I was also well aware that old

sweaters are a finite commodity. There are lots of crafters competing for the wool in thrift shops. If I was ever going to leave teaching, it wasn't going to be for mittens. There were just too many
variables that could lead to failure. I also knew that I couldn't turn
sewing into something I needed to do for profit when I so often
needed it for my sanity.

At the same time, I was starting to get a lot of feedback on
social media from my interviews. People seemed to like me. They
liked the fact that I wasn't turning my newfound fame into a cap-
italist venture. They liked the fact that I appeared normal and
kind. There's a real need in our society to combat greed. I told
reporters that I wasn't going to throw away the quality of my life
to chase after money. I had a five-year-old daughter and a wife. I
wanted to spend my spare time with them, not making mittens
for the masses. People were cheering for me. The sensitive part
of my heart was overjoyed that people I didn't even know liked
me. It felt like I was being given a big thumbs up in a world that
sometimes leads with a different finger. The ex-president was
gone, Biden was now president, and somewhere in a little corner of Vermont, there was a teacher telling everyone that when
you already have everything you need, more money doesn't make
you more happy. I was surprising myself. Sometimes I would
look back at my interviews and think, is that really me? Who is
that thoughtful person with such a clear vision of what it actually
takes to create a joyful life?

On the Friday after the inauguration, I sent my students home
with the report cards that had been my albatross. With a head
finally clear enough to think, I realized that I was at the end of my
rope. I needed advice on how to proceed. I knew this situation

was full of potential, but I was out of ideas. I pulled into my drive-way and a reminder popped up on my phone about scheduling an appointment to get our taxes done.

Linda! I'm not sure if I yelled it out loud or if it was just a really loud thought in my head. Linda is our extremely smart accountant. I unbuckled Helen from her car seat and sent her inside to Liz.

"Tell Mama I need to make a phone call in the car."

"Okay Mommy!" Helen grabbed her princess backpack and ran down the driveway towards the back door. I shivered, hurried back to the driver's seat, and turned the car back on. A wave of heat blew out of the air vent on the dashboard and I turned it up while dialing Linda's number.

I was so grateful when she picked up the phone. Linda is a practical, kind, soft-spoken lesbian who knows every aspect of our family's finances. She had filed my taxes on the mitten busi-ness for many years. Linda was also an old friend. When I first moved back to Burlington after leaving North Carolina, I lived in her barn apartment. Her partner, Steph, and I used to jam on our guitars. Just hearing her voice brought my blood pressure down.

"It's the famous mitten lady!"

I rolled my eyes.

"Yup."

"How are you holding up?"

"Not good. It's too much." I held my free hand up against the heat.

"I was wondering about that. What are you going to do with all of it?"

"I don't know, but honestly, I just want it to go away. I can't handle the pressure."

"Every interview I've seen of you looks like you're weathering it pretty well."

"I'm faking it."

"Ah. Well, what do you want to do?"

I leaned my head against the steering wheel. When I lived at Steph and Linda's in my 20s, sometimes I would sit with Linda on her side porch while Steph obsessed over the roses growing up the side of their picket fence. Linda was always good for a heart-to-heart chat.

"That's why I'm calling. I don't know what to do." I let a silent tear fall from my eye. I didn't want Linda to know I was crying, but it was hard to hide.

"Have people been reaching out to you to help make the mittens?"

"Yes, hundreds. My inbox has thousands of messages from people asking for mittens. More than I could ever make. And there are business offers and people wanting to give me sweaters. I don't know where to start! I just want to get rid of it. I want someone to swoop in, and handle it all without me."

"Why don't you sell it?"

I picked my head up like Linda was sitting in front of me and gave her a surprised look.

"Sell what?"

"Sell your business."

"I don't have a business to sell! I've been trying to get out of the mitten-making business." I raised a frustrated hand in the air to emphasize the point. Every year when we sat down with Linda to do our taxes, she asked how much money I had made from the mittens and despite my efforts to downsize, I always made something.

"I know, but can you sell the pattern?"

"I don't own it. It's all over the internet. I've changed it, but I can't patent what I didn't create."

"Well, think about what piece of this you do own. What piece of this is yours?"

I sucked in a long breath and thought for a minute.

"Well, I own my name, my fame, and a really long list of people who want to buy mittens." I laughed at myself, Linda patiently listened.

"I own the fact that I made the most famous mittens in the world right now." I laughed at myself again. The thought of being mitten famous was so ridiculous.

"There's value in all of that, Jen." Linda has the sweetest way of saying my name. The intonation always starts low then goes high—as if she is breaking my name into two syllables. In that moment, just hearing her say my name grounded me in the present. "Do an email search for business offers and look through them. See what stands out to you. Pick a few companies, reply to them, and see what they're offering." She was gentle and practical. "There are lots of great Vermont companies. What about Darn Tough or the Johnson Woolen Mill?"

I nodded my head. This was solid advice from a wise woman. Ideas were pinging around in my brain. We said our goodbyes and I went inside to find my laptop. A quick email search revealed hundreds of business inquiries. There was one from someone at the Vermont Teddy Bear Company. My friend Jessie used to work there and she loved that company. I starred that email then scrolled down a little further to find one from Darn Tough, a Vermont sock company. There were a lot of companies I didn't recognize, but I had easily found two Vermont companies with which I was familiar. Linda was right, and the offers to collaborate were already in my inbox.

I decided to call Darn Tough. They seemed like a good fit to me. It was almost five o'clock, and the customer service line was about to close. When I explained who I was, the woman who picked up the phone told me that my call had come in just under the wire. It was the last one of the week, and she was psyched she'd taken it.

"I feel like I'm talking to a celebrity!"

I let out an uncomfortable half-laugh. I didn't feel like a celebrity on the inside. Celebrities were always walking around on red carpets, looking beautiful, and waving at the cameras. I was just sitting on my couch. Fame is such a strange smokescreen. Maybe we're all just really skilled at pretending fame is good.

The salesperson immediately offered to send me some free socks. I was delighted by that offer because I seriously love their socks. She was so kind and helpful. It is really a rare treasure in business these days to call a company and have a person pick up the phone. Not only was I speaking to a person, but she was a nice person. I later learned that all of Darn Tough is like that. They have an impeccable customer service team, and they actually care about and value their customers. I explained to her that I was reaching out to form a partnership and that someone had emailed me. The salesperson explained that she needed to pass this offer on to someone higher up, and since it was a Friday, I might not hear back until Monday.

"That's totally reasonable. I don't expect people to work on the weekends," I said. After hanging up, I immediately felt some of the stress and pressure drain out of me. I had done something, I had taken a step forward, and it felt like the right thing.

Within an hour, Courtney from Darn Tough called me back. She was ecstatic that I had reached out to them. Her enthusiasm and energy lifted my spirits. We talked for a long time. She told me a little more about the company, then she told me about her family, then we were just talking about our lives. I was at my wit's end that evening, and she treated me like I was her long-lost best friend. It was such a shame that Courtney and I couldn't meet in person due to the pandemic. I could have talked to her forever. We set up a Zoom call for 2:00 the next afternoon, when her two-year-old son would be napping. My friendship with Courtney turned out to be one of the best things that came out of the mitten fame.

That night I lay awake in bed for hours, unable to sleep. I could hear Liz tossing and turning on her side of the bed. She sniffed a few times and sighed. I didn't want to wake her up, but I was pretty sure she wasn't asleep.

"Are you awake?" I whispered.

"Yes."

"I can't sleep."

"Neither can I."

I rolled over and curled up next to her.

"I feel so much anxiety about this. I don't know what to do." I laid my head on Liz's chest and could feel the steady beat of her heart. We snuggled there together for a long time, playing out possible scenarios. I could reach out to some friends who sewed and we could make some mittens and start fulfilling orders. I had the whole weekend stretched out before me. For how much would I sell the mittens? Would I pay my friends? Should I open an Etsy shop? Many people were offering to help me. Despite the prospect of something great coming out of my meeting with Courtney, I couldn't stop considering other options.

In my late-night spiral of self-judgement and angst, I talked myself into making some mittens to sell. Maybe all the people who were encouraging me to capitalize on the moment were right. I was being foolish to delay. Everything in my being told me not to do this, but I pressed override. I got up and sent an email to Lise-Anne and my good friend Jenny, who also sews and is an avid crafter.

"I've decided to go ahead and make some mittens to sell," I told them. "Will you help?"

On Saturday morning I shuffled into the family room with my coffee to find Liz and Helen already knee deep in a Magna-Tiles building project.

"Look at this," Liz said, pointing to her phone. "Meet the Queer Schoolteacher Who Made Bernie's Mittens!" It was an online article from *The Advocate*, an LGBTQ magazine.

"How on earth do they know I'm gay? They didn't even ask me for an interview!" I sat with this news for a moment. I never think about my sexuality as being a noteworthy or "newsy" thing any more. The fact that I made Bernie's mittens had absolutely nothing to do with the fact that I'm gay. Truthfully, there is still a little piece of me that is protective of that part of my identity. I came out in the 90s, before there were many protections for gay people. Anyone who has ever had to hide their sexual orientation in order to stay employed understands the deep-rooted fear that comes with being outed. Even though I could no longer be fired for being gay and my marriage was now legal in all fifty states, fear of homophobia is a trauma that lingers. It seemed like *The Advocate* was sensationalizing my sexuality. I didn't understand why they hadn't reached out to me first and given me a voice to out myself. I was trying to remain level headed, but *The Advocate* had just outed me to the whole world.

"Are you mad?" Liz asked.

"Kind of." I was so full of self-doubt about the whole situation that I wasn't even sure if my anger was warranted, but I did feel mad. "Why would anyone care that I'm gay? It has nothing to do with me sewing mittens."

"People are going to say all kinds of things about you. If you talk to the reporters, you're feeding the fire." I rolled my eyes. Liz was now making it *very* clear how she felt about all the attention we were getting.

I didn't want to feed the fire, but I did want to remain in control of my story. If this conversation was going to become one about my sexuality, I wanted to have a voice in it. I began to think, *what if I took control of that story too?* No one else could out me by surprise if I was already out. That's when I had the idea to donate a pair of mittens to Outright Vermont, an organization whose mission is to give queer youth hope, equity, and power. What I had in my possession was the ability to make mittens that thousands of people wanted. What I could do for queer justice was to give those mittens to Outright to be auctioned off.

If someone wanted to spend an outrageous amount of money on a pair of mittens, I felt that it should go to a good cause. I was beginning to realize that this media frenzy could be used to do something powerful. All the reporters wanted a good story, so I decided to give them a story worth writing about. You don't have to respond to fame with greed. You can take the spotlight and cast it on those who need it. If there was a queer kid out there who was feeling lonely and ostracized, I wanted them to know about Outright. I wanted to use my fame to give them a huge shout-out in a bleak time.

Liz had a friend on the Outright board of directors and she immediately got on the phone to offer them a pair of mittens. Donating mittens to Outright was something tangible that I could do right then. It was another step forward, and I needed to take it. Then it occurred to me that maybe I could make another pair to donate to another organization to create a second auction. It was all kind of spur of the moment, but I looked over at our mutt Danny, whom our vet calls her "Southern Special," and thought, he's one of the best things that has ever happened to us. So, I reached out to a dog rescue called Passion 4 Paws Vermont and offered them a pair too. Why not?

That Saturday morning, I made three new pairs of mittens. Two of them would be for the organizations listed above, and the third was for an anti-racism group I had contacted, but not yet heard back from. Just the act of sitting down at my sewing machine and piecing together the wool gave me the peace I so desperately needed. I became lost in the creative flow. I realized that in order to remain sane during this media blitz, I was going to have to sew, but I was not going to sew for the tens of thousands of people who reached out to me. I was going to sew at my pace, and for organizations I cared about. I texted Lise-Anne and Jenny and told them to forget about my previous email. I didn't want to make the mittens to sell. I wanted to make them to donate.

All morning Helen had been lumbering around the house, sighing. She had built a castle with her Magna-Tiles, drawn a picture of our family with heads, arms, and legs, but no bodies—her signature portrait. Then she'd played with her stuffed animals and occasionally commented on the mittens I was making. The excitement of being on TV and in the spotlight had worn off. She wanted things to go back to normal and her patience for my sudden fame was gone. She looped her arm around mine and watched me sew the last few stitches in my third pair of mittens.

"Why don't you go pick a craft from your playroom and I'll put all of this away for the afternoon?" Her brown eyes lit up and she scurried out of the room.

I turned off my phone and we sat at the dining room table crafting with her Perler Beads. This is a craft where you place small plastic beads on a plastic peg board using tweezers. Once the beads are placed in the design you have chosen, you iron the whole thing and peel it off the board. Liz had become an expert at ironing these creations during the pandemic. A global quarantine is the perfect time for an esteemed doctor of English Literature such as Liz Fenton to hone her skills at ironing kids' crafts.

While Helen and I worked on our creations, my mind was wandering. I couldn't stop thinking about what to do. My mother had been trying to call me all morning. Apparently when they couldn't reach me, a reporter had tracked her down in Maine and convinced her to ask me for an interview. The reporter worked for MSNBC. I was sick of interviews and didn't want to do any more. I was delaying responding to my mom, or the reporter. I was so flooded with my own thoughts that I hadn't even noticed that Helen was struggling to place a bead in the corner of her design. All of a sudden she burst into tears.

"It's just so hard right now!"

I opened up my arms and she moved over for a huggle-snuggle in my lap. She sobbed and sobbed.

"I know, honey, it's hard right now. Mommy's doing the best she can." Helen cried some more. I rubbed her back. It broke my heart to think that my preoccupation with the mitten frenzy had caused her such stress.

"It won't be like this forever, honey. It's just busy right now. People will forget about the mittens soon and we can go back to our regular lives."

Helen cried until she ran out of tears and then she took in a deep breath.

"It's just," *sniff,* "I can't get that orange Perler Bead in the last peg! It keeps popping off." Then her tears started again and I had to laugh at myself. I was so consumed with my own drama that I assumed her tears were about *my* stress. I took in a deep breath too. This media frenzy had left me self-absorbed and raw. I wished I could open up the floodgates and have a big Perler Bead cry of my own.

At 2:00, I brought all my mom-guilt, sleepiness, confusion, and angst to the computer in the guest room and joined a Zoom call with Courtney from Darn Tough. She appeared on the screen with a big smile and a friendly warmth. I needed a helper in that moment. I needed an open door, and that is what Courtney provided. We talked for two hours. She told me that she worked with Lance Pitcher, the father of two of my Westford students whom I particularly adored. Apparently, Lance had already vouched for me. Vermont is a small place, and just about everywhere you go, someone knows you, or knows someone who knows you. Lance's children were now in high school, but when they were in first and second grade, I had both tutored and mentored them. I knew Lance was grateful for this, and now I knew that he was behind the scenes trying to help me.

Courtney and I discussed all the possibilities. Could Darn Tough sew the mittens? Their knitting machines were really only set up to knit the tubular shape of socks. Could they utilize their fleet of sewing machines? They'd bought the machines at the beginning of the pandemic and sent them home with their employees to sew face masks for the essential workers. Could I train their staff to sew the mittens at home? Where would we get the material? Was there something else they could make? Could they make a Bernie's Mitten sock? We brainstormed many possibilities, intermingled with other conversations around family life. She was seven months pregnant with her second child. It turned out that we had lots of other interests in common.

At one point she said, "I feel like I'm actually talking to myself!"

I had to agree.

It was so refreshing to meet someone new during the pandemic. We had been sequestered in our little pods for so long, we barely interacted with friends. Courtney was a breath of fresh air and the promise of a new, true friend. I hadn't instantly connected with someone like that in a long time. At the end of the conversation, we agreed that she would present all the ideas to Ric Cabot, the CEO, and see what he wanted to do with them. We also agreed that once her baby was born and we were both vaccinated, we would meet up for margaritas somewhere. I emerged from my conversation with Courtney a little stronger than before.

Chapter 16
Bought and Sold

A s soon as I agreed to the interview with MSNBC, I regretted
it. Millions of people would be watching, and unlike my
other interviews, it was going to be live. My only motivation for
agreeing to participate was to publicize the auctions. I put out a
quick Twitter post telling everyone that I'd made three more pairs
of mittens and they should tune in to MSNBC to find out where
they could get them.

The rest of Saturday was taken up with playing Guess Who
with Helen, giving more interviews and helping Passion 4 Paws
and Outright set up their auctions—which mainly consisted of
offering them pictures of the mittens so that they could post them
on their online platforms. Outright created a new website for the
auction. It had the ability to accept donations from people who
wanted to contribute but couldn't afford to bid.

I waited and waited to hear back from the anti-racism group. I
felt strongly that I wanted to include them, but it wasn't until the
end of the day that they returned my call. They let me know that
they made all their decisions by consensus and wouldn't be able
to meet for another week to discuss whether or not to accept the

donation. I was disappointed, but I understood. I deeply respect their organization and told them that I would use the mittens for something else, but the offer would stand forever. If they wanted to auction mittens off in a year, or ten years, I would make them a fresh pair.

I managed to fall asleep for a few hours, but once again, I awoke in the middle of the night, my mind racing over the MSNBC interview. What if I said something stupid? What if our internet failed? What if they asked me a question I couldn't answer? My jaw ached from grinding my teeth, which I used to only do at night, but since the inauguration, I'd started grinding all day too. I tried to lie quietly and not wake Liz up, but again, I realized she was awake as well.

"Do you want to cuddle?" I whispered.

"I thought you were awake." Liz rolled over and extended her arms to me. I nestled in the crook of her shoulder. "Are you nervous about your interview?"

"Yes." I wrapped my arm around her waist. "I wish I'd never agreed to a live interview. My mind is racing about all the things that could go wrong." She scratched my back a little.

"You'll do fine. You always do. You give a good interview."

"But what if this time I don't? What if I say something so stupid and hate myself forever?"

"You won't. Trust yourself."

I was trying to figure out if Liz really believed what she was saying or was just trying to say the right thing in that moment. The burning fire of anxiety pulsed down the veins in my arms again. Why did my nerves cause my circulatory system to feel like an acid reflux cycle? The situation was already pretty tough, but to top it all off, I was annoyed at my own anxiety.

"And if you mess up, I'll still love you," Liz continued. I half expected her to make a joke here, like follow it up with a *maybe*, but she didn't. She was 100 percent serious, and I knew it was true.

I hugged her a little tighter. Just being this close to her body had steadied my breathing.

"Thanks. What should I do about the third pair of mittens? They're the really cute red and rainbow striped pair."

"Keep them for yourself?"

"The last thing I need is more mittens. I have such a huge opportunity to publicize them; I should do something with them."

We lay there in silence for a few minutes. "What if I auction them off for Helen's college fund? Do you think people will think I'm being selfish?"

"There's no way people will think you're being selfish. You are literally being selfless right now. Why shouldn't we benefit from this too?"

This was a valid enough point. Liz kissed my forehead and I rolled back over to my side of the bed. Buoyed by her unconditional love and acceptance gave me enough peace to fall back to sleep until my alarm went off at 6 am. I showered, tried to eat a piece of toast, and got myself ready for the interview.

Our guest room is in the original part of the house and has never been updated. It's a pretty room with maple floors and two big windows. I turned the space heater on to fight the chill. The oldest part of our house doesn't have insulation in the walls, and it was particularly noticeable that January morning.

I logged on to the link sent to me by the producers and they put me in the virtual "Green Room." I wasn't sure if the camera was on or if anyone could see me, so I just sat there watching the blank screen. My segment was supposed to air at 8:10, but that time came and went. By 8:30, I was starting to worry they'd forgotten about me. I had to pee, but was afraid to get out of my seat. What if they started filming while I was gone? It all felt so awkward.

"Ok, Jen?" The voice of the producer brought my mind into sharp focus and turned my knees to Jell-O.

"Yup?"

"You'll be on in forty-five seconds. Are you ready?"

"Yup."

I looked at myself in the camera reflection. I looked tired. I don't usually wear make-up, and even though I had some, I'd decided not to put it on. There was no sense in pretending to be someone I wasn't. If people didn't like my face as is, I had already decided I didn't care.

"And you're on in 3, 2, 1 . . ."

The background music began, and a voice started talking to me, but I couldn't see anyone's face. The screen remained blank. The producer had forgotten to turn on the studio camera. They could see me, but I couldn't see them. It was very awkward. I had no idea who I was talking to. Since the interview was live, there was no way to tell the news anchor that I couldn't see her. Then a man's voice chimed in and I realized there were two anchors. I decided to just smile and be as pleasant as possible. There was really nothing else I could do. They asked a few of the familiar questions and I tried to answer clearly and pleasantly. I was operating on pure adrenaline. It was such a strange experience. I felt like it wasn't even me to whom they were talking. It was like I had sent them my calm and confident field rep.

At the end of the interview, the female voice told me she had brought a hat that she had knitted and asked me if I liked it. I couldn't see it, but assured her she had done a fine job while simultaneously thinking: *do people really still think I knitted Bernie's mittens?* The interview ended and the screen went black. The producer said a quick goodbye. Then there was silence. I stood up and my head started to spin, so I flopped myself down on the guest bed and took some very deep breaths. My knees had gone from Jell-O to completely numb and so had the tips of my fingers. *Have I been holding my breath? Why can't I feel my limbs?* My heart was racing, and I vowed never to give a live interview again.

We scheduled the auctions to begin as soon as the MSNBC interview aired. As tempting as it was to plant myself in front of my computer screen all day and watch the bids come in, I knew I needed to do something productive.

I decided to send an email to the man who had reached out to me from Vermont Teddy Bear. I'd been thinking about emailing him all weekend, and hadn't had a chance. I didn't know what would come of my conversation with Darn Tough, but I knew there could be more than one opportunity to connect with local businesses. My inbox had now swelled to 18,000 emails. I did a quick search for business offers and waded through about a hundred new ones since Friday night. I found one from Hayes at Vermont Teddy Bear and began crafting a quick reply.

Danny walked into the living room from the kitchen. His claws made a click, click sound on our wood floors. He walked up to me, sat down, and put one paw on my knee—his signature move. His brindled coat shone in the morning sun that spilled in through the window. I ignored him for a second while I finished my email to Hayes.

"Himmmmm," Danny let out a high pitched, barely audible whine to get my attention. I knew he needed some exercise and some fresh air would do me good as well.

"Ok, who wants to go for a walk!" Danny jumped up and ran for the door. No one else was quite as excited, but I managed to convince everyone that we should go.

We got in the car and headed to the Indian Brook Reservoir, leaving our phones at home. We laughed as Danny pummeled through the snow. Inside our house, he was the perfect gentleman—a quiet, serene dog;—but outside, he was one click away from being a wild animal. He ran so fast, we didn't know how he managed to avoid hitting the trees. The Indian Brook Reservoir has a two-mile path leading all the way around it and by the end, we had a tired five-year-old, two sleep-deprived moms, and a dog who looked like he could go around five more times. We managed to corral him into the car and drove home in silence. Liz set the kettle on for tea and we both sat down and opened our phones.

I pulled up the auction for Helen's college fund. It was already over $2,000.

"Oh my gosh, do you see that?"

"The Outright Auction is at $3,000!" Liz looked up from her phone, both of us reeling. This is what I wanted to happen, and it was electrifying to see it in action.

Bids poured in all morning. I was glad we had seized the moment to go for a family walk when we did because once we realized how fun it was to watch the auctions blowing up in real time, we couldn't stop. Every time we hit refresh, the total had risen another hundred dollars for each pair. Sometimes one pair would take the lead with a big bid, then another would catch up. It was completely thrilling. Meanwhile, I received a response from Hayes at Vermont Teddy Bear. It was Sunday, so I was surprised to hear from him. He asked if we could meet on Zoom that afternoon.

I felt such tremendous guilt about my level of preoccupation with the whole ordeal that I had promised myself to carve clear boundaries around when I would give interviews and hold meetings. I told Hayes I was committed to spending the day with my family and I'd be willing to meet after Helen's bedtime.

In the midst of the excitement, I got a text from Liza Driscoll, Bernie's daughter-in-law and the owner of Essex Hollow Playschool. "Jen, would you be free for a phone call from Bernie at 4:30?" *I guess I can make an exception to my "clear boundaries" for Bernie.* I laughed at myself.

"Oh my god, yes!" I replied. "I'll turn my ringer on."

I went into the craft room, turned on the space heater, and sat down in my office chair at the sewing table, which was just a folding table from Costco. I shivered. The craft room was just as cold as the guest room. It was painted dark purple and was kind of a mess. I was glad this was going to be a phone call, not a Zoom call. I took some deep breaths, then looked down at my hands, which were shaking, then at the clock. It was 4:27, and of course, I had to pee. Did I have time? What if he called and I didn't pick up the phone in time? Was he going to call me from his personal cell phone? Would that mean that his phone number would be in my phone? I held my hands up next to the space heater and decided to stay where I was. I could hear Liz and Helen playing in the living room.

At 4:30 on the dot, my cell phone rang, and Senator Sanders was on the line.

"How are you doing with all this media?" His voice was gruff, New Yorky, and instantly recognizable.

"Well, it's kind of overwhelming. I'm all over the internet." *I'm on the phone with Bernie! I'm on the phone with Bernie!*

"My best advice to you is, don't look online and don't read everything people write."

"That's probably a good idea."

"I wanted to tell you myself that my campaign ran a sweatshirt sale, and as of now, we have raised almost two million dollars for Meals on Wheels Vermont. This isn't public knowledge yet, but I wanted you to know."

Bernie sharing insider info with me made me feel pretty special. I smiled to myself while trying to keep breathing and remain cool. It was totally normal to be talking to Bernie Sanders in my messy, frozen craft room. *TOTALLY NORMAL.*

"Really? That's amazing! My grandmother got Meals on Wheels. That's a great organization!"

"I understand you're raising some money too."

"Yes, I donated mittens to Outright and Passion 4 Paws, to be auctioned off."

"Both excellent organizations."

The conversation was polite and straightforward. I was so excited to be talking to him. I wanted to tell him everything about the auctions and the partnerships. But before I knew it, he was wrapping things up and it sounded like the conversation wasn't going to be the big heart to heart with my favorite senator that I hoped it would be. It was a Sunday evening and he was probably about to sit down to dinner with his family.

"I noticed the tack on your mitten cuffs has come undone, do you want me to fix that?"

"No, thanks. They're good."

"This was all very unexpected."

"Yes, it was." I could have talked to him all day. "Well, goodbye now, and thanks for the mittens."

The call ended. I sat there, stunned and a little crestfallen. Two million dollars. He said "goodbye now" just like my dad. *Two Million Dollars!* I felt light headed and giddy. One hand was frozen from holding the phone to my ear in the sub-zero craft room, while the other hand was numb because I'd been sitting on it.

When I returned to the living room I sat down on the hearth in front of the fireplace, which was burning brightly. Liz gleefully informed me of the stats on the auction sales and I swore her to secrecy about the two million dollars.

I followed Bernie's advice and didn't google myself, but I couldn't stop googling him—or rather, memes of him. It had been five days since the inauguration, and the meme explosion hadn't died down in the least. Although lacking in sleep and nutrition, every meme someone texted was a different kind of fuel. There were other funny things, too. The Holderness Family, an online singing and comedy group, released a parody called "These Are a Few of my Favorite Memes," and several other comedians and songwriters reached out to me with little ditties and videos they made about the mittens. One of my favorites was from a high school student named Cordelia, who was making videos during the pandemic about the Danish practice of celebrating all things cozy. She called it "The Hygge Corner." In the most adorable form of tongue and cheek humor, she gave an in-depth commentary on Sanders' fashion choices on Inauguration Day and a detailed analysis of the Nordic print on his mittens. She pointed out that the white pattern across the back was actually meant to be *fleurs-de-lis*. I was very impressed. I'd made the mittens and hadn't noticed that! These little gifts were inspiring and funny. Each one made my day, and even though I wasn't able to respond to every sender, I appreciated them.

On Sunday night, I returned to the guest room and logged onto the computer to meet with Hayes on Zoom. The fact that he was using weekend time to connect with me was a good indicator that he was serious. It was also a tell-tale sign of dealing with a Vermont company. A lot of business in Vermont happens at the picket fence, between neighbors, or on the ski slopes. I'm sure business happens on the golf course too, but it was the dead of winter in a pandemic. We had to work with what we had, and what we had was weekend Zoom calls.

Hayes had taken the job of Head of Product Development at the Vermont Teddy Bear Company the previous summer and was Zooming in from Rhode Island because he had not yet moved his family to Vermont. He appeared as a happy, red-haired man, a little older than me. Hayes's focus was more specific than Courtney's from Darn Tough. He wanted Vermont Teddy Bear to make the mittens. They had all the sewing machinery set up, connections to acquire the materials, a customer service department, and basically everything I lacked as a part-time crafter. Hayes explained that the mittens meshed with their business plan to market and sell things in the line of "cozy."

Hayes and I talked well into the night about the many possible ways we could collaborate. I could go to the factory and train the design team on how to make the mittens. I could share with them my email list and they could manage it and harness it for sales. I explained to Hayes that I hoped there would be some portion of the profits from the sales of the mittens that would go to charity. I had mentioned this to Courtney too. I recognized that this was an opportunity to use the wealth generated for more than corporate profit. They both agreed. Hayes and I ended our Zoom meeting with a plan to be back in touch. He needed to consult with members of his team, and I needed to go to bed because I would be back in my classroom bright and early to start another week of teaching.

Two great connections with Vermont businesses had transpired over the weekend and three auctions were underway. Linda's advice had propelled this situation to a new level. I was excited to see what the businesses would come up with and what their offers would be, and I was also a little nervous. What if they both wanted to make the mittens? Vermont Teddy Bear was obviously better set up to do it, but I had an instant connection with Courtney. I knew that in business you had to put your practical mind in front of your heart, but that was exactly why I wasn't in business. I am a person who makes decisions based on gut instinct and human connection. If both companies exclusively wanted the same thing, it was going to be a tough choice.

I didn't have much time to dwell on it, though, because other things were still brewing. I didn't want to do any more interviews, but if I was going to broker a business deal with a Vermont company, I needed to maintain some level of visibility to keep them interested in working with me. The internet is fickle, and just as quickly as the spotlight had appeared on me, it could turn off. I lined up TV and news interviews for every night after Helen went to bed and for every lunch break at school the next week. Some of the interviews were even going to happen after school in my classroom while Helen played quietly with the doll house in the corner, just off camera.

My mom-guilt was a constant strain, but I held on to hope that things were heading in the right direction. If I sold my mitten-making business and the mitten auction was successful, I could secure a better future for Helen. Plus, I loved connecting with people. It was one of my strengths in the sudden burst of fame. I didn't have all the answers, a game plan, or a business model to follow; but what I did realize was that on the other line of every interview, Zoom call, or even at the other side of every proverbial virtual table, there was a person, a real human being. They showed up with their own worries and struggles. They were pregnant, could only talk during nap time, or were grappling with huge decisions like whether or not to move their family to a new state. I realized that if I could connect with people on a human level, if I could find common ground with them on the important things, like family and friendship, then the other things would fall into place. What really matters in this world is not how much money you have, how many big deals you have brokered, or how powerful you are in the business world. The most valuable thing about you is your kindness and your honest connections with other people.

Courtney from Darn Tough got back to me by the end of the day on Monday to let me know that Darn Tough couldn't make the mittens. It just wasn't in their wheelhouse and not the direction in which they wanted to move. They did, however, want to make a sock! Since they steer clear of politics, they wanted to call it the Jenerosity Sock instead of the Bernie sock. The thought of having my name in a sock label was surprising and strange. They wanted to honor my request to benefit charity by giving 100% of the profits from this sock sale to the Vermont Food Bank. Not only that, but they wanted to include me in the design process. While I was a little disappointed that they didn't want to take on the mittens, the thought of them making a sock for charity was such an incredible turn of events. It also cleared the way for me to move forward with my collaboration with Vermont Teddy Bear.

After an exhausting day at school on Monday, I finally realized I could not go to work on Tuesday. I needed to sleep, I needed to find some more help, and I just needed some peace and quiet without Helen at my heels. I was in over my head and was trying to do everything and too much all at once. I sent an apologetic email to the parents of my students at around 3 am that Tuesday morning, six days after the inauguration, and another equally apologetic one to my principal. Then I spent the next hour or so writing detailed lesson plans for my sub. Substitute lesson plans are almost always written by a teacher who has a fever, is experiencing a miscarriage, has just had a death in the family, or in my case, hasn't slept through the night in almost a week. It's a monumental task that always comes at the worst time.

Then I went to bed, and I slept. I deeply and completely slept. By the time I awoke, five hours later, Liz had already taken Helen to school and the house was quiet. I got up, showered, and sat down with pen and paper in hand to make a list. Taking in a deep breath, I asked myself: *What do I really want to come out of all of this?* This is what I wrote:

1. Keep connecting with Vermont businesses to make mitten-themed products to benefit charity.
2. Keep making mittens to donate to charity.
3. Find someone to manage the media.

I put out a simple plea on Facebook. This is what it said:
Hey Facebook Friends, I probably should have asked this days ago, but I was just so shocked by all of this attention and I kept

thinking it would go away. But who do I know who can help me manage this going forward? I'm not even sure what I'm looking for, and I haven't made any money off it yet so I can't promise to pay anyone up front, but what should I do? Let me first say— that I don't want to go into the mitten business full time. But I could make some more mittens. What should I do with them? I also want to be sure to include charities.

There were fifty-four responses to this post. Most of them were overwhelming to read.

People were suggesting lawyers, branding specialists, and trademarking. Lots of people had follow up questions to which I didn't have answers. Some of the people offering to help were not actually helpful, though I knew they meant well. Then there was a private direct message from my old friend Deb Flanders:

Hi Jen, I'd be interested in helping you out since I've set up a business and I have experience in managing multiple details. My tour and travel business has come to a complete stop. I'm also a seamstress, have been for years. I sew with my grandma's Singer!! Anyway, I wouldn't expect any money at this point since I'm doing ok financially. I could help you get started. Getting a lawyer is key, and a good accountant. I work with 2 good ones. Let me know what you think. Deb

Deb! My heart glowed thinking about her. She was a kindred spirit, and I hadn't talked to her in years. Deb is a friend you never forget: a serious person, in her late fifties. She has thoughtful, kind eyes, and feathered, windswept brown hair. Deb is a person who understands people who are struggling. She is a rock, and I needed her.

Deb ran a successful travel agency called Goodspeed & Bach. I'd met her years before when we sang in the Bella Voce Women's Chorus together. I knew she was extremely smart and diplomatic.

I also knew that she would not be overwhelming to work with. I called her right away and accepted her offer. I explained to her what I was hoping for in a media manager, and she said she could do all of it. I must have thanked her a dozen times, but before she hung up she said,

"You don't know how much I needed this, Jen. My whole life has been on hold because of COVID-19. I'm languishing. This is a gift."

I was stunned. Deb? Languishing? It seemed impossible. Deb had her finger on the pulse of life, how could she be languishing? And how on Earth could the annoying tasks I was asking her to help me with be a gift? The answer came in gentle waves of support and care. Deb is a doer, a caretaker, a helper. She was just the right person at just the right time.

Deb created a web page that day. She told me exactly what she needed for copy and pictures and as soon as I sent things to her, they appeared neatly and beautifully online. I shared with her all the little details. I didn't know how to negotiate the business contract with Darn Tough or Vermont Teddy Bear and needed a good lawyer to handle that for me. Several people had reached out to me asking to make documentaries about the mittens, or to write children's books about it. I wasn't sure if I should agree to let them tell that story, or if I should write it myself. A friend of mine told me that as soon as someone published my story, they owned it. That scared me. How could someone else own the story that was playing out in *my* life? I soon learned that I needed an entertainment lawyer too—something that doesn't exist in Vermont despite our bustling entertainment industry.

The stress of how I was going to pay for the lawyers, Deb's assistance, the web page, and all the other incidental things that might come up was a whole new headache. I resented Bernie a little when I thought about it. He expected media attention and was prepared. He had people to manage all of these things, and professionals raising money to pay for it. I didn't know yet if I was going to make any money from this experience, so Deb suggested a Go Fund Me to prevent me from going into debt.

I handed over my Gmail account password and let her take the lead managing the thousands upon thousands of requests. She helped me open a post office box so that I could have a public mailing address that kept my home address a little more private. She began vetting media requests and scanning my email for business offers. Over the next few months, she became my sounding board, my right-hand lady, and most importantly, my close friend.

Hayes got back to me that afternoon with a business proposition, and we began negotiations for a partnership. Vermont Teddy Bear would make the mittens. I would meet with their design team, give them my tips and tricks, and help them with advertising. I agreed as part of the deal not to disclose the details of our arrangement, but I felt that the terms were fair and equally benefitted us both. The best part of our arrangement was that Vermont Teddy Bear agreed to always donate a generous portion of the sales to a non-profit. This was incredibly important to me. There are so many organizations doing powerful work in Vermont. I wanted the mittens to bring joy and financial support to as many people as possible.

The auctions, meanwhile, were set for five days each. That meant they would close on Thursday at 8 am. I obsessively checked on the auction for Helen's college fund and took great delight in seeing the numbers rise. It was thrilling to follow. Throughout the week there would be little bidding wars, and people would text me to tell me that a certain pair had just hit three or four thousand dollars. *Incredible*, I thought. Just last year I was selling them for thirty dollars!

I noticed that other people also started auctioning off mittens they had purchased from me. One of my co-workers even texted me to ask if I would mind if she auctioned off mittens she had purchased from me the year before.

"I would rather you not do that," I responded. I don't know why it bothered me to think of people making money for themselves over this. Obviously, people would see this as an opportunity to make a quick buck. I just felt like it was a little underhanded for my own friends to start auctions that competed with the ones I was sponsoring.

Lance, the father of my former students, texted me on Tuesday night to ask if Darn Tough could do a photoshoot with me on Wednesday. He wondered if we could use my classroom. There were very few places we could go in the height of the pandemic, and I definitely didn't want a photo shoot to happen at my house, so I agreed. I had to get special permission from the superintendent of our school system in order to let the photography crew into the building. We decided to meet up at the school at 8 pm, after I had put Helen to bed, and after all the basketball players who used the gym in the evenings had gone home. The school was empty and eerily dark.

I parked in the dark parking lot and walked up to the truck parked outside my classroom door. They were ready for me. It was heartwarming to see Lance after so many years. His long, beautiful hair and stoic demeanor framed his handsome face. He looked ready to pose for an 80s heavy metal band photoshoot at any time. Lance is the kind of person who speaks his mind, which makes some people angry, but I find it refreshing because I always know where I stand with him. The last time I talked with him, he had recently harvested a deer that had been killed by a car. I asked him for his number. I love deer and would be devastated if I hit one with my car. The least I could do if that happened would be to call Lance so he could make use of the meat. I affectionately call him my "Dead Deer Guy."

The crew made quick work of moving every piece of furniture

in my classroom to set up an elaborate cave of reflection sheets and lights. I busied myself removing children's names and images from anything that might appear in the photographs. Everything took a long, long time, and I was fading fast. I sat down at my desk and pulled up my school email. My school inbox now had several thousand messages from people who had looked me up online. As I was browsing through the queries, the words Disney Channel Interview Inquiry flashed onto the screen. I clicked on the email. A producer from the show *The Nook* with Ariel Martin and Chandler Kinney was asking if I would like to do a paid segment for their Earth Day Show.

"You're not going to believe this, Lance, the Disney Channel wants to interview me!"

"Of course they do. You're a celebrity."

Lance didn't even look up from the lighting he was setting up. He was like one of those informants on Law and Order being interviewed by the detectives while continuing to fix the plumbing below a sink.

"But I'm actually not."

"Well, we don't set all this equipment up in the middle of the night for just anyone. Can you come sit over here?" I sat down in my wooden teaching chair, a relic from my Montpelier classroom that was gifted to me when I left. My mind was spinning. The Disney Channel felt like a really big deal.

The photographers tested out all the flashes, and then took a hundred pictures, at least. Inside, I was trying to remain level-headed, but in that moment, I did feel a little bit like a star. Then Lance said,

"Ok Jen, look directly into the camera and give me your best deadpan." Click click. "That's our money shot, it's a wrap."

All that for one shot where I look expressionless into a camera?

After the film crew left, I put everything back to its original place in my classroom and proceeded to disinfect every surface.

That was the agreement I had with the superintendent. It was 11 pm by the time I pulled away from the school parking lot and headed home.

When Helen and I walked back into the school building at 7 am the next morning, I groaned. It felt like I'd never left.

"Ahhhh, warm Westford!" Helen exclaimed. She loved the way the heat piled up in the entryway to the school and greeted her like a hug. Our house was so drafty, Westford must have felt like a summer day to her.

When my class went to Art, I briefly checked my phone and found ten new messages. The mitten auction for Helen's college fund had exploded. In the last two hours it was open, it had gone from three thousand to six thousand dollars in a bidding war. I hadn't even thought about the fact that the auctions had closed at 8 A.M.

"I can't believe you're going to practically double Helen's college fund with the sale of one pair of mittens!" Liz had texted. The thought of putting that much money into Helen's college fund felt like a big life win. Liz and I didn't have college funds when we were kids. Our parents helped us as much as they could when the time came, but we both graduated college with enormous debt. I wanted Helen to have more options than we'd had.

"It's unbelievable," I texted back.

I had loads of work to do during my planning period, but I couldn't help but look online to see what the totals were. The Passion 4 Paws mittens had sold for $3,500, the Outright mittens had sold for $7,100, and the mittens I was selling for Helen went for $6,100. It seemed like such an enormous amount of money. I was floating on air all day.

By Friday, Darn Tough was ready to launch their limited run of the Jenerosity Sock. I had spent the week talking to their design team about colors and patterns. I'd actually sent them the hygge video from Cordelia because her insights on the design were so accurate. I also had continued my talks with Hayes from Vermont Teddy Bear. Our conversations and negotiations often went well into the night. We were working out all the details of a contract for our collaboration. It was big and amazing. They had been looking to expand their business, and the mitten idea was the perfect fit. It was Vermonty, it was charitable, and it was fun.

Courtney and I decided that a Friday night release would be best for the launch of the Jenerosity Sock. I asked Vermont Teddy Bear to hold off their announcement of our partnership until after the sock sale was underway. I didn't want to have competing news stories. The Jenerosity Sale went live at 4 pm on January 29, 2021. It was now nine days after the inauguration, and the global fascination with mitten memes was seemingly endless. News of the sale instantly went viral. I tried to help with the publicity by tweeting to my now twenty-two thousand followers. Online articles were popping up everywhere. By 7:30 pm here were the stats:

First 10 minutes: 78 pairs

First 30 minutes: 800 pairs

First hour: 2,000 pairs

First two hours: 3,400 pairs

First three hours: 4,500 pairs.

By 8:00 the only states without orders were Wyoming and Hawaii. By 10:00, they had sold over 6,000 pairs. The original run was supposed to be 8,000. Courtney texted me at 10:30 to tell me that she and her coworkers were placing internal bets on whether they would sell out before or after midnight. At some point in the night, Ric Cabot, the CEO, decided to raise the number of socks they would sell to 9,000.

The first message I read on my phone on Saturday morning was from Courtney. She texted to tell me that Darn Tough had sold out of the Jenerosity Sock. They had never sold that many pairs of a single design in such a short time frame. It was a record-breaking night. Darn Tough never announced the amount of money they made from the fundraiser; they converted the total into meals instead—a classy move in my opinion. In one night, they had raised enough money to provide 294,111.79 meals for Vermonters in need. I jokingly texted Courtney that I felt bad for the person who only got 79% of a meal!

I went downstairs and poured myself a cup of coffee. Liz was already up and Helen was in a grumpy mood. It was a stark contrast from the delightful way that *I* had woken up. I read the room: It was five degrees out and there would be no outside play. We faced another frigid pandemic day with just the three of us, stuck in our house. I just wanted to go somewhere, *anywhere*, but the pandemic left us with limited options.

"Oh my god."

"What?" I asked. Liz was looking at her phone.

"The winner of the Outright Mittens donated them back, and they've offered them to the next highest bidder. Now their auction is over $20,000!"

"Wow!" This morning was shaping up to be quite the rollercoaster. "Wait, I thought their top bid was $7,100?"

"It was, and the second highest bid was $7,000. The rest of the money is from donations!"

I logged onto their website and noticed that several people had donated other items to also be auctioned off, one of which was an adorable, crocheted Bernie doll wearing mittens. It was astounding. Outright had harnessed the mitten donation in a truly spectacular way. They wrote on their website that the money they raised would go to adding a second week to their summer camp program.

Then, Liz called to me from the kitchen with the exciting news that our friend Susanmarie had made homemade bagels and was going to drop some off for us. Great news was happening, and bagels were on the way! Then it got even better. Liz made a plan for Helen to go to her aunts' house for the day. Liz's aunts were in their seventies and lived on the other side of town. They were the only people in our pandemic bubble. They thoroughly doted on Helen, and she was more than happy to spend the day at their house. I felt terrible guilt for feeling such glee at sending my own child away for the day, but I needed a break. Mom-guilt makes every break you take from your children a little bitter.

After Helen left, I finally felt like I had the head space to sit down and look at the eBay auction site. On Friday morning, I'd received a desperate email from the top bidder of $6,100 asking to cancel his bid on Helen's college fund mittens. He explained that his young son had gotten into his account and bid on the mittens without his permission. I knew he must be panicking over this, so I wanted to figure out how to cancel his bid that morning. Being an eBay novice, I couldn't easily figure out how to do it. Liz took a look at the site and couldn't figure it out either.

"Why don't you ask him to cancel it from his end."

"Can he do that?"

"He should be able to."

I sent him a quick message before heading to school on Friday. It was a weird task to delegate to a stranger, but I really didn't have the time to deal with it until the weekend.

When I opened my eBay account on Saturday morning, I sleuthed around looking for the information on my auction. The interface on eBay was so difficult to navigate that I clicked on several different links before I was finally able to see the results. It very clearly listed that frantic father as the top bidder. I rolled my eyes. He hadn't followed through and canceled his bid. That meant that the 2nd place bidder of $6,000 probably thought they had lost, and moved on. I wanted to quickly cancel that father's bid. I clicked "cancel this bid" and nothing happened. There was no response. His bid was still there. So, in a split second, I clicked "Cancel bid and relist." And just like that, with that tiny mistake, a message box appeared on the screen that said "This auction has been canceled," and the entire list of bids disappeared.

I screamed. Liz had just returned from dropping off Helen. She ran into the room. "What?"

I immediately started trying to back track. I pressed the back button. eBay sent me to a blank screen with a message, "You cannot use the back button." I tried to use the forward button "You cannot do that either." I clicked back to the main page and tried to remember how I had found my auction in the first place. Meanwhile I kept screaming.

"Tell me what happened!" Liz cried.

"I deleted the whole auction."

I started pleading with the eBay interface as if it was a person, to just let me figure out where the mitten auction had gone. The more frantic I became, the more wrong buttons I pressed. Every time I tried to press the back button, it brought me to a blank screen, requiring me to log in and start all over again. My hands were shaking. I couldn't believe that in one mistaken click, I had just lost over $6,000.

When I finally found my way back to the listing, it said, "Jen Ellis Authentic Bernie Sanders Mittens, starting bid $30." The original auction was gone. I started to cry. Not cry; sob. Liz wanted to help, but there was nothing she could do. I was hysterical.

"Please! Let me help!"

I choked out a "No!" I didn't know what she could do to help. I was so upset that I couldn't begin to explain.

"There isn't anything you can do!"

"Fine, I'll be in the office." She huffed out of the room.

I searched the eBay site for any way to contact them and eventually figured out how to chat with their customer service team. After clicking through several filter questions, I was directed to an automated chat. I explained what had happened, they responded with an automated explanation of how to cancel a bid. I explained that I needed to reinstate my auction, they responded with how to set up an auction. Finally, I wrote "Can I please just talk to a person?" Another automated response: "A customer service team member will be available to chat with you in 3 minutes." I looked down at my hands. Hives had formed and were starting to climb up my arms. I was crying so hard, I couldn't catch my breath. My whole self was in pieces.

I recognize now that this was an extreme reaction. The ten days since the inauguration had left me depleted. I hadn't eaten or slept properly and my mind was spinning from all the interviews and attention. I try to have some compassion for myself when I think back on how upset I was in that moment. I am not a person who is cut out for that kind of stress. Liz tried to calm me down by reminding me that it's only money. *I knew that*. But in all of this mitten frenzy, it was the only thing I had asked for myself. It was the thing I wanted the most, because it was for Helen.

I checked in on my new listing and it was already up to $100. Those 3 minutes felt like an hour. Finally, eBay Brian showed up for an online chat. I again explained the problem and he responded "Your product has been relisted and you now have a new auction."

"I know that, I want the old auction reinstated. I canceled it by mistake!"

"I'm sorry, we cannot reinstate auctions that you cancel," and he disappeared. There was nothing left to say.

I searched the site again, looking for a place to talk to an actual person. Tucked at the bottom of a very long page of explanations of everything, there was a small button to request that a customer service representative contact me by phone. I pressed it, confirmed my phone number, and received another automated response.

"Your customer service call will begin in approximately 6 minutes." I took some deep breaths and tried to pull myself together. *I need to think of some positive self-talk*. I put my thinking cap on, but nothing came to mind. I was so furious with myself that whatever was left of my spirit from the roller-coaster of emotions and recent events was shredded.

The new customer service agent came on the line and as I explained who I was and what had happened, I again began to cry.

"I love your memes!" she said as I sniffled on the other end of the line.

"Can you help me?" I must have sounded desperate, and in that moment, I was. When I thought about how long it would take me to save $6,000 on my teaching salary, I gagged. It was such a tremendous loss. I have always tried to be careful with money. I was raised to save money and spend it wisely. I felt stupid for making such an enormous mistake.

"I'm sorry, I cannot reinstate an auction that you have canceled." The exact words that Brian said to me on the chat.

"There's nothing you can do?" It seemed impossible to me that with all the technical advances of the 21st century, eBay was unable to help me.

"No, I'm sorry, I'm unable to assist you. I see that your new online auction is gaining interest, you're now up to $250. Is there anything else I can help you with today?"

I was completely defeated, starving, thirsty, exhausted, and in a quiet voice of resignation I whispered "No."

I found Liz in her office, on her bike trainer. She took one look at me and dismounted.

"I lost it all," I sobbed, "and eBay says they can't help me get it back." We stood in the office, holding each other. I was sobbing into her sweaty workout clothes, and she was trying every possible combination of words to console me. The last time I had cried like that in front of her was the night we lost our first pregnancy.

Liz talked me into taking a shower and cooling off. As soon as I turned on the water, though, I started sobbing again. This time it wasn't even about the $6,000. It was for everything I had lost.

My time, my privacy, my anonymity, the ability to ever sit at a craft fair again and sell my sweet mittens to my community. I now knew that if I ever did that, someone would just buy them all and resell them for their personal profit.

After my shower, I composed myself and poured another cup of coffee. I wished I could travel back in time and undo my mistake. I wondered what I would be doing right now if Bernie had never worn the mittens in the first place. Maybe we would be eating chocolate chip pancakes and settling in for a family game day or a cozy movie. I missed my old life. Once again, tears began to well up in my eyes. The only thing I could think of to do next was to call Deb.

Deb always keeps her phone on. She has people who call her with some regularity just to talk to a calming voice. I didn't know this about her until I needed it, but Deb was an actual lifeline for people. I explained the whole morning to her. I cried, she listened. I tore myself apart, she told me all the good things she loved about me. I was unreasonable, she was a voice of reason. By the time I was done talking to her, I was ready to have a bagel and move on with my day. I can't remember exactly what she said, but she blew some wind into my sails and convinced me to try to forgive myself.

A few minutes after I got off the phone with Deb, I got a text from Jackie, my contact person at Passion 4 Paws. She was excited to mail out the mittens to the winner of their auction and asked if she could stop by. I reluctantly agreed. I looked at myself in the mirror. My eyes were puffy, and I looked sad and pathetic. This was the lowest point of the whole Bernie's Mittens affair. I found a cold wash cloth and sat with it on my eyes until Jackie arrived.

She pulled up in a car full of barking dogs, some of whom she owned, some for whom she was trying to find homes. I handed her the mittens and we took some pictures. She was so cheerful.

She gave both Liz and me Passion 4 Paws hats. Just moments before, I had been so uncontrollably sad, but handing the mittens to Jackie gave me enormous joy. We talked for about thirty minutes in my front yard. I was certain that if we met again under different circumstances and not in the depths of a pandemic, we would be fast friends. I walked away from that conversation with some true happiness in my heart. It didn't erase my feelings of disgust with eBay or with myself for deleting the auction, but it was something to hold on to.

The joyousness of the fundraising returned later that day, when the partnership with Vermont Teddy Bear was announced. People flocked to their website to order mittens, but they didn't have a prototype yet, so they provided a place for people to join an email list.

I checked back in with the new eBay auction a few times throughout the week and it was growing steadily. It rose to over $1,000 in the first two days. I reached out to all the people who had bid on the previous auction, explained the situation, and asked them to bid again. Some of them did and I was very grateful to them. It was another five-day auction, and on the day before it closed, another bidding war ensued and the end total was $2,500. I was pretty happy with that. If you subtracted out the false bidding war that the twelve-year-old boy had created, the original auction would have net about $3,500, so I felt like $2,500 was at least more than half of what I would have otherwise gotten. This time I immediately contacted the highest bidder to close the deal, and he immediately emailed me back.

"I'm so glad I won! Thanks! I actually don't want the mittens, I just like to win eBay auctions."

My jaw dropped. I was so confused by his message. Why would he bid on them if he didn't want them? Who does that?

"So, you don't plan on paying for them?"

"That's correct. I'm not going to pay for them."

I looked up at Liz, silently shaking my head in disbelief.

"What?"

There were no words to describe how I felt. Was this a joke? Was I on the Truman Show? It was so ridiculous it was almost funny. Almost.

Sometimes I look at Helen and think: *she's completely guileless.* She doesn't even register when other kids are being mean to her. It's so far from her realm of existence. This moment with the second auction made me wonder if Helen's innocence was a spin-off of my own. I just never think people will be so thoughtless and inconsiderate, until they are, and I'm shocked.

I went to delete his bid, and again, almost deleted the whole auction. I had to call someone in customer service at eBay to walk me through how to delete it, step by step. It was the most counter-intuitive process. I never would have been able to figure it out.

I went into the system and offered the mittens to the next bidder. Twenty-four hours went by with no response. I reached back out and asked the bidder to respond so that I could offer it to the next bidder on the list if they didn't want it. Another twenty-four hours went by. I finally just offered it to the next bidder, then the next, then the next. Some of the bidders got back to me and said they no longer wanted them; others just didn't respond. I eventually gave up. It was now two weeks after the inauguration and the partnership with Vermont Teddy Bear had been announced. As part of the deal, I had agreed to stop selling the mittens. So, the red mittens with rainbow stripes you see me wearing while posing in front of the University of Vermont for professional pictures became mittens that I just kept.

I'm not sure what the lesson was for me in all of this. Stay humble? Cut your losses? One might think that becoming instantly famous for being the maker of Bernie's mittens went to my head, and once in a while it did, but then things like the eBay auction took me right down to ground zero. The whole hurricane of emotions left me drained and spent. It was time to move on. I deleted my eBay account and never looked back.

Chapter 17
The Imposters

2011 AND 2021

I came home from school one chilly February day in 2011 to find a pink card in my mailbox from my dad. It was my birthday, and true to form, his card arrived right on time. It was about a year after Liz and I had bought our house, and the sight of our address on the envelope still made me smile.

Our house was a 1940s style cape that had been owned by the same family for over sixty years. By the time we bought it, practically every inch of it needed some sort of repair. In the eight months since we'd bought the house, we'd spent every dime we had (and then some) fixing it up, and it still had a very long way to go.

As soon as I pulled it out of the mailbox, I had a funny feeling that something was amiss with the birthday card. It looked like it had been opened and then resealed with tape. I could feel that there was the cardboard shape of a gift card holder inside. My dad must have sealed the envelope and then remembered that he wanted to include a gift card, so opened it back up. His taping job was excessive and sloppy.

I went inside, opened the envelope, and realized that the cardboard gift card holder was there, but the actual plastic gift card had been removed. On the cardboard it said, "A little extra for your new house! Love, Dad" In the corner was written, "$200."

"Look at this, my Dad sent me a Home Depot gift card for $200!"

"Wow, that's a lot!"

"I know, but I don't see the gift card."

We inspected the birthday card and envelope. Someone had clearly opened up the envelope and stolen the gift card from inside. The only thing I could think of was that maybe the mail carrier had stolen it. It seemed like a ridiculous thought. Essex Junction is a very small place where everyone knows everyone else. A mail carrier would probably not commit such a crime. I called the post office anyway, just to be sure.

The voice on the other end was curt and annoyed.

"Our carriers would never do that. Mail theft is a federal offense, and your mail carrier has been on your route for fifteen years."

I had to agree with her. It was probably not the mail carrier. I decided to call my dad. His house was in a quiet neighborhood and his mailbox was at the end of his driveway. It would be easy for someone to steal from a card if he had left it in the mailbox with the little red flag up overnight.

"Do you think someone might've tampered with the mail on your street?"

"No. I mailed that card in the mailroom at work." My dad worked in a large hospital. "I dropped it in the plastic bin for out-going mail. I bet someone took it from there. Let me check with the mailroom clerk and see if we can figure it out."

A few days later, Dad called me back to say that over 50 people had used their key-codes to get into the mailroom the morning after he dropped off the card and before the mail went out. There was no way to figure out who it could have been, and there were no cameras.

At the time, I had been watching a lot of *Law & Order* on TV, and the mystery of my missing gift card intrigued me. I wanted to catch the guy who stole it from me, so I started sleuthing. My dad had purchased the gift card on his credit card, and the gift card number was listed on the receipt. I had him read it to me over the phone, then got to work.

The next day, I called Home Depot national headquarters in Atlanta. I explained to the sweet southern gentleman on the other end of the line what had happened and asked him to look up the number to see if it had been spent and where. Indeed, it had been spent the very same day that it was stolen, at a Home Depot not far from my dad's hospital. They were able to give me the exact time and register where it had been used.

My next step was to call the Home Depot store and speak to a manager. I think both the Home Depot employee in Atlanta and the one near my dad's work must have been watching crime shows on TV too, because they were more than willing, and I would venture to say even excited, to help me get to the bottom of this. I kept joyfully humming the *Law & Order* theme song in-between phone calls.

"You're ridiculous," Liz said as she rolled her eyes at me.

"I know," I replied with a grin.

When I reached the manager at Home Depot, I asked him if they had cameras in their store that looked out over the registers.

"We do," he said. "And we keep the footage for at least a few weeks, so let me see what I can find, and I'll get back to you."

"I should have been a detective," I bragged to Liz when I hung up. "We're going to nail this crook. He should know better than to mess with my birthday card!" Liz was dutifully amused by my investigation. I was clearly bored with life to pursue this with such vengeance.

The next day, the manager from Home Depot called back to inform me that they did have a video of the transaction, and his next steps would have to involve the police.

A local police officer called me later that week to ask me a few questions and take a statement. I then connected him with my dad. I had set the police up with all the evidence they needed. The investigation could continue on without me at this point.

Dad called me the next day to tell me that he and the manager of the mail room at his hospital were going down to the police station to meet up with the manager of Home Depot and watch the surveillance video to see if they could identify the thief. I was thrilled that my detective work was paying off. I secretly hoped my dad was proud of my clever problem solving too. A few days later, he called me back.

"Well, Jen, we watched that surveillance video at the police station and right away we knew exactly who the thief was. It was very clear."

"Really? Who was he?" I asked.

"It wasn't a *he*, it was a woman who works in the mailroom. She was with her boyfriend. The mailroom manager thinks that the boyfriend put her up to stealing the gift card and has been taking advantage of her access to the mail."

My heart sank.

"The woman was working in the mailroom as part of a work program for people with various levels of ability," my dad continued, "and she has been fired. She's in a lot of trouble."

"Oh, crap." I took a deep breath. I never imagined this outcome. "Let's not press charges, Dad. I mean, I want to drop it." The $200 gift card really wasn't worth pursuing any further.

"We can't drop it, Jen, it's out of our hands. She's being charged with a federal offense."

"That's horrible." My cheeks felt hot and flushed with embarrassment that I had gleaned any joy from pursuing this. I started grasping for any possible way to resolve the situation.

"What did she buy with the gift card anyway? Could you see in the video? "

"It was household goods, an ironing board, a mop, things like that."

"Well, could she return them and give me my gift card back for a lesser sentence? Can we give her a chance to make it right?"

"Jen, there's something else."

"What?"

"On Friday, after she was fired from the mailroom, she went home to the house she shared with her mother and in a freak accident, her house burned down."

"Her house burned down?? Are you kidding me? Is she ok?" This situation was becoming epically worse.

"It was an electrical fire; it had absolutely nothing to do with the other events. It was just a weird coincidence that all of this happened on the same day."

I thought about the twisted karma that had befallen this woman. It ground my spirit all the way down. Why couldn't I have just let it go? Why did I have to play detective? I felt such unbelievable guilt for playing any part in the terrible events that wrecked this woman's life.

"I'm sorry, Dad," was all I could think of to say.

"Me too. You know, this was not your fault, right?"

"It kind of feels like it was a little bit."

"I know, but you need to let it go."

"Ok Dad. I love you."

"I love you too, Jen. Goodbye now." My dad always ended his conversations with, "Goodbye now." It was endearing and it made me feel like he probably wasn't mad that I had dragged him into this terrible story. I hung up the phone and explained what happened to an equally stunned Liz.

"That is not usually how things go on *Law & Order*," she admitted.

"I think I'm done with *Law & Order*."

It's been many years since that happened and I still think about that woman. I wonder what she's doing now and whether her life has improved. I like to imagine that her boyfriend is in prison for being an asshole, but I know it's unlikely. I carry a lot of guilt about that time and wish that the whole thing hadn't happened. I learned the hard way that the person behind a crime isn't always the criminal you want them to be.

When a lawyer from the Vermont Attorney General's office called me at school about a week and half after the inauguration to tell me that people were impersonating me on the internet, and trying to sell mittens they claimed I'd made, I didn't want to get involved. It was almost exactly ten years to the day after the terrible gift card incident.

"It has come to our attention that at least three different websites are claiming to be you. They're using your name and likeness to sell mittens." I had less than zero energy or time to devote to this. "We were wondering if you have a minute to answer some questions for our investigation."

"Investigation?"

"Yes, we are pursuing this as a criminal case." His voice was deep and very official sounding.

"Honestly, I really don't care. If those people want to sell mittens, let them."

"Well, they probably aren't selling anything. They're probably just scamming people, and they're using your name to do it."

"Oh. Well, I don't have the money to hire an attorney."

"You don't have to hire anyone. We want to pursue this on your behalf as a resident of the state of Vermont."

"I don't really have the time to get involved in this."

"Well, It's part of the responsibility of the attorney general's office to stop fraudulent behavior and prosecute identity theft on any scale."

The word "theft" hung in the air.

"Will you help us with this investigation?"

I felt the familiar acid reflux feeling in my veins. My whole body was saying *no*. I did know that people were impersonating me online. Several of my friends had emailed or texted me over the last week. I just didn't have the time to think about it. I was under so much pressure that I'd asked my friends not to tell me things like that. I wasn't able to take on another drama in this already outrageous experience.

"I can't help you, I'm sorry, and . . ." I thought back to the terrible feeling I had when my dad called me to tell me about the woman who'd stolen my gift card. "When you find these people, please don't destroy their lives. I have a lot of compassion for them. This is a really bad time for everyone."

"You're very thoughtful, Jen, but the people who are getting ripped off may turn around and blame you. They think they're buying mittens from *you*."

"Look, I've told every reporter, newspaper and magazine, Twitter and Facebook that I don't make the mittens anymore. I can't imagine anyone will actually think that's me selling them."

"But they do think that. That's why they're buying them. Right now you have a very public profile and that's a dangerous position to be in."

I considered his point. I didn't want people to start coming after me, looking for mittens I didn't have and didn't sell to them. I didn't want my name and image to be dragged through the tabloids in scandal. It all felt like such an enormous hassle.

"Ok. What do you need from me?" I had taken this call in the main office at school, and I looked over at Betty who was sitting nearby. She gave me a sympathetic look.

"We need a list of anyone you think might be impersonating you."

I doubted I would follow through, but I wanted to get off the phone with him.

"Ok. I'll see what I can do." The lawyer gave me his email address and I told him I'd *try* to be back in touch. I emphasized try.

When I got off the phone, Betty was shaking her head.

"Did you catch that?"

"I caught enough of it." She rolled her eyes.

"Honestly, Betty, why can't people just behave themselves?"

She chuckled.

"Well, they're about to get a pretty big discipline referral from the State of Vermont, I'd say." That sounded accurate.

The conversation with the attorney general's office left me shaking and light headed. Just when I thought the mitten frenzy was winding down, a new tornado had arrived to spin me around. I didn't want to be involved in this one, but in the end I figured it would be best to actually try to help the lawyer. I knew that these kinds of scammers were particularly effective at ripping off older people. My unending affection for my grandparents, even though they had been gone for many years, led me to change my mind.

There was no possible way that I would have the time to travel down the rabbit hole of searching for shady internet imposters, but I had another idea. Many, many people had reached out to me asking if they could help in any way. They offered to sew mittens, find wool, and set up a website. Most of the help people were offering I didn't need. But when this happened, I decided to reach out to some of the helpers to see if they would take this on. I created a Google Doc and sent it to two friends who I thought might enjoy an internet investigation of this sort. One was bored at home recovering from cancer and the other just loved sleuthing. They happily agreed to do a deep dive on my behalf. After two days, they had compiled a very thorough list. They seemed to enjoy the thrill of the investigation, as I had many years before. I forwarded the document to the attorney general's office in Montpelier without even looking at it.

Sure enough, about a month later, I started getting irate emails from people who were looking for the mittens they'd ordered from me. I kindly explained to each of them that I no longer sold the mittens. Then I forwarded their messages on to Montpelier to add to the investigation. It was too bad that the actions of just a few dishonest people cast a shadow on the Bernie's Mitten Meme extravaganza. In the end, I never did look at the websites of the imposters. I intentionally avoided anything having to do with the ugly underbelly of the internet. I didn't want to invite anger and frustration into this experience. I listened to Bernie's helpful advice not to Google myself. It may sound naïve of me to think this way, but the only way I could sleep at night was to recognize that these imposters were probably miserable, suffering people and I just needed to forgive them and move on.

I reached out to Jack Thurston from Channel 5, the same reporter who had interviewed Helen and me on our front lawn on Inauguration day, and asked if we could do a news story warning people about the imposters. I reached out to some of the people who had contacted me about being ripped off and they agreed to let me connect them to Jack for the interview. Jack also interviewed Vermont Attorney General T. J. Donovan. I pasted a link to that news clip on every piece of social media I could think of and asked people to share it.

About a month later, the lawyer from the attorney general's office called me to give me an update. They had managed to get the imposter sites taken down. It turned out that they were all linked to one person.

"So, what will happen to him?"

"I can't give you any more information at this time, Ms. Ellis, but I do appreciate your cooperation."

For months afterward I received letters and emails from people looking for their mittens or a refund of their money. I sent them the link to the Jack Thurston news report and explained that they had been scammed. They needed to fight the charges through their credit card companies. In May, I received a letter at home that was addressed to: Jen Ellis, The Mitten Lady, Essex Junction, Vermont. I had to laugh at this. You didn't even need to know my address to send me mail anymore. It wasn't fan mail though, just another person looking for a refund. She included all the correspondence she'd had with the company, the bill of sale and everything. They were offering discounts and free shipping. Every correspondence was signed "—Jen." It was very disturbing.

I never knew what happened to the thief. After reading countless appeals from people asking for their money back, I didn't actually feel as much compassion for this guy as I initially had. I hoped whatever consequences he faced would lead him to stop being a crook, but I doubted it would. I was thankful to the State of Vermont for taking on this case, though, and stopping him.

I tucked the internet imposter away in my mind with the same guy who bid on my mitten auction just to win. This is a category of people who I will never understand. I was trying to hold on to the guileless innocence I saw in my daughter and might still be sparkling somewhere inside of me, but it was getting harder and harder. The world was showing more of itself to me than I had ever noticed before, and at times, it was surprisingly terrible.

Chapter 18
Vermont Teddy Bear

2021

About a week after the initial verbal agreement and big announcement of my partnership with Vermont Teddy Bear, I spent a day at the factory showing their design team how to make the mittens and discussing all the tips and tricks for selling them. I felt the need to move quickly with them because I wanted the mittens to sell, and didn't want to lose the momentum of the inauguration. Hundreds of people were still reaching out to me each day asking for them.

After the design meeting, weeks went by with no word from Hayes, who was my main point person. I worried that they were going to back out of the deal. Critical time had passed, and I wasn't sure if I could get another business partnership with a different company to make the mittens. I began to put pressure on Vermont Teddy Bear to shore up the contract and start making the mittens.

I didn't realize at the time that creating a whole new product from concept, to design, to hiring and producing would take so long. After all, when Lise-Anne and I decided to make mittens, I popped in to the Salvation Army, found an old sweater and made a pair that night. When the contract was finally finalized at the end of February, I hoped the mittens would be well underway, but they weren't even close. There was a steep learning curve between small-town crafter to large factory production. I experienced it and I think Vermont Teddy Bear did too.

Vermont Teddy Bear and I saw eye to eye on many things. We agreed that a portion of the proceeds should always go to charity. We agreed that calling the brand "Vermont Mittens" would fit well with their other product, "Vermont Teddy Bears," and we agreed that they would offer the mittens to the twenty-two thousand people who had reached out to me, or had signed up for the waitlist on the company's website.

As with all strong partnerships, though, we had our growing pains. The biggest difference was whether to keep the mittens as "sweater mittens," or to source virgin knit material and try to replicate the Bernie pattern for mass reproduction. I was in favor of the latter. From my ten years of making "Swittens," I knew that sweaters could be hard to come by. They were also time consuming to wash and cut. Because every sweater was knit with different thicknesses of yarn, the stretchiness and bulkiness of each pair of mittens would make for a wide array of end-product sizes, even if every mitten was made with the same pattern. It would be nearly impossible to produce a consistent product. Even if they had to invest in a knitting machine, I felt that it was worthwhile to have a uniform product. Hayes felt strongly that we should keep the theme of upcycling by using repurposed wool sweaters.

I didn't entirely disagree with him. The sweater mitten is a really neat idea, and it's fun. But even as I pushed for a streamlined product, it became clear that because of the pandemic, materials were hard to come by, as supply chains were blocked and companies were frequently waylaid by COVID-19 outbreaks. Hayes was able to secure a supplier for used sweaters and Vermont Teddy Bear moved forward with that idea first. I had my doubts that it would be successful, but was pleasantly surprised when the mittens hit the market. They sold so fast, Vermont Teddy Bear could barely keep up with production. The Vermont Mitten was a huge hit. I learned later that the new mitten line had endeared itself to the employees on every level. It was exactly what Vermont Teddy Bear was looking for at exactly the right time.

Since every mitten would be different, Vermont Teddy Bear made three color categories on their website for people to choose from, and the rest would be a surprise. I thought that was a fun idea, too. Hayes was confident that the Vermont Mitten would go through many different iterations, and that using repurposed wool sweaters was just the first one.

About a month after production began, Hayes invited me to the Teddy Bear (and now Mitten) Factory in Shelburne, Vermont to see production first hand. I was struck right away by a beautiful mural of Bernie wearing his mittens. It was the first thing most people would see when entering the building. Any lingering doubt I had about their commitment to this project was assuaged. As I admired the mural, at least three sets of tourists stood in front of it to have their pictures taken with our famous senator and his infamous mittens. There was a white folding chair strategically placed nearby so that people could assume the Bernie pose. Even after several months, it brought people so much joy. It was spectacular.

The factory is open daily to the public and is a popular tourist destination for families visiting Vermont. Excited children were buzzing around in the Make Your Teddy Bear corner, and the mood was lighthearted and cheerful. It wasn't entirely unlike the happy vibe of the craft fairs where the mittens started. The director of manufacturing, Donna, met me in the lobby and we began our tour.

As we walked back into the factory, I began to notice little things I had missed before. There were gender-neutral bathrooms, gay pride stickers on doorways, and a designated nursing/pumping room for breastfeeding mothers. When new mothers needed to pump breast milk at my school, we had to lock our classroom door during our twenty-five-minute lunch break and hope no one unlocked it to let in a student who'd left something behind, like a water bottle. Even though my school was a very gay-friendly place to work, there were no rainbow ally stickers on my colleague's doors. Donna had been working at Vermont Teddy for a long time, and I could see why. This company took care of its employees.

Walking through the factory, off the beaten path of the hourly tours, was a little like being in Willy Wonka's Chocolate Factory. Everything was colorful, larger than life, and so fascinating. Donna showed me enormous shrink-wrapped cubes of used wool sweaters, just waiting to be processed. I met the men and women who had been hired to wash, dye-cut, and match the mittens. Then we headed onto the factory floor, which is on display for the tours to watch. A lively group of families passed by on the elevated walkway that looked down into the sewing area, and that's when I saw *them*: four women sitting together at sewing machines. They were talking to each other and making my mittens with skill and accuracy.

"These women are new Americans, Jen. We created ten new full-time jobs for Vermont Mittens," Donna explained.

"They didn't work here before?"

"No, they have these jobs because of Bernie's mittens."

Rays of sunshine from the wall of south facing windows poured over the group as they laughed together while they worked and chatted in a language I didn't know. Though I didn't understand what their words meant, there was a part of me that knew exactly what they were saying to each other. They were every group of women who gathered together to sew. They were Lise-Anne and me on all those Sunday afternoons; sharing their life stories, healing from their sadnesses, recalling funny encounters, and probably gossiping, too. They were forming community and solidarity over the beautiful, creative act of making mittens.

"Do they all work full time and have benefits?"

"Yes, and they're paid a fair, livable wage." Donna took a moment to introduce each woman to me by name. As I watched, I noticed they were sewing the cuffs differently than I did.

"I never thought to do it that way," I said to one of the women.

"It's faster and easier," she told me. "I figured it out, and now we all do it that way."

It was delightful to see this new trick, and I made a mental note to try it the next time I made a pair of mittens. She had figured out a better way of doing my own craft and taught it to me! It was clear to me that these women took pride in the finished product. I won't pretend to know what it's like to be a new American or what the jobs meant to these women. But I did know that a full-time job with medical benefits and a livable wage is an empowering stepping stone in life.

It's hard to quantify the impact of the mitten meme sensation. There were millions of memes—too many to count. Upcycled mitten crafters everywhere experienced an uptick in sales. Spin-off products appeared all over the internet. Millions of dollars were raised for charity and lots of people made a quick buck. On the way home from Vermont Teddy Bear that early summer afternoon, I repeated "ten new jobs," over and over in my head. So much of the experience had been a moving target of numbers and possibilities until then. *Ten New Jobs*. I could quantify that. I had made a difference, and it meant something.

The mittens sold steadily through the summer and fall, and in October, Hayes invited me to the factory to present a check of over fifteen-thousand dollars to Make-a-Wish Vermont. This amount represented the portion of the sales we had agreed would go to charity. Hayes and I stood on either side of a giant check and posed for pictures. We had done it.

I never could have imagined taking a little craft and turning it into an entire new arm of a large company, but that is what happened. Now everyone could have Bernie mittens! And then there was another number I could quantify: Fifteen thousand, three hundred and thirty-six dollars. I'm not a person who typically deals with thousands of dollars at a time, so this amount seemed enormous to me. It was like a dream, but it was very real, and for as long as the Vermont Teddy Bear Factory made Vermont Mittens, a generous portion would always go to charity. That check was just the start.

Hayes left the company in November of 2021. He decided not to move his family to Vermont after all. His replacement was a thoughtful and collaborative woman named Cassie. She set up monthly meetings with me and the Vermont Mitten team to keep me in the loop. We decided to switch the charitable benefactor from Make-A-Wish Vermont to Outright Vermont after the first year. I requested Outright because I knew they would harness the money for something amazing, just like they had done with the mitten auction. At first, I was afraid that Vermont Teddy Bear would shy away from a partnership that might be viewed as controversial by some, but Cassie reassured me.

"I love this company because we walk the walk. We're allies and we're not afraid." I'd trusted my gut when I entered into the partnership with Vermont Teddy Bear, and my gut was right.

When we met with the directors of Outright to tell them we wanted to give them the charitable donation, I learned a surprising new fact about the original mitten auction. The donations had continued to stream in over the last sixteen months and the grand total ended up being just over $56,000. The second week they added to their summer camp had doubled the number of LGBTQ kids who could attend. This new partnership would help Outright to continue offering two weeks of camp each summer. *Two weeks*. I could quantify that too.

Chapter 19
Teachers

My Pandemic Class referred to me as their "Famous Teacher," and constantly made me laugh with their antics and giddiness over my notoriety. I guess fame still seems glittery and wonderful when you are young and don't know how stressful it can be. Then the packages started arriving. It was slow the first week, a letter here, a small gift there, but by the third week after the inauguration, multiple packages started arriving for me at school every day. My classroom phone was eventually turned back on because most of the TV and radio reporters had moved on. The ones who still wanted to find me were just emailing. Each day I would get a phone call from Betty, in the main office.

"Your mail is here!"

"Oh my. I'll come get it."

Some days there were so many packages that I had to make two trips back to my classroom to get them out of the office. Betty was an incredibly good sport about it all. I think she found it amusing. Who would think to send the maker of Bernie's mittens fan mail? But lots of people did. Maybe people wanted to participate in the gift giving. After all, it was a gift that started the whole thing.

The things people sent were incredible, especially the gifts of books and classroom supplies. We had lost so many supplies in the rain and weather in our outdoor classroom. I didn't know how I was going to replace it all on my classroom budget. Children's book publishers sent me whole boxes of new release books. One company in California sent me a sample of every leveled reader they had and a gift card to buy whole sets of them for my reading groups. I handed the books out to the class and we spent an afternoon reading them and voting on the ones we should buy.

Lots of people sent notes and cards. I would read their words and feel like a bit of an imposter. I didn't feel that I deserved their praise. People told me that I inspired them. They confided in me about their battles with depression over the winter and how my mittens and the memes had lifted them out of a funk. People told me that they had dusted off their old sewing machines and rediscovered crafting. Teachers wrote to me to tell me that they saw me on the news telling MSNBC that my teaching job was more important than the mittens, and that I wouldn't abandon my class and my colleagues mid-year to start a cottage industry and capitalize on the event. They were reminded about the enormous impact of the teaching profession. Even Ms. Alfaba, my fourth grade teacher who caught me sneaking out of the bus line, sent me a card with a copy of our class picture and a blue facemask with little Bernies on it. Someone had actually printed a Bernie's mitten meme fabric.

Before the inauguration, the only thing that came up when you googled my name was a school picture from five years before. My only public online identity was "Jen Ellis, second grade teacher, Westford School." The easiest way to find me was at school. I assumed that was why the packages went there first. Soon they started arriving at my home too, which I'll admit, was a bit creepy. It is so easy to find people on the internet.

My students began returning from lunch full of anticipation for what packages we would receive. We started opening them together. I would read the letters out loud and then we would celebrate every kindness from every stranger. One day a few weeks after the inauguration, we were having a gratitude circle in our outdoor classroom. We bundled up in our snow pants and winter clothes, and I made a fire in the fire pit. As we sat around the crackling flames, we shared the things we appreciate about our friends, our school, and our community.

Vermonters were now getting the vaccine. Some of my students' parents were health care providers and they were first in line. Their grandparents had their first shots, too. There were many offers of thanks and praise for the vaccine and hope for the end of the pandemic. When we got to Grace, she was introspective and kind as she said,

"I'm thankful Ms. Ellis is our teacher."

"Thank you, Grace," I said.

"Yeah, we get so much cool stuff now that you're famous, Ms. Ellis!" said Jack. He always made me laugh with his frankness and honesty.

"That's not why I'm thankful for her, Jack," said Grace. In the way that small towns in Vermont are very small, Grace and Jack were cousins.

"I know, I was just kidding. We're thankful for you because we love you, Ms. Ellis." There were nodding heads and hand signals of connection from nearly every student. It was one of those teaching moments that takes your breath away.

The truth is, I loved them too. I loved all my students, but I especially loved *this* group of students. I was so thankful for each of them during the mitten frenzy. They made my days easy with their lightheartedness and joy. They made me smile. They made me feel excited to come to school each day just by being the amazing people they were. Grace always said, "I wish that I could hug you, Ms. Ellis," and I wished that, too. I wanted to hug all of them. We came together in the midst of the pandemic and worked together to create a classroom community with the most indomitable spirit. We found freedom and friendship in the vast forest of our outdoor classroom. They had given me the gifts of their wild and untamed spirits, and I had given them the gift of setting them free in the wilderness. That school year was the most joyous one of my career.

In the months after the inauguration, I did a handful of podcast interviews. Each one veered away from the mittens and seemed to center on my career as a teacher. As a society, we seem to have endless reviews of this profession. We are either praising teachers for their selfless calling or ripping them apart for their flaws. Our memories of teachers are augmented through the lens of time and the emotions of nostalgia. We remember the names of every teacher who wronged us and every teacher who saved us, and virtually no one in between. After the inauguration, I was constantly referred to as "The Vermont Teacher Who Made Bernie's Mittens." I couldn't help but wonder what the headlines would have said if I had been an accountant, a botanist, or a warehouse manager. The fact that I was a teacher became critical to the story.

When I refused to give up teaching and make mittens full time for the tens of thousands of people who immediately wanted them after the inauguration, everyone assumed that I loved teaching too much to stray from the path. News reporters mused that teaching was my vocation, my true passion, my dedication. While some of that was true, the extent to which it was advertised made it false. What became clear during the mitten fame was that I wouldn't like running a mitten business full time. It was really that simple.

Over the years, teaching had given me wonderful opportunities. I recognized that many of the teachers of my childhood were part of the successes I experienced in my classroom. I enjoyed carrying on some of the treasured lessons I had learned in school. Some of the best things I did as an educator were reincarnations of projects and class sessions I remembered from my youth. When

I started teaching in North Carolina, my favorite high school English teacher, Susanne MacArthur emailed me her entire curriculum: every test, quiz, lesson plan, vocabulary list and assignment. I began my career by stepping into the footsteps of a truly masterful teacher. Every Valentine's Day I did an Exotic Fruits Taste Testing. I got that idea from my seventh-grade teacher Mr. Towle. We often did experiments rubbing fresh bread around our classroom, then letting it mold in plastic bags to see what colors it would turn. That one came from my second-grade teacher Ms. Smith. Sometimes when I was stuck on a particular lesson, I would think back to Ms. Alfaba and try to remember how she taught it. Even though Mr. Hunter didn't teach much, he was fun and caring. There was something of him in my teaching too. Then there was Mrs. Collett.

I still think about Mrs. Collett every time I sew. In 2016, I tracked down her address and sent her a beautiful pair of my hand-made mittens. I remembered that she was a petite woman, so I made them extra small. I wrote her a card and thanked her for giving me the gift of sewing, then tucked it in the package with the mittens. I told her that I had also become a teacher, knowing this would bring her great joy. It is never too late to thank a teacher for teaching you something very important.

Most of my teachers came and went from my life and I never saw them again. After I sent Mrs. Collett the mittens, she wrote me a thank you note and I believed that was the last I would ever hear from her. But it wasn't. Like so many wonderful things that emerged from the Bernie mitten meme sensation, Mrs. Collett returned to my life, making a brief but lovely cameo appearance, three decades later.

Hundreds of reporters reached out to me in the weeks after the inauguration for interviews. Most of them I never responded to. But one interview I did accept was with the Portland Press Herald. I knew instantly when I saw the request that this story could not be complete without Mrs. Collett. In the same creepy way that dozens of people had found my address online, I easily found her home phone number. A few days after the inauguration, I called her.

I explained that a reporter wanted to interview me and that I wanted to include her. We talked for a long time about her career and the importance of home economics classes. Towards the end of her career, Mrs. Collett taught a very successful quilting class at the high school. She told me with some sadness that when she retired in 2017, they retired the entire program, and home economics is no longer offered in the South Portland School system. Mrs. Collett was delighted to hear about my teaching career, the success of my outdoor classroom, and my love for quilting. She was as full of wisdom as ever. She said, "All children want is to know that you care about them, even just a little. If they think you like them and care about them, they will do anything for you." I had to agree. This was a teaching skill I had worked especially hard on over the past few years. The children who needed love and approval the most were often the ones who asked for it in the most unlovable ways.

"Do you remember how much I loved your class, Mrs. Collett? I just wanted to sew all day long."

There was a pause, and then she said, "I have to be honest; I know you were in my class but I don't remember you exactly." She asked me who else was in my class and I listed some of the more notable students. She did remember them. It didn't bother me that she didn't remember me. She had taught thousands of students just like me over the years. She also met me at a time when I had perfected the art of disappearing.

"So, is this reporter interviewing you because of your teaching?"

"No, he's more interested in the mitten thing."

"What mitten thing?" This made me laugh. I had been talking to Mrs. Collett for thirty minutes and she had no idea why the reporter wanted to interview me. It was such a humbling moment. For days I had been feeling so exposed; I was all over the internet and TV news. Here was my former teacher, completely unaware that I had become strangely famous. I was so wrapped up in my own whirlwind, I hadn't even thought to explain to her why I had called.

"Well, I made Senator Bernie Sanders a pair of mittens, like the ones I made for you, and he wore them to the inauguration, and now . . ."

"Oh yes! I have seen some of the funny pictures of him, sitting in his chair."

I took a moment to explain the rest of the situation and why I wanted to include her in the interview. I think I was equal parts relieved and shocked that there was at least one person I knew who had no idea I was connected to the Bernie memes.

Mrs. Collett agreed to the interview, so I called the reporter from the Portland Press Herald to set it up. I was certain that this article would be the most meaningful one yet. It included all the warm fuzzy elements of a feel-good story. But when it came out, I realized that the reporter had mainly stuck to the facts and didn't really take the time to listen to Mrs. Collett and her infinite wisdom about teaching. I was disappointed that he hadn't told the story with the heartfelt words I felt it deserved. Since it was hidden behind a paywall, most people I knew didn't get to read it anyway.

I don't keep in close touch with Mrs. Collett, though she is with me every time I thread my sewing machine. I hear her home economics teacher voice in my head sometimes when I'm cooking, saying "Read the whole recipe and gather ALL the ingredients before you begin to mix." "Gently fold the blueberries into the muffin mix, don't stir, or your batter will turn green." "Scrape the peeler away from yourself when you peel a carrot." Thoughts of her always bring a smile to my face and a deep sense of calm and control.

I never told her about the perverted old man in my neighborhood who molested me when I was in the fourth grade. I would venture to say that most people in my life probably don't know that happened to me. Mr. Johnson died when I was still in elementary school. Though his house still stands in my old neighborhood, the rest of his existence has disappeared. I once looked up his obituary on microfiche in my hometown library, and it said very little about him. If he had lived long enough, I might have pressed charges against him when I got older; then again, I might not have. Men like him are rarely punished for their crimes. Stories like mine dangle in history with unwritten endings. There is very little justice for the crimes against girls and women. The fact that that terrible part of my childhood so gently led to my love for my home economics teacher and for sewing is, in itself, a kind of gift. I arrived in Mrs. Collett's sixth-grade classroom searching for something, and she helped me to find it. Fabric was not the only thing she taught me how to mend.

One thing I have learned about healing is that you always need to look for an open door. For some people it's running, for others it's talking to a friend. I know people who heal through writing, going on long drives, watching movies. I heal by sewing. That is the door Mrs. Collett opened for me. When everything else is falling apart, sewing is how I put it back together. When the World Trade Center fell, I sewed my grandmother's quilt. When we lost our first baby, I made mittens. When the COVID-19 quarantine tethered us to our homes, I cut up my wedding dress and all my grandmother's old clothes and sewed my magnum opus—a quilt for Helen. When my neighbor molested me, I threaded my first sewing machine and have been stitching the pieces of my life together ever since.

After the inauguration, one of my childhood friends made a meme of Bernie Sanders sitting in our old home economics classroom. He looked so funny on the teal and white checkered tile floor with the metal, pastel cabinets and enamel countertops in the background. The room hadn't been updated in fifty years. Just the picture of that space evoked the smell of cinnamon twists in the oven and the hiss of a steaming iron on the board. A teacher's classroom is the stage for the epic daily performance of their wisdom and care. I was flooded with love and nostalgia when I saw that meme. Deep inside me there will always be a repeating whisper of gratitude: "Thank you Mrs. Collett."

Chapter 20
Unexpected Joy

I stepped onto the plane on a warm May morning, found my seat towards the back, plugged in my headphones and began listening to my favorite podcast. Ira Glass's voice was quirky and curious as he introduced us to "Act One of today's episode, Act One." Something about that second "Act One" really sealed the deal. I looked out the window at the fresh green trees and the blooming Vermont landscape. Four months had passed since the inauguration, and things had calmed down considerably. Even though the mittens still crept into my life on a daily basis in one form or another, I was mostly able to carry on as I did before.

Today was an exception. I was on my way to Los Angeles to be a guest on a game show. I signed about a hundred nondisclosure agreements before my appearance, so even though it is readily viewable on YouTube, I can't mention the name of the show in this book.

The plane was tiny, as are most planes leaving Burlington, Vermont. It was only three seats wide. I had seat A, which meant no one was sitting directly next to me. As we took off, I studied the landscape. Lake Champlain was completely still and glistening in the morning sun. Flying out of Burlington always made me a little sentimental. I had lived so much of my life in this town. Sometimes I felt like I had lived more than just my own life here as well. My dad grew up on Farrington Parkway, and he liked to tell me stories of the times he and his friends would sneak past the fence at the old meat packing plant to go swimming at the beach that is now Leddy Park. We teased him, "So *that's* what's wrong with you, Dad! A childhood spent swimming in salmonella!"

My memories of Burlington are both personal and generational. Looking down at the University of Vermont campus, I could see Ira Allen Chapel and the parking lot where Dani Comey told me everything I needed to know about being a lesbian. I spotted the library where my parents met in 1970 and the hospital where Helen was born.

Even though it's only seven miles from our house, sometimes it seems like a faraway place full of nostalgia. I rarely go there anymore, and during the pandemic I never went. It felt like I was looking down at an old friend from the steadily climbing plane. As we crept up into the clouds and the lake below disappeared, I settled back into *This American Life* and was thankful for the peace and quiet to catch up on all the podcasts I had missed.

The game show I was heading to first aired in the 1950s and had been on and off the air ever since. When the casting agent reached out to me on my website, Deb vetted her and forwarded the request on to me. Deb had grown adept at filtering out the scams and finding the invitations that would be most in line with my mission.

When I arrived in Los Angeles, a driver showed up to transport me to my hotel in the fanciest hotel transport I had ever seen. It was a souped-up SUV with leather seats and complimentary bottled water. He brought me to a swanky hotel near Universal Studios, and I was escorted to my room where I was told to stay put until my designated time to be COVID-19-tested in the morning. I ordered room service, watched cable TV, and did some school work. I was supposed to quarantine for four days in the hotel room before filming, but by the second day, I was so bored, I started looking for local attractions to which I could walk. The Brady Bunch house was less than a mile away, so I set off on foot to check out one of my favorite childhood movie locations.

Of course, none of the Brady Bunch was actually filmed there, and there was a security detail out front, so I just walked by *really* slowly and gawked for an appropriate amount of time. At the end of the street, I turned around, took my sweater and hat off and walked back in the other direction, pretending to be someone else. I don't think they fell for it, but since their windows were tinted, I couldn't tell if they even noticed me. I gave up all pretense on the second pass and took some legit touristy pictures before hustling away. Do you know what is shocking about that house? There is a polluted, concrete-lined waterway that runs directly behind it that never appeared in the show.

Hollywood is one layer of smoke and mirrors on top of the next, and television corporations are serious about keeping it that way. As I was escorted through the studio premises on an extra-long golf cart on the day of filming, I just wanted to take pictures of everything, but I was trying to play it cool, like this was *totally* normal for me. I was also afraid they would confiscate my phone. The different buildings were labeled with the names of the show sets inside. There were lots of trailers and little houses where the stars spent their time when they weren't filming. I had already experienced the feeling of fame, but this felt like *movie star* fame, which was a different brand altogether.

When I got on set, I had my own dressing room with my name on it and a private bathroom. They asked me to bring at least three outfits to choose from and when I met with the wardrobe designer she told me what to wear. We spent most of the day rehearsing what we were going to do during the taping. The producers had a very specific vision for how everything should go. I felt again that

I wasn't really playing myself, it was some other version of me that they wanted. It was me through a funhouse mirror, mixed with Hollywood dazzle.

Artists who had worked with hundreds of stars did my hair and make-up. By the time they were through with me, I hardly recognized myself. I could have sat in their studio salon chairs all day and chatted with them. Their lives were exciting and filled with creativity. The other contestants were lovely too. At every turn I met fascinating people. The game show itself wasn't nearly as fun as the social scene off-set. I also met a bunch of extremely famous people. Not surprisingly, their lives were not as glamorous as you might think. They were friendly, but they looked tired and one of them had on extremely uncomfortable looking shoes and tight clothes. I didn't envy them.

The game show was full of bright lights and loud music. It went by very quickly. After the whole day of prepping, we were on camera for less than ten minutes. Every second of the show was carefully planned out. The team of people who pulled it off reminded me of well-choreographed dancers. Each person played a small part, and the way it all came together was beyond my imagination. I felt like a star for the day, and then it was over. The hype and pomp of the whole experience left me feeling exhausted. In the end, I was ready to go home. I missed my family, and I missed Vermont, where the pace was slower and everyone wore less make-up.

The day after the taping, I got up very early to head home. On the way to the airport, I asked the driver if he had ever driven any stars around.

"All the time."

"Who've you met?"

"I can't say."

"Were they nice?"

"Some."

"Were they happy?" There was a long pause here.

"It's hard to say. They spend a lot of time working out and they don't eat very much. I think it makes some of them grumpy."

"That would make me grumpy too." I left that conversation feeling thankful that my fame was minimal ... and fleeting.

In some ways, the pandemic made all of the publicity easier to handle because aside from the game show trip, no one expected me to travel for interviews. All I had to do was find a quiet spot in my house with a blank background and log in to a Zoom call. Also, the fact that I didn't Google any of the people I was talking to after the inauguration and wasn't caught up on news-culture spared me from a lot of angst. One time Liz came into the living room and said,

"Did you talk to Katty Kay?"

"I think so, is she with the BBC? I talked to them this morning."

"One of my friends from work just heard that interview. She said you did a good job. Katty Kay is really famous."

"Hmmmmm, yes, she seemed nice." Liz gave me an annoyed look like I wasn't as excited about the famous people as I should have been. I think she found me a little exasperating during that time.

The Disney Channel interviewed me at home that spring. It wasn't until months later that I actually looked up the two young women who hosted the show. One of them was Ariel Martin from the Disney movie *Zombies*. I found her on YouTube and discovered that she also was a singer and had released a bunch of hilarious music videos. She was not only an actress and musician but had an enormous social media presence and ran an anti-bullying movement called #ArielMovement.

The other was Chandler Kinney, who was also in *Zombies*. She was a terrific dancer and singer. I'm glad I had no idea who they were before the interview because I might have been nervous. These women were all over YouTube and social media, being positive and encouraging role models. I instantly looked up to them, even though they were half my age. Famous people intimidate me a little. I think it's because I am always afraid I'll say something stupid in front of them. I try to remind myself that they're just people who also say stupid things and probably have their own social fears.

Once the initial mitten media frenzy passed, offers emerged for more in-depth podcast and talk show interviews. I loved these opportunities because they were relaxed, and the questions were more diverse. After a while, it seemed like every news reporter just asked me the same thing. I wanted to say: haven't your listeners already heard this? But the podcasts in particular, were different. One interview I did was for a podcast called, *The Best Worst Thing*, with Josh Walehwa. At the end of the interview Josh said,

"Tell me something in your life that was the best thing, and then I am going to ask you about a worst thing."

"It's funny how the best things can also be the worst things. Bernie Sanders wearing those mittens was definitely a 'best/worst thing," I told him. It had turned my life upside down, put a strain on my marriage and family life, and had frequently caused me severe anxiety. It had also connected me with hundreds of people to whom I never otherwise would have met. I had also made some money from the advertising and my TV appearances. I didn't set out to get rich from this experience, but the flow of income was helpful. We were able to buy a new (used) car that spring.

One of the strange and unexpected perks of my fame was the continued fan mail. The letters arrived for months after the inauguration. One day a package arrived and it was full of letters and a $300 gift card to Target. The letters were from a company called Love Woolies in Utah. Their business of making accessories out of repurposed wool had blown up after the inauguration, and they were able to hire and train over fifty previously unemployed women from across the country to sew for them from home. Each one of them had written me a personal note telling me what their new jobs had done for them. One was paying back medical bills, one was able to catch up on her rent, another was able to pay off student loans. Their words were so kind.

People sent me wool sweaters, mitten shaped earrings, art, pottery, tee-shirts, and mugs. There were so many gifts that I ran out of thank you notes and then ran out of time to send thank you notes. I felt guilty about that and hoped people would understand that I was thankful, and also overwhelmed.

One of the best packages I received was a brand-new industrial strength Singer sewing machine. Steve from Singer Worldwide interviewed me right after the inauguration and published a two-minute video called "My Singer Story" on social media and YouTube. It was such a sweet little video, and he contacted me later to tell me that they wanted to give me an upgrade. I was still using the Singer Sewing machine my mother had given to me for my twelfth birthday thirty-one years before. When the new machine arrived, I was almost afraid to open it. It was so nice; I didn't want to break it.

It wasn't until the summer that I finally pulled it out and set it up. It was computerized, you didn't even need a foot pedal to operate it. You just pushed a button and the fabric easily slid beneath the needle leaving strong, even stitches behind. It was so quiet, I thought it wasn't working at first.

There were some strange gifts, too. My student Charlotte's mom sent me a Bernie Sanders night light. When you plugged it in, the image of Bernie, looking kind of grumpy, glowed throughout the room. I wasn't really sure anyone would want that night light shining on them in their sleep, but I kept it for laughs. I knew that it would be useful at some point. I did have the forethought to know that someday this would all be a distant memory and we would tell people about it and laugh. This sort of thing happens just once in a lifetime. No doubt it would morph into an epic tale.

We would say to Helen's children, "You see that night light over there? The one with the grumpy man? That was Bernie Sanders!" The thought of telling this story sometime in the future to people who had not experienced it gave me great joy.

Great things continued to happen around the mitten frenzy all year. I reconnected with dozens of people from my past throughout this experience. As a young singer, I had attended the Tanglewood Institute the summer I was sixteen. Back in 1994, we didn't have easy access to the internet or email. I didn't even own a computer. In those days, you made wonderful friendships and met kindred spirits at summer camp. Usually when you said goodbye, you never spoke again. It was easier back then to accept that connections were not forever. However, the Bernie's mitten frenzy put my face right into the living room television sets of all my old friends from that summer. I reconnected with a group of women with whom I had spent a wild summer of singing, sneaking out of our dorms, and getting drunk for the first time.

I continued to make the mittens for charity, including a campership fundraiser for a summer camp I attended as a kid, Camp Takodah. They were trying to build up a scholarship fund for kids attending camp whose families needed financial support. When all the tickets were sold and they had raised $1,540 for the campership, they drew the name of the winner. It was none other than my old camp friend Lael. I had forgotten when the drawing was going to be held and I missed the live broadcast. When I opened my phone one day to the message, "I won!" I didn't know what Lael was talking about, but then I realized she had won the Bernie mittens!

About a month later, the director of Camp Takodah invited me to come to camp and speak to their staff at the end of staff training. I put together a presentation with slides and music. As I drove onto the camp property in southern New Hampshire, I was flooded with memories from happy childhood days spent swimming in

Cass Pond and singing camp songs in the dining hall. Going to summer camp was my favorite childhood experience.

The dining hall at Camp Takodah was full of eager young camp counselors in their late teens and early twenties. They were coming off a year of online school and quarantine, and I could tell they were so glad to be together. I told them a little about the Bernie's Mitten Meme fame, but mostly I talked to them about the lessons I've learned from working with kids for the last twenty years. I showed them pictures from my career and told them stories. I told them that they have the power to make a child's life better. I challenged them to find the one child in their cabin who is probably the least popular kid in their school and befriend that kid. Teach them how to be a friend. That's what I learned at camp. That is their Bernie Mitten. It's a gift they can give that will keep giving in phenomenal ways. It is the first domino in a chain of events that ends in joy.

When I was done with my talk, the staff erupted into applause. Then they all stood up with their hands clasped in the air. They gave me a silent standing "O," the highest honor given at camp. Tears streamed down my face. For all the anxiety, fear, and trouble the mitten frenzy had caused, here I was, in the heart of my favorite childhood experience, receiving an honor I could only have ever dreamed of as a kid.

That summer, the Michaels Corporation, a crafting supply company, invited me to run an online class instructing people how to make the mittens. I couldn't do that because I had an exclusive contract with Vermont Teddy Bear, but I offered to do a quilting class instead. Quilting was really my first love. On a dreadfully hot July afternoon, I signed on to my Zoom class and taught three hundred strangers from across the globe how to turn sweaters into lap quilts. It was so much fun that I offered to come back and teach more online classes for Michaels. They agreed to donate one dollar for every sign-up for the class to the Boys and Girls Club. Of my TV and online appearances, Michaels was the first corporation that willingly donated to a charity at my request.

Another amazing thing that happened the summer after the inauguration was that Lise-Anne opened a studio/store. I had had a few conversations with Lise-Anne throughout the spring. Things felt a little strained between us. The mitten business was originally her idea, and here I was gleaning tons of attention for it. I felt a little guilty, like she was the one who should have been given all these accolades. When I mentioned this to her in a phone call, she brushed it off.

"I didn't give the mittens to Bernie, you did."

It was gracious of her to view it this way. We hadn't spent any time together in several years. Her children were now in college and high school. She never stopped by the Westford School anymore. I missed her, and yet, I understood that amazing people come and go in life and it's impossible to maintain every important friendship.

After the inauguration, and before I connected with Vermont Teddy Bear, I suggested to some people that they could get Bernie mittens from Lise-Anne. I had to be cautious about this suggestion because even though I know she wanted *some* business, she didn't want to spend all her days making mittens either. She was a talented crafter who made lots of beautiful things. She later told me that before long, her inbox filled with thousands of requests that she was also unable to fulfill.

Some of those requests were also business requests. Whereas I didn't want to give up my teaching job to make mittens, Lise-Anne was in a different position. Her love for repurposing material and her savvy business sense made her an appealing business partner for a California-based sustainable clothing company called Outerknown. With their support and collaboration, she opened Outerknown Project Vermont, a studio/store in St. Albans. She employs fourteen crafters and sewers, mostly women. They design and craft onsite, repurposing all kinds of materials from denim to plaid. They also mend garments and donate items to local and national causes.

When I saw Lise-Anne later that year, she looked happy. She told me that opening a store had never been on her radar before.

"Really? I feel like I suggested this to you lots of times."

"Maybe you did, but I never really considered it."

We were standing in a parking lot half-way between our two houses, loading boxes of sewing materials someone donated to me into her car. It was far more than I needed and I knew she would put all of it to good use.

It was a windy evening and her hair kept getting stuck in her glasses. I actually hadn't seen her in person in several years. She took her glasses off and cleaned a speck from them with her shirt. We both had aged but her lovely spirit was just the same. She was eager to show me some pictures of her studio and I showed her pictures of Helen. It was a little heartbreaking to think of all the life we had lived since we parted ways. There was a time when I thought I would like to ride shotgun in her SUV forever.

"I bet you're an amazing boss."

She gave a modest half-laugh.

"Well, I have some amazing employees."

Lise-Anne told me that her employee's ages ran from 19 to 75. Many of them were looking for purpose or a new path, and working with her at Outerknown had given them hope and direction in a dark time.

"I can see how sewing with you might help someone through a dark time." She gave me another awkward laugh that left me wondering if she even knew how special she was to me.

Lise-Anne isn't an overly sentimental person, but of course I was tearing up a bit as I said this to her. The wind had picked up and I pretended it was making my eyes water. But really, my thoughts were transported back to the days after the miscarriage when my life felt so dark and hopeless. Sewing at a table across from Lise-Anne was a magical thing for me then. It was part of what saved me. When you sew with Lise-Anne, she brings all her gifts to the crafting table. She holds a lot of space around her for people to show up as they are. She is a powerful person, an anchor, and a true friend. When I think of her now, I smile. I am cheering for her. Always.

The Bernie's Mitten Fame gave me a platform to share with thousands of people the lessons I had learned as a teacher. It gave me a chance to teach crafting classes, reconnect with long lost friends, build business relationships, and help my family financially. It also impacted countless other crafters. Lots of people needed a boost in the winter of 2021, and the mitten meme sensation was a gift that kept giving.

The summer after the inauguration went by faster than any previous break. Before I knew it, we were back at school, sitting through endless meetings at in-service. I wasn't ready to start all over again. It filled me with dread to think about building another classroom community after the magical year spent with my Pandemic Class. My new students arrived with a set of unprecedented challenges. They had never experienced a normal school year. Their kindergarten year was cut short in March of 2020, and their first-grade year was marked by constantly changing education models and COVID-19 outbreaks.

In addition to the stressors within the classroom, there were additional outside pressures. The previous spring, the Vermont state treasurer, supported by several legislators and senators, rolled out a plan to address the pension deficit at the state level. Despite the fact that teachers and state employees had worked relentlessly during the pandemic to keep our communities afloat, we were told that we would likely need to work at least five years past the age when we thought we could retire. In addition, they wanted us to pay more now and receive less later. None of this made sense to me because I knew that teachers and state employees had always paid every penny into the pension system that we were supposed to pay. It was deducted from our salaries. The shortfall had been caused by lawmakers repeatedly shortchanging the pension system for decades with little thought to how that deficit would multiply over the years. The fact that anyone thought this deficit should be resolved by teachers and state employees paying more was just insulting. This was a debt created at the state level, it should have been resolved at the state level. Yet, all year, educators and state employees received updates about the negotiations around our pensions, and in the end, our pensions were reduced, and we had to pay more.

Educators were overwhelmed with district-wide demands too. There was a sense of urgency in our school district that teachers needed to make sure the students made up for lost time. When we expressed how stressful this was to hear, administrators told us, with the same urgency, that we needed to simultaneously practice self-care. Meanwhile, more and more tasks were put on our plates each day.

The pandemic had taken its toll on everyone in millions of ways. Addressing all the new struggles our staff was facing on a daily basis was like trying to stop a waterfall with a cotton ball. To top it off, we were perpetually short staffed. We used to have dozens of applicants for every teaching position, but now we were lucky to get five. Our school had vacant positions all year. Marcie scrambled to find coverage for anyone who had to be out sick. She often pulled support staff from one classroom to sub in another. There was a clear unspoken message that we needed to come to work, even if we were ill or needed a mental health day. We had sick and personal days in our contract but couldn't use them. Staffing shortages were a constant strain. I don't think you could have mopped our morale off the floor, it was so low.

In the second month of school, I had to give up my outdoor classroom because my class needed more support, and that support was inside. The outdoor classroom had become my favorite part about teaching, and as soon as we moved inside, little by little, piece by piece, every last shred of love I had for my profession slipped away. No amount of self-care could fix the daily grind of standards and behavior referrals. I would gaze out the window at the changing seasons and feel like we were all missing the point. All I had to do was open the fire door and set us all free, but as close as we were to the great outdoors, there was no way to get back out there given the constraints of our school system.

As the pandemic gradually turned endemic that school year, we stopped wearing masks, and most people, including myself, got COVID-19. We had avoided it for so long, but it was inevitable. Our society was unable to eradicate it with vaccines and masks. We had an incredible opportunity to make big, positive changes in our school system as a result of the school closings. Every structure that locked us into the old way of doing things broke apart and we could have built it back better. But we didn't. The school year dragged on and it was clear that what we were striving for was to get back to "normal." And normal meant, the way things had been before.

There was a time when I really did love teaching, even before the outdoor classroom. Being a teacher made me feel like I was an important person in our community. I had been teaching for so long that it defined a very large piece of my identity. I was a teacher before I was a lot of other things in my life: before I was a partner, a mother, and before the strange identity of Bernie's Mitten Maker landed in my lap. When I was in my twenties, teaching was so much of my identity that it was the greatest source of meaning I had in my life.

I had been a public-school teacher now for seventeen years and I *always* had hoped that it would get better—that I could be part of making it better. But in the year following the pandemic, I lost hope. I stopped believing that I had what it took to make positive change. It started with the hits to our pension, and continued with our staffing shortages. The last straw was losing my outdoor classroom. And so, one sunny day the spring of 2022, I resigned.

Chapter 21

The Craft of Connecting
to the Past

M y grandmother reclined on her 1980s tweed couch at her home in Guilford, Vermont, and I sat at her card table with my laptop open. She gently opened an airmail envelope and pulled out the thin paper letter inside. It was the summer of 2005, and Grandpa's letters from the European theater of World War II were now over sixty years old. His writing was illegible to me, but Grandma adjusted her glasses and began to read.

We had been working on the project of typing up Grandpa's letters for seven years, and in that time Grandma had grown thinner, and her life had shrunk with her declining body. Her mind was sharp though, and her memories vivid. "*Letter number 71,*" all their letters began this way. They wrote to each other every day, and usually their correspondence started with a list of the letters they had received that day. Many of the letters never arrived because mail planes were shot down or the mail ship torpedoed.

Somewhere in France February 26, 1945
Darling,
Say, I think maybe pretty soon I'll get some mail. Two of the

boys got some tonight, so I figure there is some down at head-
quarters. It's six or seven miles down there, and a blackout
drive too, so I'm not going to get it tonight. I hope to get it first
thing in the morning.

Honey this has sort of been blue Monday for me. It was a
dark, cold day, and nothing much going on. Then to top it off
the boys have been giving me trouble. Oh honey I didn't mean
to tell you I was blue, but I guess you would know it before I
finished this letter. Sweetheart all that I live for is the day that
I get back to you.

Grandma had become skilled at reading the letters at just
the right pace for me to type them. When we started this project, I didn't even own a laptop. We had to borrow one from her
investment banker. After the war, my grandfather had been a
small-town doctor in Brattleboro, Vermont, and had delivered
many of the babies born in that area between 1946 and 1976. He
had delivered all three of the banker's children. People never
forget those moments. Grandpa bought a jeep when he returned
from the war. He drove it all over the county delivering babies at
home and visiting sick and elderly patients. Back then, a small-
town doctor covered everything from birth to death. I imagine
he passed through the front door of every home in the area,
paying a visit of one kind or another. The banker told me when
I went to pick up the device that loaning us a laptop to preserve
the legacy of Dr. John P. Lord was the least he could do. I didn't
understand then what I understand now, about the profundity of
those raw and salient life events, like the birth of a child or the
death of a parent. Communities are full of interconnections that
carry us through time.

Grandma looked up from the letter.

"You're smiling."

"I love it when he says stuff like that. He 'lived for the day' he would get back to you. It's so romantic." With a soft shake of her head, she continued. My grandparents had only been married for two months before Grandpa shipped off to war. His letters were fascinating, heartbreaking, and sometimes funny. He often asked her to bake him chocolate chip Toll House cookies. If Grandma brought the letters where he had requested things to the post office, she could send the items for free.

Grandma often stopped reading the letters and told me side stories about the people mentioned and what happened to them after the war. It was unbelievable to me how this horrific experience happened in our world. Millions of lives were destroyed and disrupted by it all. Yet, there was my grandpa, the same age as I was then, twenty-seven, carving out a daily existence in the midst of all that destruction. Each night Grandpa sat down and poured all his thoughts out to Grandma on the page. I imagine it helped him clear his head enough to be able to sleep after the events of the day and the atrocities he'd seen as a battalion surgeon. This particular letter went on for three pages and came to a close on a small quarter sheet of paper. I'm sure Grandpa saved the rest of that piece for another day. Not a single thing could be wasted during the war.

We read a lot about how poorly equipped the Germans are and how low their morale is. That may be, but they certainly are stubborn fighters. They do fall back, but they cause a lot of trouble before they do it. They make the infantry work mighty hard for every inch of ground they take. It amazes me where they get all their strength. It seems as though they must throw in the sponge pretty soon. Sure hope this spring drive will finish them off.

Well darling I guess I'll close now as it is getting late. Sweetheart I love you with all my heart. It thrills me to address letters to Mrs. J.P.Lord. It just doesn't seem possible that we belong to each other. It will be so wonderful when we can be with each other again.

All my love,
John

Grandma closed her eyes, the letter rested gently on her chest. I wasn't sure if she was taking a quick nap or just remembering something from long ago. I studied her face for a moment, the way her skin sagged off her cheeks and her wisps of gray and black hair brushed back off her forehead. I loved everything about her and already had begun to grieve the day she would leave me. I gazed out the window at Grandpa's old gardens. His apple orchard was now overgrown with tall grass, and the asparagus had gone to seed. The old blueberry bushes were over six feet tall. Grandma had paid her helper, Arlene, to drape netting over the frame around the blueberry patch to keep the birds out, so that the grandkids could pick the berries. The truth, though, was that the grandkids were all grown and didn't come around much anymore. Most of those berries would rot on the bush.

Grandma's eyes fluttered open.

"Oh, I must have dozed off for a bit. I think we should be done for today." Our letter-typing sessions were getting shorter and shorter. Sometimes we would only type one letter before she needed a break.

"Grandma, do you think I could dig up one of Grandpa's blueberry bushes to transplant in my backyard in Winooski?"

"I don't see why not. There are some shovels and pruning shears in the shed below the garage."

I walked out into the high summer humidity. The cicadas buzzed in the fields. A car barreled down the dirt road, barely kicking up dust in the heavy air. The shed beneath Grandma's garage was dark and cool. Its rich, earthen smell was a cross between something sweet and something old. I stood for a moment and looked around while my eyes adjusted. Grandpa's tools hung from pegs on the beams that supported the garage, adorned with cobwebs. I chose a few that looked sharpish and headed back out into the heat.

The blueberry patch was steeped in memory for me. I lifted a round river stone off the gauze netting to make an opening for myself. My mom, Grandma, and I used to pick these blueberries for hours. We had old lunch pails strapped to belts around our waists. At first the blueberries would make a little plunk-plunk sound as they hit the bottom of the metal pails. Then the sound would dull to a softer thump as the pails began to fill. My grandmother stored the berries in her deep freezer in the basement, and all winter she turned them into muffins or pancakes. I used to pour them on my Frosted Flakes when I was little. It's funny what memories cling to you over time. I still remember the way the milk would freeze onto the berries and the sweet crunch of Frosted Flakes mixed with the tartness of the fruit. I haven't had Frosted Flakes with frozen blueberries and milk in decades, yet I can still conjure up the sensation of them in my mouth.

Inside the blueberry patch, the bushes were huge and over-grown. They scratched at my legs and arms as I made my way to the back of the frame. I wanted to take a bush that wasn't visible from the house, so Grandma wouldn't have to look at a hole in the patch. These bushes had been transplanted from the house where my mother grew up on Spruce Street in Brattleboro. They had to be over 50 years old.

It was even hotter in the patch than it was outside. The netting that kept the birds out boxed me in and stifled whatever breeze had been circulating through the valley. I found a healthy bush on the back edge and started to dig. The roots were so thick beneath the ground that the shovel barely scratched the earth. I took out the pruning shears and began cutting them, trying to free enough of a bush to give it a chance at surviving the transplant. Sweat dripped off my forehead as I fought with that bush. I tugged and dug, clipped, and chopped. This bush had pulsed through the soil tilled by my grandfather for my whole life, and it really didn't want to leave. In the end, I was able to secure a pathetic, tangled mass of roots that I stuck in a five-gallon bucket. A few blueberry limbs stuck out the top. I dragged it up to the garage and was relieved to walk back into Grandma's air-conditioned house.

As I drove away later that day, Grandma stood in the window waving to me. She used to wave from the driveway, then she waved from the porch, now she laboriously stood up and with the help of her walker, made it to the window. I wondered if it would be the last time I saw her. Lately every visit ended this way. I would gently hug her boney frame and tell her I loved her, fighting back tears; then drive away down the dirt road, weeping all the way to Brattleboro. I simultaneously wanted her to live forever and recognized that her quality of life was poor. I didn't want her to be lonely or to suffer.

I planted Grandpa's blueberry bush in a sunny corner of my backyard and watered it every day. It looked healthy and strong as the autumn approached, but the Vermont winter was brutal, and the little bush was nothing but a skeleton of branches by the spring. I left it there for most of the summer, hoping it would come back to life, but it didn't. On the last day I mowed the lawn the following September, I pulled what was left of the blueberry bush and tossed it on top of a pile of leaves headed for the dump. I knew I wouldn't try to dig another bush out of that tangled mass at Grandma's house. It was a grand effort—though in the end, literally fruitless.

One twisted and mangled blueberry root stood up from the overturned bush in the pile. I took my garden shears and cut it off. It was about eighteen inches long. I ran it under the hose and scrubbed off the dirt. It was strangely beautiful and had a sweet smell. I stuck it on the windowsill above the kitchen sink and left it there.

My grandma lived for three more years. We typed the letters every chance we got. I'm not sure why I held on to that blueberry root, but when I moved to Burlington the next year, I stuck it in a box and brought it with me. While I was unpacking in my new apartment, my yellow lab, Joey, found the root in the box and brought it to me, tail wagging.

"That is not for you!" He seemed to smile and ran away. I managed to save it from him with only a few bite marks. After returning the stick to the box, I put it in storage. The years passed.

A few months after Grandma died, I met Liz. I have always wondered if Grandma had some sort of cosmic influence over our meeting. She would have loved Liz. She loved smart people. Everything that was Grandma's became a treasure after she was gone. I inherited many lovely things from her, just in time to start my new life with Liz. We bought a house and filled it with a combination of things from both of our apartments and from my Grandma's house. When we were moving in, I happened to find the blueberry root, and told Liz the story. She rolled her eyes.

"You never throw anything away, do you?"

"Yes, I do . . ."

"Like what?"

"Like things that have no use."

"Then why do you still have a dirty old stick you dug out of the ground five years ago?"

"I don't know why. Someday I think it could be something beautiful."

"Like what?"

"I don't know yet." And that is how many of our conversations about my boxes of things went. Liz brought large trash bags of junk to Goodwill, and I built more shelves in the basement for sentimental things with which I couldn't bear to part.

My friend Mary's mother knitted two wool sweaters for her grandsons when they were children. After Mary's mother died, she asked if I could turn the sweaters into hats and mittens for her family for Hanukkah gifts. The sweaters never fit the boys. They were thick and scratchy, and the arms were long and too skinny. Her sons were teenagers now, anyway, and too cool for Fair Isle sweater patterns. She couldn't part with them though, and I understood why. Somewhere in my basement lay a blueberry root for the same reason.

Most of the sweaters I cut up to make mittens were from popular stores and had been mass produced. I would make a set of mittens from a Woolrich sweater with a Nordic pattern one year, and the very next year I would find the exact same sweater at a yard sale and make another beautiful set just like the first. It was kind of fun when that happened, but my favorite sweaters were the sentimental ones. There was something almost magical about cutting up a sweater that had been hand knit. I wondered whose hands had labored over each stitch, the conversations they might have had while their knitting needles rhythmically clicked, pulling and pushing the wool in and out in an intricate wave of knots.

Mary's sweaters were thick and small. I was extra careful with them because I didn't want to waste a single piece. They had a charming smell of old lady perfume. When I gave the mittens to Mary, she cried so hard that I started crying too. I didn't even know her mother. It was one of the first times, pre-Bernie, that I realized the power of the mittens. Mary's mother had carefully knitted every stitch of those sweaters. She chose the patterns and the colors. The oils from her hands blended with the fibers from the wool. I felt the same way about turning those sweaters into mittens that I felt about turning my great-great-grandmother's quilt face into a finished quilt.

I don't believe in ghosts, but I do believe that something of a person's spirit is left behind when they go. I have often sat down at my sewing machine to repurpose something made or owned by someone I have never met. I can't say that this process leads me to "know" them very deeply. I may be able to make assumptions about their skill level or how careful of a crafter they may have been, but I never feel that I know them when I'm finished. What I do feel is that I've met them. I sat down with whatever ounce of their spirit inhabits the thing they left behind, and my hands took over where their hands left off. In that way, we touched each other through time.

When I was finishing my great-great-grandmother's quilt, I marveled at how small some of the pieces of fabric were. She saved and repurposed every inch of unused material from her other sewing projects. I wondered what other clothes she made from those fabrics. Sometimes I looked through old family photos to see if I recognized any of the patterns on their clothes, but I never did. I admired her small, even stitches while simultaneously admonishing her for smoking. She left little cigarette burns on her work. I imagined her anticipating the birth of my grandma. Time is so long when you're waiting but so short when you are remembering. It was in the act of crafting while waiting that I met my great-great-grandmother. She was waiting for Grandma to arrive and I was waiting for her leave. She wanted to speed up time, and I wanted to slow it down. And in the middle of all that time, there was a quilt.

There was a woman in Westford named Missy whom I really admired. The first year I taught in Westford, Missy and her husband Bill adopted a six-year-old son from Serbia. The next year, he was in my second-grade class. I loved this little boy. He was so delightful and happy. Each week I would write out pronouns and verbs in different tenses and post them near his desk to help him learn English. "I run, you run, they run, he runs, she runs, I ran, you ran, they ran," etc. He was easy to teach and eager to learn. The next year, Missy and Bill adopted another son from the same orphanage, and I did the same thing for him. A couple years after that, they adopted a daughter, too. I worked closely with Missy to help each of her children in school. I loved them for everything they were and for the marvelous life they were building as a family.

Not long after I started teaching, I opened a Facebook account exclusively for my professional work. This is how I learned that Missy had taken up the hobby of turning wood into pens on a lathe. She posted pictures of pens that she had crafted out of cherry wood, apple trees, and lilac bushes. It was now 2019, and the last of her kids was in my second-grade class. She was selling the pens at a local craft show, and I really wanted to buy one, but I also had a craft fair that day at a different venue. The next time I saw her at school, I stopped her in the hall and struck up a conversation about the pens. Missy told me about a pen she made from a branch that fell off her apple tree, and I remembered the blueberry root. I had no idea if I even had it anymore. I hadn't seen it since we moved into our house almost a decade before. I told her about it and she said if I could find it, she could make it into a pen for me. We parted ways, and I kind of laughed at the thought. What were the chances that the old root was still kicking around?

But it was still kicking around. Just like my great-great-grandmother's quilt face had landed in a box in the basement, so had the blueberry root. I called Missy and offered to trade a pair of mittens for a pen. The truth was, she probably would have made me the pen for free just because she's generous like that, and she was grateful to me for teaching her children—even though that was my job. I also knew that she probably would not accept my money, but the mittens were not money. They were a barter, which was more valuable than money, because it was more personal. Bartering is the economy of the industrious crafter. There are things that have so much value, the money it takes to buy them can never match the meaning and heart it took to make them. Money is a cheap trade for craft. But craft is an equal trade for craft. It says, the value of your creation matches the value of mine. Something is built between humans when they barter: a bridge, or a path, or maybe it's just an understanding.

I made Missy a pair of mittens from a sweater with a Celtic design because I knew she loved Ireland and had visited there with her family the year before. She made me not one but *four* pens from the blueberry root. When the root was lathed, sanded smooth, and polished, it had a soft, blond color with dark brown striations. They were twist pens. The top part turned to reveal the pen beneath the lower part. They wrote in black ink, nothing fancy, and yet everything seemed to bear greater meaning when I used them.

After my grandmother died, her house was sold. I don't know what the new owners did with the blueberry patch. Good luck to them if they ever tried to dig it up! My mother took the box of letters and keeps them in the coat closet of her house. Sometimes, when I am visiting her, I take them out and hold them. They are brittle and fading, but the past radiates from them. My grandpa once held those pieces of paper. He moved every stroke of the pen that told the story of his life in World War II. Every coffee stain and smudge was his. When Grandma held those letters, she was connected to her memories of a distant time. A time, when, as a young woman, she loved a man who went to war, and hoped he would someday return to her. When she read those letters to me, she gave me a past that was not mine. She gifted those memories to me. She gave me time and stories, sighs, naps, and words. She gave me sunny afternoons, and history beyond my imagination. I knew my grandfather as an old man who died slowly of Parkinson's disease, but through our days of typing up his letters, Grandma introduced me to him as a young man. Through those letters, I met a man in love, trapped in a brutal war.

Part of the reason I had no mittens for sale after the inauguration was that I had spent the fall and early winter of 2020 making six lap quilts for my friend Mindy, whose mother had also died. Someone in their family owned a cashmere factory and her mother left behind dozens of extra small cashmere sweaters. Some of them had stains on the chest where food often lands, and some had old deodorant stains. I cut out all the imperfections and used the beautiful material to sew the softest quilts I'd ever made. I looked through Mindy's pictures on Facebook and saw lots of pictures of her mom. She had a radiant smile. Somehow, I knew that about her from her sweaters. They were cheerful colors; they had been worn to parties. There were make-up stains and wine stains. She was fun and she was loved. All of this emanated from her clothes after she was gone. I never met her in person, but I knew some part of her.

A crafter can turn the line that connects one person to another into a triangle with space in between, and that is where the story resides. Mary's mother knitted sweaters that I turned into mittens for Mary's family. I entered that memory and pulled it into a new thing of beauty. My great-great-grandmother stitched a quilt for my grandmother that I finished. We triangulated five generations into one work of art. Mindy's mother left behind cashmere sweaters that I turned into quilts and returned them to her family as something warm and useful. I gave my favorite senator some mittens, and they connected us both to a world of memes and laughter.

When my grandfather returned from the war, he planted some blueberry bushes. He and Grandma started a family. They picked blueberries with their three daughters and five grandchildren. They laid the roots for my family tree and the roots of their garden. They left behind a history rich of writing and loving. My grandfather died in 1993. It was a cruel ending for a great man. He never met my friends or my wife, but in the strange way that things hold memories, my friend Missy met him when she took the root from a bush he had planted and cultivated for decades and turned it into a pen. A pen with which I sat down to write her a thank you note. Many years later, when I had another story to tell, I took the pen and began a book.

Chapter 22

The Final Stitch

I often think about the whale my brother Ryan and I encountered beneath our canoe in Alaska back in 2009. It swam away
that day, without incident, and Ryan and I paddled safely to the
shore. We enjoyed the bounty from his shrimp pots that night and
agreed that in the future, a canoe was probably not the best vessel
for shrimping. The image of that giant, ominous figure gliding
beneath our boat returned to me often in the wake of the inauguration. It was an enormous, beautiful, scary thing that happened
to me. I frequently felt like I was gently paddling with trepidation
above a dark and unpredictable force. It was a stunning experience
to be near the center of the joyousness that the world experienced
because of the mittens I made for Bernie Sanders.

In the end, I too managed to navigate my way through those
months without becoming the target of too much negative media.
The world can be a fickle place, but maybe, just maybe, people
recognized that I was doing the best I could in an unexpected
situation. And maybe they also knew that I was trying to harness
the experience for the good of many.

One cold night, at the end of 2021, I was walking to my car with my friend Kathryn. We'd had a great night out and were saying our goodbyes. She was shivering and brought her bare hands up to her mouth to warm them with her breath. I was wearing the red and rainbow striped mittens that never sold in the ill-fated eBay auctions.

I turned to Kathryn and said, "I want you to have these mittens." It was a split-second decision, but I knew right away it was a good one. Her face lit up. It was as if I had given her a car or something. She immediately put them on and brought them up to her cheeks to feel how soft they were. Then she gave me a giant hug. It was clear that the mittens meant so much to her. I hope it was also clear to her how much her friendship meant to me.

Giving Kathryn that particular pair of mittens felt like the gentle closing of a door. I would always be Bernie's Mitten Maker, but it was time to let go of the strife it had caused. Perhaps those red and rainbow striped mittens were never meant for some random person to buy on eBay. I don't believe that everything happens for a reason, in fact I hate that saying. But I was willing to let the fact that Kathryn didn't have any mittens to wear on that blustery winter night be the reason why the eBay auctions for my daughter's college fund had fallen through. Why not? It made for a better ending to that bitter part of my story.

In earlier parts of my life, I used to equate generosity with giving money and material things away, and when you give things away, you don't have them anymore. In essence, I equated generosity with loss. I was wrong about that.

Generosity is about so much more than money and material things. Generosity was the patient companionship of my grandmother at family gatherings when she loyally sat with me to keep me company, instead of joining the other adults. Generosity was my kind and loving home economics teacher who was determined to teach every child in South Portland, Maine, to sew. Generosity was my students who loved me with abandon in the depths of the pandemic. Generosity was my old friend Deb who reappeared in my life to help me navigate a dizzying burst of unexpected fame. Generosity is not loss.

When I go back through the salient events of my life and pick out the moments of astounding joy, at the root of each there was generosity. When Helen shot into the world, fist first, it was because a man who would never be her father donated sperm to make that possible. When I stood in front of my family and friends and married Liz in 2011, it was because she generously loved me despite all of my shortcomings. The fact that our marriage later became legal in all fifty states was because generations of gays and lesbians had generously given of their time and safety to fight for the rights of people to love each other openly.

I gave Bernie Sanders a gift that miraculously ended up as the focal point of millions of memes and countless moments of joy all across the world in the middle of the pandemic. No one could have predicted that. You never know what will happen with the crafts you send out into the world. They begin as humble pieces of beauty, made by hand. Some travel the world and remain unseen; others have a different fate.

When people think about Bernie's mittens, they might think about the memes and the inauguration. They might recall the pandemic and our bitterly divided country. But when I think about the mittens, I think about Lise-Anne inviting me to sew with her at her house and Mary trusting me with the sweaters her mother knit. I think about all the connections I've made at craft fairs. I think about the many ways that creativity has brought healing and peace to my life. I think about the generations that came before me, and the ones that will come after me, and the many threads that will connect us through time. Tomorrow I will sit down with Helen to create something that didn't exist today. Together we will push and pull the yarn, and that is where a new story will begin.

Acknowledgments

I would like to thank Adam Schear for being one of the first people to believe in this book and encouraging me to keep writing it and Kaomi Taylor Mitchell for being the first reader. Thank you to Vermont Teddy Bear Company, Darn Tough, and Physician's Computer Company for their endless support and sponsorship. To Amanda Feller, Grace Kennedy, and Julianne Harris—you were the best cover design team ever. Thank you to Scott Stoll and Susanna Badgley Place for the space and time to write at the Cove. Thank you to my early readers: Jennifer Smith, Ruthie Mason, Sara Solnick, Jane Perlmutter, Harry Goldhagan, Jacqueline Weinstock, Jill Entis, Christa Champion, Lauren Starkey, Danielle Friedman, and Kathy Blume. Thank you to Gretchen Legler and Ruth Hill for encouraging me to boldly speak my truth. Thank you to Jessica Moreland for the early writing coaching, Shelley Brander for the publicity coaching, and Deb Flanders for managing all the chaos. Thank you to all the friends who read chapters along the way, and to my launch team for helping me with publicity. Thank you to Green Writers Press for taking a chance on me and to Rose Alexandre-Leach and Ferne Johansson for being excellent editors. Thank you to the kids in my Pandemic class for your endless sense of wonder. Thank you to my parents and my chosen family for loving me. A huge shout out to the Gayborhood and the NICE Neighborhood for being a wonderful community. Thank you to Helen for being the best kid ever. Mostly, thank you to Liz for reading every draft, encouraging me, loving me, and laughing with me. My world is complete because you and Helen are in it.